Queer Adolescent Literature as a Complement to the English Language Arts Curriculum

Queer Adolescent Literature as a Complement to the English Language Arts Curriculum

2nd Edition

Edited by
Paula Greathouse
Henry "Cody" Miller

ROWMAN & LITTLEFIELD
Lanham • Boulder • New York • London

Published by Rowman & Littlefield
An imprint of The Rowman & Littlefield Publishing Group, Inc.
4501 Forbes Boulevard, Suite 200, Lanham, Maryland 20706
www.rowman.com

86-90 Paul Street, London EC2A 4NE, United Kingdom

British Library Cataloguing in Publication Information Available

Library of Congress Cataloging-in-Publication Data

Names: Greathouse, Paula, editor. | Miller, Henry "Cody", 1989– editor.
Title: Queer adolescent literature as a complement to the English language arts
   curriculum / edited by Paula Greathouse, Henry Miller.
Description: 2nd edition. | Lanham : Rowman & Littlefield, [2022] | Includes
   bibliographical references and index. | Summary: "This text offers secondary ELA
   educators guided instructional approaches for including queer-themed young adult
   (YA) literature in the English language arts classroom"—Provided by publisher.
Identifiers: LCCN 2021036211 (print) | LCCN 2021036212 (ebook) | ISBN
   9781475861860 (cloth ; alk. paper) | ISBN 9781475861877 (paperback ; alk. paper) |
   ISBN 9781475861884 (epub)
Subjects: LCSH: Homosexuality in literature. | Young adult literature—Study and
   teaching. | Gays in literature. | Lesbians in literature. | LCGFT: Literary criticism. |
   Essays.
Classification: LCC PN56.H57 Q4415 2022 (print) | LCC PN56.H57 (ebook) |
   DDC 820.9/353—dc23
LC record available at https://lccn.loc.gov/2021036211
LC ebook record available at https://lccn.loc.gov/2021036212

♾ ™ The paper used in this publication meets the minimum requirements of American
National Standard for Information Sciences—Permanence of Paper for Printed Library
Materials, ANSI/NISO Z39.48-1992.

Contents

Introduction

Henry "Cody" Miller and Paula Greathouse

The teaching of LGBTQ young adult literature is invaluable in creating affirming classrooms for LGBTQ youth. And the need for this affirmation is urgent. Since the publication of the first edition of *Queer Adolescent Literature as a Complement to the English Language Arts Curriculum* (Greathouse, Eisenbach, Kaywell, 2018), attacks on LGBTQ books have remained constant. For instance, books that feature LGBTQ characters continue to occupy the bulk of the most frequently banned book lists in the United States (Villarreal, 2020). Subsequently, new measures to deny LGTBQ youth their humanity in schools continue to take shape. At the time of this writing, several states have enacted or are in the process of enacting anti-transgender student legislation that will cause immense harm to K-12 transgender students (Burns, 2021). Our work as English teachers in affirming LGBTQ youth cannot be overstated. Teaching LGBTQ young adult literature can braid the goals of affirming LGBTQ students with the aim of addressing homo- and transphobic beliefs many non-LGBTQ students may hold (Malo-Juvera, 2016). Though such teaching is not done without navigating barriers.

We know that English teachers who profess support for LGBTQ youth and political causes may have trepidation when it comes time to teach LGBTQ texts and curricular material (Greathouse & DiCicco, 2016; Thein, 2013). This hesitancy comes as a result of many factors, including tension around parental and administrative pushback. Thus, the chapters within this edition illuminate the teaching of LGBTQ young adult literature through the lens of core English language arts practices such as narration, writing, reading instruction, and multimodality, among others. This emphasis on English language arts content as a focus for teaching LGBTQ young adult literature marks a shift from the first edition. Framing the teaching of LGBTQ young adult literature in the language of content area standards and practices can be a valuable method of negotiating institutional barriers and tensions (Miller, 2019). Collectively this book imagines an English classroom where LGBTQ young adult literature is integral to English language arts curriculum. Then, it offers pedagogical and instructional moves to concretize that imagining.

The work of creating affirming schools for LGBTQ youth must be vigilant in understanding and tackling interlocking systems of oppression such as racism, classism, ableism, sexism, and other harmful ideologies and social forces (Blackburn & McCready, 2009). Unfortunately, LGBTQ young adult literature has predominately spent its attention on white characters at the neglect of LGBTQ characters of color (Garden, 2014). Inclusion of LGBTQ content without a critical analysis of *who* is being included and *how* will only "reinforce the optimization of some LGBTQ students' well-being to the detriment of others" (Kokozos & Gonzalez, 2020, p. 1). For instance, many characters of color are still relegated to superficial love interests for white protagonists in LGBTQ young adult literature (Monet, 2019). It is important for educators to highlight LGBTQ young adult literature written by and centering LGBTQ people of color in English classrooms.

Approaching narratives by and of LGBTQ youth of color through an intersectional lens can help students understanding how race, gender, and sexuality are "constructed by the individual characters, by the group or cultural communities to which they belong, and by the institutions with which they interact" (Durand, 2016, p. 77). Equally important, centering young adult literature by and for LGBTQ people of color can support teachers in balancing the need to "address the very real challenges our students [of color] face due to their undeserved oppression" while being "mindful that this is not the only story we tell to and about them" (Reid, 2020, para 14). Several chapters in this second edition of *Queer Adolescent Literature as a Complement to the English Language Arts Curriculum* offer pedagogical approaches rooted in an intersectional analysis of LGBTQ young adult literature centering protagonists of color. These chapters provide illustrations of how teachers can teach about systemic oppression while also honoring the resistance and joy LGBTQ youth of color experience and enact daily.

We also want to acknowledge our limitations. This edition does not include chapters dedicated to teaching literary works by Asian American Pacific Islander or Indigenous LGBTQ authors. Those absences reflect a serious limitation of this edition. We as educators must continue to amplify and honor LGBTQ people across racial identities and ethnicities, especially communities who have been neglected by publishers and curriculum in the history of LGBTQ young adult literature.

We present this second edition of *Queer Adolescent Literature as a Complement to the English Language Arts Curriculum* as a way to integrate a multitude (though still limited) of LGBTQ experiences, narratives, and voices into current and longstanding approaches to English curriculum. Such an amalgamation of LGBTQ material with the curriculum is much needed to affirm and support LGBTQ youth (Miller, 2016). As history and current sociopolitical happenings illustrate, movements and attempts to create more affirming realities for LGBTQ youth require a constellation of actions and actors, which include secondary teachers. In offering approaches for teaching LGBTQ young adult literature through English language arts content area skills, educators can construct classrooms that begin to realize the goal of affirming and loving spaces for LGBTQ youth.

ORGANIZATION

This edition of *Queer Adolescent Literature as a Complement to the English Language Arts Curriculum* opens with "The History of Queer Young Adult Literature" by Michael Cart and Joan F. Kaywell. This chapter, which also appeared in the first edition, takes readers on a chronological journey of the history of queer young adult literature as it began and transformed through the decades. Beginning in the 1970s to the present day, the authors spotlight the growth, change, and innovations of queer young adult literature.

Each chapter that follows is organized with an introductory section, a summary of the text, and then instructional activities for before, during, and after reading and extension activities that move beyond the text. In many cases, activities build on each other, and in other cases, they exist independently, allowing teachers to pick and choose which fits their students best. Although the chapters in this edition illuminate the teaching of LGBTQ young adult literature through the lens of core English language arts practices, we have organized the collection thematically. In doing so, readers are exposed to a multitude of practices that can be utilized when reading thematically similar texts.

In chapter 2, LaMar Timmons-Long offers approaches for exploring a "memoir-manifesto" that details the author's life growing up as a young Black queer man in New Jersey. Through the suggested approaches, educators can guide students through the process of conducting a rhetorical analysis to understand how Johnson uses language to construct a queer Black narrative.

The next two chapters in the volume spotlight graphic novels. In chapter 3, René M. Rodríguez-Astacio offers approaches for teaching characterization and symbolism through a close emphasis on the manner in which the graphic novel presents both traditional, comic-book storytelling and illustration that is valuable in class discussions due to its prominent themes on queer and adolescent identities. Chapter 4, by Nicole Ann Amato and Jenna Spiering, offers instructional approaches to teaching narrative structure through an exploration of the author's choices regarding structural elements (i.e., color, panel structure, manipulation of time) within the graphic format, while developing student's understandings of gender and sexuality and their relationship to romance and kinship. Both these chapters provide a model for how queer content and graphic forms are not in fact at odds with ELA standards and instruction.

The next chapter grouping shifts in focus to spotlight verse novels. In chapter 5, shea wesley martin centers queerness and verse as the key to dreaming and going "beyond." Building on queer and liberatory pedagogies, they offer a blueprint not only for teaching the text, but also for cocreating a container with students that centers joy, wholeness, and the brilliant nuance of our students. In chapter 6, Ryan Burns offers approaches for using Candice Iloh's *Every Body Looking* as an exemplar to teach narrative structure that resists and breaks from the predictable pattern of linear unfolding of narrative so often seen in literature. To highlight Iloh's threading of narrative strands from different time periods and moments in the protagonist's life, the strategies included in this chapter invite students to identify, describe, and discuss the social worlds in which they participate.

From graphic novels to a play, chapter 7, by Terri Suico, offers approaches for examining issues of inclusion while also introducing or reinforcing ELA content such as symbolism and point of view. Additionally, the chapter shares adaptations of *The Prom* in different media as a means to provide opportunities for students to consider how each adaptation shapes and changes the story based on the medium's capabilities and intended audience.

The guiding theme of the next four chapters is magical realism and mystery. In chapter 8, Summer Melody Pennell suggests approaches for exploring the author's craft, imagery, and the analysis of a fairy-tale retelling and remix. In chapter 9, Scott Storm focuses on building close reading as literary practice. Included are activities such as a cognitive apprenticeship, queering the Socratic Seminar, academic literary conferences, a speculative worlds' fair, or a Fascinators-inspired drag ball. In chapter 10, Danelle Adeniji, Brittany Frieson, Tatyana Jimenez-Macias, Kristin Rasbury, Kyle Wright, and Amanda E. Vickery bring together abolitionist orientations of teaching, centering Black queer voices, and disrupting traditional notions of English language arts through activities that explore characterization, the historical basis of spiritually and astrology, and advocating for queer intersectional identity safe spaces. Lucy A. Garcia and Megan Lynn Isaac close this thematic grouping with "*Felix Ever After*: A Mystery in Progress." In chapter 11, students learn about the genre of mystery and how the tools employed to solve mysteries can also be used to deepen literary analysis. Special attention is paid to allusions, foil characters, and first-person narration.

Our collection ends with chapters that explore the theme of identity. In chapter 12, Gabriel T. Acevedo Velázquez guides students through the difference between identity markers put upon us by others and how we can navigate in self-discovery. In chapter 13, Anthony Celaya and Joseph D. Sweet highlight the dangers of assumptions and stereotypes to frame student analysis and offer approaches that guide students in the exploration of different multimodal texts they consume and produce in and out of school. Closing out this volume is chapter 14 by E. Sybil Durand. This chapter highlights multiple ways that students can engage the sociocultural contexts of a story by focusing on the literary elements of characterization and setting. Through this focus, students consider the characters' identities as multidimensional and contextual, encouraging them to reflect on and analyze the intersections of sexuality, race, socioeconomic class, religion, and mental health.

A NOTE TO READERS

Throughout this collection, authors use the term *secondary* as opposed to middle school or high school, this is intentional as even though some YA literature is often associated with specific grade levels, we have known many teachers who have used these texts across all grade levels. We also refrain from specifying specific reading levels for any of the texts discussed as we have found assigning Lexile and grade levels to be restrictive without adding any benefits. We intentionally leave those types of decisions to our teacher readers who know their students best. Similarly, although the pedagogical approaches offered within chapters align with current English language arts and Literacy standards, we eschewed referencing any specific ones as lists of standards can become unwieldy in texts and because teachers can easily determine how activities meet their local requirements.

REFERENCES

Blackburn, M. V., & McCready, L. T. (2009). Voices of queer youth in urban schools: Possibilities and limitations. *Theory into Practice, 48*(3), 222–230.

Burns, K. (2021, Mar 31). The Republican attack on trans kids' health care, explained. *Vox*. https://www.vox.com/22360030/trans-kids-health-care-arkansas-explained.

Durand, E. S. (2015). At the intersections of identity: Race and sexuality in LGBTQ young adult literature. In D. L. Carlson & Linville (Eds.), *Beyond borders: Queer eros and ethos (ethics) in LGBTQ young adult literature* (pp. 73–84). Peter Lang Publishing.

Garden, N. (2014). LGBTQ young adult literature: How it began, how it grew, and where it is now. *The ALAN Review, 41*(3), 79–83.

Greathouse, P., & DiCicco, M. (2016). Standing but not delivering: Preparing pre-service teachers to use LGBTQ young adult literature in the secondary English classroom. *Study and Scrutiny: Research on Young Adult Literature, 2*(1), 35–52.

Greathouse, P., Eisenbach, B., & Kaywell, J. F. (2018). *Queer adolescent literature as a complement to the English language arts curriculum.* Rowman & Littlefield.

Kokozos, M., & Gonzalez, M. (2020). Critical inclusion: Disrupting LGBTQ normative frameworks in school contexts. *Equity & Excellence in Education, 52*(4), 1–14.

Malo-Juvera, V. (2016). The effect of an LGBTQ themed literary instructional unit on adolescents' homophobia. *Study and Scrutiny: Research on Young Adult Literature, 2*(1), 1–34.

Miller, C. (2019). Being a radical pragmatist: Reflections on introducing LGBTQ YA lit to an ELA department. *English Leadership Quarterly, 41*(3), 5–8.

Miller, S. J. (2016). Why a queer literacy framework matters: Models for sustain (a) gender self-determination and justice in today's schooling practices. In S. J. Miller (Ed.), *Teaching, affirming and recognizing trans and gender creative youth: A queer literacy framework* (pp. 25–45). Palgrave.

Monet, A. (2019, Nov 04). Queer love interest of color and the white gaze. *Medium.* https://ashiamonetb.medium.com/queer-love-interests-of-color-and-the-white-gaze-8928b7b5e6ad.

Reid, S. (2020, Oct 15). There's more to our lives: Reflecting on the materials we select to "culturally relevantize" our curricula. *Green Schools National Network.* https://greenschoolsnationalnetwork.org/theres-more-to-our-lives-reflecting-on-the-materials-we-select-to-culturally-relevantize-our-curricula/.

Thein, A. H. (2013). Language arts teachers' resistance to teaching LGBT literature and issues. *Language Arts, 90*(3), 169–180.

Villarreal, D. (2020, Sep 29). LGBTQ themes found in half of the past decade's twenty most-banned books. *NBC.* https://www.nbcnews.com/feature/nbc-out/lgbtq-themes-found-half-past-decade-s-20-most-banned-n1241353.

Chapter 1

The History of Queer Young Adult Literature

Michael Cart and Joan F. Kaywell

The field of young adult (YA) literature with lesbian, gay, bisexual, transgender, questioning or queer, intersex, asexual, and so on, standing for all of the other sexualities, sexes, and genders not included in LGBTQIA+ content, began with the publication of a single book, John Donovan's (1969) *I'll Get There. It Better Be Worth the Trip.* Coincidentally, Donovan's novel was published in the same year as the Stonewall Riots, which launched the Gay Rights Movement. The story of two thirteen-year-old friends—Davy, the book's protagonist, and Altschuler, his schoolmate—offers a tentative examination of their relationship, which includes a kiss and perhaps more, though the latter is carefully veiled. This was true of any sexual content in early queer YA literature. Subsequently, Davy's beloved dog Fred is run over by a car, and Davy blames his activity with Altschuler as being the cause. Fred's fate and Davy's reaction introduce an unfortunate leitmotif that haunted early queer YA literature: death—often in an automobile accident—and the seeming punishment of the presumably gay or lesbian character for his or her actions.

1970s' YA QUEER BOOKS: DOOM, GLOOM, OR "IT'S JUST A PHASE"

The publication of Donovan's novel, while historic, did not open the floodgates to queer YA literature, and only eight such novels appeared throughout the entire decade of the 1970s. Perhaps the most significant of these was Isabelle Holland's (1972) novel *The Man without a Face*, the story of fourteen-year-old Chuck who develops a crush on his gay tutor, Mr.

McLeod. The "man without a face," later played by a resolutely straight Mel Gibson (1993) in the film of the same name, was badly disfigured as the result of, yes, an automobile accident in which one of his male students was killed. The unfortunate implication when reading this novel is that the only good homosexual is a dead one. Sandra Scoppettone's (1974) *Trying Hard to Hear You* has a gay character involved in a scandal who also dies in a car crash. Rosa Guy's (1976) *Ruby* introduced another unfortunate theme that would haunt the literature for at least another decade—the notion that homosexuality is nothing to be concerned about because "it's just a phase." Aside from this dubious distinction, the novel is significant for two other reasons: it is the first to feature a lesbian relationship and the first to feature characters of color, something that would not recur for some fifteen years until the publication of Jacqueline Woodson's (1991) *The Dear One*. Again, "it's just a phase" is the message in Mary W. Sullivan's (1976) *What's This about Pete?* Another vehicle accident is the denouement of Lynn Hall's (1977) *Sticks and Stones*, though the person killed this time is not the gay character but, rather, his tormenter. Scoppettone's (1978) second novel with queer content *Happy Endings Are All Alike* also features violence perpetrated on a homosexual character, a lesbian this time, who is savagely raped because of her sexual orientation by a clearly sociopathic teenage boy. Deborah Hautzig's *Hey, Dollface* (1978), featuring two girls exploring their feelings for each other, is the same old story: are they gay or is this just a passing phase—probably the latter. Finally, the other significant novel in this decade is M. E. Kerr's (1977) *I'll Love You When You're More Like Me*. Here the gay character is not, for the first time, a troubled protagonist but an out, well-adjusted gay secondary character, the best friend of the straight protagonist. Such a relationship would not recur to any degree for some decades. The second significant feature of this book is its humor, the first to feature such a tone, the other novels of the 1970s being largely distinguished by their *Sturm und Drang* content and tone. It would be eleven years before humor would again distinguish a queer book, Ron Koertge's (1988) novel *The Arizona Kid*.

In retrospect, the novels of the 1970s established the situations and attitudes that would become stereotypical in the years to come: it is dangerous to be queer, one is punished for being queer, queer relationships are bound to end badly, being queer is just a phase, and so forth. The condition of being queer was, to put it simply, a problem and the novels featuring such protagonists quickly became one-issue problem novels as evidenced in Hanckel and Cunningham's (1976) article, "Can Young Gays Find Happiness in YA Books?" These stereotypical situations would continue until the publication of Aidan Chambers' (1982) work of literary fiction, *Dance on My Grave*.

Chambers' novel was a bit of an anomaly, since few other novels to follow could claim that literary mantel; it was not until the publication of Chambers' (1999) novel *Postcards from No Man's Land* that non-stereotypical literary fiction became a staple part of queer literature.

1980s YA QUEER BOOKS: LOVE, QUEER ADULTS, AND SECONDARY CHARACTERS

Significant advances marked the decade of the 1980s in queer literature. The number of titles published, for example, increased appreciably to thirty-six, though the quality of content did not necessarily match this increased pace of publication. Two exceptions stand out, however: Chambers' *Dance on My Grave* (cited above) and Nancy Garden's (1982) groundbreaking, now classic *Annie on My Mind*, the first lesbian love story with a happy ending; indeed, the first queer novel to dramatically demonstrate that homosexuality is not simply about sex but also, more importantly, about love. Another distinguished novel that stressed the aspect of love appeared at the end of the decade with Francesca Lia Block's (1989) luminous *Weetzie Bat*. In this one, the eponymous protagonist's best friends, Dirk and Duck, are in a love relationship that, though challenged, ends happily, making it the first novel in which a gay (male) relationship ends on a positive note.

This decade also marked the first appearance of queer adult characters, both parents and teachers. In the 1970s, with one exception, it was always the protagonist who was struggling with his/her sexuality. In the 1980s, however, it was, as often as not, a secondary character who was queer and often that character was an adult. The context for the parents' coming out was usually an acrimonious divorce that left the always straight teen protagonists caught in the middle as in Norma Klein's (1980) *Breaking Up*. As for teachers, their appearances were stereotypical as in Gary W. Bargar's (1981) *What Happened to Mr. Forster?* where the teacher is fired for being gay; also note that two female teachers in *Annie on My Mind* were also fired.

Two other noteworthy firsts marked this decade: the publication of the first queer sports story, Anne Snyder's (1981) *Counter Play*, and the appearance of the first AIDS novel, M. E. Kerr's (1986) *Night Kites*. Another first that became a common trope of queer YA literature in the 1980s was the female protagonist who discovers that her boyfriend is gay. This revelation would not be dealt with equanimity until the twenty-first century. As for the "Ls," in LGBTQIA+, lesbians did not fare well in the 1980s. They are represented in only nine of the decade's thirty-six queer YA novels and of that number, only one, *Annie on My Mind*, treated them positively.

NINETIES YA QUEER BOOKS: SECONDARY CHARACTERS, COMING OUT, AND BISEXUALITY

The 1990s also saw a significant increase in the number of queer YA novels published, seventy-five to be exact. Virtually, in the majority of these novels, the "problem" encountered by the closeted queer characters was always whether or not or how to come out; this would remain a fixture of the literature throughout this decade. Interestingly, in only twenty books was the protagonist the character dealing with this issue; the rest were supporting characters. Indeed, of the seventy-five books with queer content, fifty featured secondary characters and only eighteen of the seventy-five featured lesbians; unfortunately, this disparity has continued to the present day. Aside from the sheer volume of queer YA books published, the 1990s largely replicated the issues and tropes of the 1980s. The decade was distinguished, however, by the publication of a handful of significant titles worth mentioning: Jacqueline Woodson's (1991) *The Dear One* (see above); Kate Walker's (1993) *Peter*, the first queer novel to be imported from Australia; Marion Dane Bauer's (1994) *Am I Blue?* a landmark collection of sixteen short stories with queer content; Theresa Nelson's (1994) *Earthshine*, one of the small handful of exemplary AIDS novels; Francesca Lia Block's (1995) *Baby Bebop*, which presents the queer character Dirk's back story; R. J. Hamilton's (1995) *Who Framed Lorenzo Garcia?* the first queer novel with a Latino character; M. E. Kerr's (1997) *"Hello," I Lied*, the first novel with a bisexual character; Stephen Chbosky's (1999) *The Perks of Being a Wallflower*, a tender epistolary novel that has become a cult classic; and Ellen Wittlinger's (1999) *Hard Love*, which was selected as a Printz Honor title the first year this prestigious award was presented.

YA QUEER BOOKS IN THE TWENTY-FIRST-CENTURY COME OF AGE

At the turn of the century, the larger field of YA literature entered a new golden age and many of its distinguishing hallmarks were replicated in queer YA literature. Among the hallmarks: Crossover titles, books that appealed to both teens and YAs in their twenties, began appearing. Linda Newbery's (2002) *The Shell House*, Garret Freymann-Weyr's (2002) Printz Honor winner *My Heartbeat*, and Peter Cameron's (2007) *Someday This Pain Will Be Useful to You* fall into this category. Another singular book belonging in this category is David Levithan's (2003) *Boy Meets Boy*, a lovely novel positing a wonderfully offbeat world in which homosexuality is simply accepted as a matter of no consequence.

Following the larger YA field's lead, an impressive total of thirty-six novels came to America from abroad. Most came from Anglophone countries, that is, England, Australia, New Zealand, and Canada, though one came from Germany—Andreas Steinhofel's (2005) *The Center of the World*—a novel that also was an example of both literary and crossover fiction.

Numerous historical novels with queer content began appearing, too: Catherine Jinks' (2004) *Pagan in Exile*, set in the twelfth-century France; George Ella Lyon's (2004) *Sonny's House of Spies*, set in the 1950s America; and Pat Lowery Collins' (2009) *Hidden Voices*, set in the eighteenth-century Venice, to name a few. Queer novels in verse also began appearing, examples being Sonya Sones' (2004) *One of Those Hideous Books Where the Mother Dies* and David Levithan's (2004) *The Realm of Possibility*. Finally, the first transgender character also emerged with Julie Anne Peters' (2004) publication *Luna*.

As all of these categories suggest, queer YA fiction was flourishing; its number alone—252 such novels were published—is impressive. While many of these remained traditional coming-out stories, a growing number of queer books described life after coming out and featured characters who "just happened" to be gay and whose homosexuality was only one aspect of their character. Queer fiction does not exist in a vacuum; it reflects the changing realities of life in the real world. An example of this is the cautious emergence of novels featuring younger queer characters found in books like Alex Sanchez's (2004) *So Hard to Say*, which features a middle school teen and Lisa Jahn-Clough's (2004) *Country Girl, City Girl*, with a thirteen-year-old protagonist. The sexual abuse of boys emerged as a feature of queer literature, too, with five such books appearing during this period, most notably Alex Sanchez's (2009) *Bait*. Finally, novels began, for the first time, putting queer characters in a community of similar others; books like Alex Sanchez' *Rainbow Boys* trilogy, Maureen Johnson's (2007) *The Bermudez Triangle*, and Brent Hartinger's (2004) *The Geography Club* are examples of this salutary innovation.

YA QUEER BOOKS IN THE TEEN YEARS OF THE TWENTY-FIRST CENTURY: GROWTH, CHANGE, AND INNOVATION

In terms of growth, consider that the period 2010–2016 saw the publication of a prodigious total of 592 queer books, a veritable tsunami of titles. Part of this phenomenon is due to the entrance into the field of several niche publishers who exclusively feature queer books: Bold Strokes (debuting in 2010), Tiny Satchel Press (2011), and Harmony Ink (2012). The sheer number of titles shows a growing market for queer fiction and, it would seem, the ever-higher profile of queer people in the United States, much of this due to the increasing presence of television programs like *Queer As Folk, The L Word*, and, especially, *Will and Grace*. It is interesting to note that 170 of these novels feature queer characters who are already out of the closet (like Will).

This decade also featured a rapidly growing number of bisexual characters and a relatively prodigious number of transgender characters; indeed, fiction with transgender characters emerged as one of the hottest trends in queer fiction. Other innovations worthy of mention are the increasing number of novels featuring same-sex parents; often these are women but a growing handful of titles feature men, for example, Will Walton's (2015) *Anything Could Happen* and Ellen Wittlinger's (2016) *Local Girl Swept Away*. In the wake of the Supreme Court's legalizing of gay marriage in 2015, we will begin to see more examples of books like Richard Peck's (2016) *The Best Man*. There is the emergence, too, of humorous queer novels, a happy change from the dour literature of preceding years. In fact, some twenty-two examples of this trend including *The Best Man* (see above) appeared from 2010 to 2016.

Another significant trend is the growing emergence of speculative fiction instead of the traditional form of contemporary realism with queer content: examples include Andrew Smith's (2014) *Grasshopper Jungle*, Rainbow Rowell's (2015) antic *Carry On* (also an example of humor), and Holly Black's (2015) *The Darkest Part of the Forest*. One other especially salutary change has been the belated appearance of characters of color; Black, Latino/a, and Asian characters are becoming fixtures of the literature. In this, we have moved beyond the tokenism of earlier years to a demonstration of embracing community. Similarly, the number of books featuring characters from abroad has continued to grow; twenty-one such books appeared during this period with characters coming from countries as diverse as Iran, Pakistan, Armenia, Germany, and more.

The continued growth of literary fiction is another feature of this period; for example, Jandy Nelson's (2014) *I'll Give You the Sun* received the 2015 Printz Award, while Becky Albertalli's (2015) *Simon vs. the Homo Sapiens Agenda* received the 2016 William C. Morris Award as the best first novel of the year. Younger protagonists continued to appear in books like Richard Peck's *The Best Man* (see above), Tim Federle's (2013, 2014) *Better Nate than Ever* and *Five, Six, Seven, Nate!*, respectively, and Alex Gino's (2015) *George*.

Unfortunately, one aspect of queer fiction has remained constant: the imbalance between gay and lesbian fiction (roughly two to one). Nevertheless, the teen years of this decade are distinguished by the salutary nature of innovations, changes, and, yes, examples of welcome continuity. Altogether, they evidence that, at last, queer literature has become one of the moment, commanding a place at the center stage of YA literature. To paraphrase John Donovan, we've gotten there and it has definitely been worth the trip.

REFERENCES

Albertalli, B. (2015). *Simon vs. the Homo sapiens agenda.* HarperCollins.

Bargar, G. W. (1981). *What happened to Mr. Forster?* Clarion Books.

Bauer, M. D. (1994). *Am I blue?* HarperCollins.

Black, H. (2015). *The darkest part of the forest.* Little Brown.

Block, F. L. (1989). *Weetzie bat.* HarperCollins.

Block, F. L. (1995). *Baby Bebop.* HarperCollins.

Cameron, P. (2007). *Someday this pain will be useful to you.* Delacorte.

Chambers, A. (1982). *Dance on my grave.* Bodley Head/Penguin Random House.

Chambers, A. (1999). *Postcards from no man's land.* Bodley Head/Penguin Random House.

Chbosky, S. (1999). *The perks of being a wallflower.* Simon & Schuster.

Collins, P. L. (2009). *Hidden voices.* Candlewick.

Donovan, J. (1969). *I'll get there. It better be worth the trip.* Harper & Row.

Federle, T. (2013). *Better Nate than ever.* Simon & Schuster.

Federle, T. (2014). *Five, six, seven, Nate!* Simon & Schuster.

Freymann-Weyr, G. (2002). *My heartbeat.* Houghton Mifflin.

Garden, N. (1982). *Annie on my mind.* Farrar, Straus and Giroux.

Gino, A. (2015). *George.* Scholastic.

Guy, R. (1976). *Ruby.* Viking.

Hall, L. (1977). *Sticks and stones.* Wilcox & Follett.

Hamilton R. J. (1995). *Who framed Lorenzo Garcia?* Alyson.

Hanckel, F. & Cunningham, J. (1976). Can young gays find happiness in YA books? *Wilson Library Bulletin, 50*(7), 528–534.

Hartinger, B. (2003). *The geography club.* HarperCollins.

Hautzig, D. (1978). *Hey, dollface.* Greenwillow Books.

Holland, I. (1972). *The man without a face.* J.B. Lippincott.

Jahn-Clough, L. (2004). *Country girl, city girl.* Houghton Mifflin.

Jinks, C. (2004). *Pagan in exile.* Candlewick.

Johnson, M. (2004). *The Bermudez triangle.* Penguin Young Readers Group.

Kerr, M. E. (1977). *I'll love you when you're more like me.* Harper & Row.

Kerr, M. E. (1986). Harper & Row.

Kerr, M. E. (1997). *"Hello," I lied.* HarperCollins.

Klein, N. (1980). *Breaking up.* Alfred Knopf, Inc.

Koertge, R. (1988). *The Arizona kid.* Little Brown.

Levithan, D. (2003). *Boy meets boy.* Alfred Knopf, Inc.

Levithan, D. (2004). *The realm of possibility.* Alfred Knopf, Inc.

Lyon, G. E. (2004). *Sonny's house of spies.* Atheneum.

Nelson, J. (2014). *I'll give you the sun.* Penguin Young Readers Group.

Nelson, T. (1994). *Earthshine.* Hachette Children's Group.

Newbery, L. (2002). *The shell house.* Random House.

Peck, R. (2016). *The best man.* Dial Books for Young Readers.

Peters, J. A. (2004). *Luna.* Little Brown.

Rowell, R. (2015). *Carry on.* St. Martin's Griffin.

Sanchez, A. (2009). *Bait.* Simon & Schuster.

Sanchez, A. (2004). *So hard to say.* Simon & Schuster.

Sanchez, A. (2010). *Rainbow road.* Simon & Schuster.

Sanchez, A. (2011a). *Rainbow boys.* Simon & Schuster.

Sanchez, A. (2011b). *Rainbow high.* Simon & Schuster.

Scoppettone, S. (1974). *Trying hard to hear you.* Harper & Row.

Scoppettone, S. (1978). *Happy endings are all alike.* Harper & Row.

Smith, A. (2014). *Grasshopper jungle.* E. P. Dutton.

Snyder, A. (1981). *Counter play.* New American Library.

Sones, S. (2004). *One of those hideous books where the mother dies.* Simon & Schuster.

Steinhofel, A. (2005). *The center of the world.* Delacorte.

Sullivan, M. W. (1976). *What's this about Pete?* E. P. Dutton.

Walker, K. (1993). *Peter.* Houghton Mifflin.

Walton, W. (2015). *Anything could happen.* Scholastic.

Wittlinger, E. (1999). *Hard love.* Simon & Schuster.

Wittlinger, E. (2016). *Local girl swept away.* Simon & Schuster.

Woodson, J. (1991). *The dear one.* Delacorte.

Chapter 2

Rhetorical Analysis of Black Queer Narratives through *All Boys Aren't Blue*

LaMar Timmons-Long

Literature is a powerful tool that can be used for students to see themselves, gain access to other worlds different than their own, and also imagine the unknown and the possibilities that can transform a young person's mind (Bishop, 1990). As such, the English classroom can be a space to read and discuss multiple narratives of Black Indigenous People of Color (BIPOC), especially BIPOC Queer narratives. Black Queer narratives convey themes like the hero's journey, friendship, self-discovery, and joy, while dealing with the intersections of Blackness and Queerness. Therefore, Black Queer narratives should be included in and studied throughout all English curriculums. Through the inclusion of Black Queer narratives, both fiction and nonfiction, teens are given an opportunity to discover and unpack the intersections of race, gender, and sexuality of Black Queer people. However, when using Black Queer narratives in the English classroom, it is imperative that teachers center the authentic experiences filled with affirmation and liberation rather than solely focusing on pain (Reid, 2020).

All Boys Aren't Blue (2020) is a young adult "memoir-manifesto" that captures the experiences of George M. Johnson as he paints a vivid picture of his life as a young Black Queer kid growing toward adulthood. Using his life as a focal point, Johnson's text provides readers with an insight into his life and identity journey as a Black Queer youth.

Since this text is nonfiction, teachers can utilize it to move students from foundational English skills toward taking a deeper look into an author's language and purpose in writing, specifically, a rhetorical reading and analysis. Through the reading of this text, students are able to reflect on, discuss, and write about the language Johnson uses to express the beauty of Black Queer voices.

SUMMARY OF *ALL BOYS AREN'T BLUE*

George M. Johnson writes his "memoir-manifesto" in first person giving a first telling account of his life growing up as a Black Queer kid turned adult with a supportive family in New Jersey. Throughout the text, he describes in detail his life growing up as Black and Queer in America. The novel starts with early memories of being bullied as a child, spending time with his family, especially his beloved Nanny. Johnson's writing directly addresses the intersections of race, gender, masculinity, and manhood throughout the stories shared in his book. Johnson is honest in discussing how he worked through his identity as a Black Queer man, discussing his innermost feeling and experiences during his lifetime. Johnson discusses moments and experiences such as spending time with his cousins, "coming out" to friends and family, and pledging his fraternity in college while using Black Queer language with phrases such "honey child." Each piece of his story is personal, giving the reader an opportunity to understand and connect to his journey as a Black Queer man navigating life in America.

BEFORE READING *ALL BOYS AREN'T BLUE*

A Note to Teachers

For years, I have used the term brave spaces (Arao & Clemens, 2013) in my classroom with my students because I want them to know that our classroom is the space to interrogate, make mistakes, and grow; it is a pro-BIPOC and pro-LGBTQ space where we intentionally listen to each other and take risk with our thinking and learning. When facilitating identity work, the educator should make the space welcoming and hold everyone accountable for the work. Therefore, establishing community norms is essential and having a discussion about those norms is necessary for the work ahead. Examples of community norms include treat everyone with respect; listen to the language of your peers; maintain and respect confidentiality; step out of your comfort zone; use "I" statements when speaking from experience. After norms have been shared, have students discuss them in small groups followed by a whole group share-out, thus, moving toward mutual respect for all learning in the space. To add, throughout the book, Johnson does discuss sexual assault in the book. Therefore, teachers should make sure they have created a space to have a conversation around the sensitive topic.

Identity Work

Throughout *All Boys Aren't Blue*, Johnson writes about his experience and journey with identity. In reading this text, it is important for educators and students to notice and interrogate their own identities and how these identities show up in the world. *All Boys Aren't Blue* works to affirm and support Black Queer youth; however, anyone reading this novel can find themselves in the characters and their own journey of identity throughout the pages. Therefore, before educators begin to read this novel with students, all parties should be aware of their own identities and the language we use to describe our identities. This activity is twofold and takes two or more days depending on how the educator would like to facilitate this process. Overall, the goal is for the students to think and reflect on their individual identities while also listening closely to others' identities. Specifically, throughout this exercise, teachers should have students pay attention to the rhetoric (language and word choice) people are using to describe themselves.

Ask students to brainstorm questions they would ask when trying to get to know something about someone whether that person be a friend, colleague, classmate, or celebrity. Then, have students consider what identity aspect each question is relating to. For instance, "what do you do in your free time?" could relate to many identities someone holds like a gamer, athlete, or artist. Then, have students consider where that identity is acted the most. For instance, a gamer identity may be most activated while hanging out with friends. Finally, have students create a wheel with all the questions, identities, and locations on it. This wheel will serve the next round of the activity.

Drawing on the community norms that have been established, students can begin to explore the identities of characters from a novel, short story, and/or film they have previously read in class or independently. Students are able to go through the identity thinking process of something familiar before they potentially work on their own identities and listen to their peers. However, students may opt out of completing a personal identity wheel. If that does happen, working a character from different pieces of literature will be just as important. Here students can notice and discuss the commonalities and differences they share. Start off with discussing something accessible such as a favorite song or personal interest. The activity can serve as an ice breaker for students to discover and hear how they are similar and different from each other. Teachers can participate in these activities as well as this work can be fun and engaging for all participants. As such, allot time and space for students to do this work individually, in partners, and in small groups. Throughout the class period, give students time to sit with themselves and complete a personal identity wheel. Once students are finished completing the personal identity wheel, place them in small groups of two to four and have them share. Teachers can follow this with a whole class share out. Some guiding questions that teachers can pose could be: *How did your partners describe themselves? What language did your partners use to describe themselves? Was this language positive or negative? How could you tell? What parts of identity were similar and different? How did you feel about sharing your personal identity?*

Teachers should express that students listen authentically and intentionally, paying attention to language their classmates have used in their responses. By asking these questions, you are preparing students for the work that is to come during the other activities for the novel because students are listening for the language that their partners are using to describe identity. Furthermore, since students are focusing on the description of language, it can help them transition to thinking rhetorically when reading *All Boys Aren't Blue*.

Once that activity is completed, students can work on their social identity wheel. The personal identity wheel may be a heavy topic(s) for students to explore; you will want to return and remind students of the community norms established as this process will follow a similar, or the same, structure as before. However, this time you want to ask students to pay attention to the rhetoric connected to social identity. Questions you may consider asking the group: *How do people talk about and describe themselves? Others? What word choices do they use? How does that word choice convey the significance and importance of one's identity?* Students can be given the opportunity to write their responses down and/or share out with the whole group. At the end of the activity, the goal is for students to be prepared to analyze and discuss social identity, which is how society identifies based on their various groups and personal identity, as well as how an individual identitifies themselves in regard to language use throughout *All Boys Aren't Blue*.

Black Queer Representation

Throughout the memoir, Johnson discusses his life as a Black Queer kid by using queer language such as "Honeychild" (p. 57), "Shade and yaaassss" (p.58), and "Black femme" (p.58) as well as share key experiences that have shaped him as a human being. Johnson gives the reader insight to an aspect of Black Queerness. Yet, Black Queer people can be seen in many different perspectives and students should be privy to their many dimensions. Therefore, to give students access to the many narratives of Black Queer people, teachers could show students clips from television shows and films. Students could participate in a jigsaw activity where they would watch various shows and films that depict the versatility of Black Queerness. Have students look closely at the language these characters use to describe, support, and affirm each other.

TV shows/Film:

- *Pose* (2019): Season 2, Episode—"Never Knew Love Like This Before"—This episode deals with the character Candy, a Black trans woman who is inferred to be murdered. It shows her community showing up and supporting her and her family. Students can examine tonal shifts for example movements of mourning at the funeral to moments of joy with her chosen family.
- *Master of None* (2017): Season 2, Episode 8—This episode discusses Denise's, a Black Queer woman and a secondary character in the show "coming out" to her family during the holidays. Students can focus on the way Denise speaks about herself compared to how her family speaks about her.
- *Moonlight* (2016): Oscar award–winning film that depicts the life of two young Black men coming to terms with what it means to be Black Queer men throughout childhood, teenage years, and adulthood. This film is connected to multiple rhetorical strategies including tone, imagery, and word choice.
- *Naz and Maalik* (2015): This film is about young Black Queer Muslim boys living in New York City as they navigate homophobia and Islamophobia while trying to come to terms with their emerging identities.

Following the viewing of these visual texts, teachers could ask students the following:

- How do these characters use language to discuss their experience as a Black and Queer person?
- How do Black Queer people build community with each other?
- How do Black Queer people view racial and sexual identity?
- In what ways do Black Queer people resist systems that harm them?
- How do Black Queer people interact with biological family and how do they create chosen family?

Students could watch their own clips individually and respond to the questions. In turn, students could be paired with groups with different clips to share their responses and discoveries followed by a whole group share-out. The class can also respond to the following writing prompt: *What have you learned about the experiences and language of Black Queer people in America?* The purpose of these activities is to foster students' critical thinking and questions they may have about Black Queer narratives. Also, students should be able to determine commonalities and notice the nuances of Black Queer lives such as the use of language, race, gender, joy, and liberation.

In English classrooms, when students are provided with clear and authentic examples of Black Queerness, the potential to engage in the internal and external work of interrogating, unlearning, and relearning the truths about this group of people has the potential to occur. Johnson references feeling "different" when describing himself; he also uses Black Queer language to describe and discuss gender and sexuality such as "Cishst" (p.58), "Queer" (p. 140), and "transgender" (p. 172). Therefore, these clips are both a mirror for Black Queer students to affirm their identity and a window (Bishop, 1990) into a world for those who are new to understanding the Black Queer community and the language used toward each other to describes ourselves and others.

WHILE READING *ALL BOYS AREN'T BLUE*

Rhetorical Reading and Rhetorical Analysis

While reading the text, the teacher should inform students that they are reading closely to determine Johnson's purpose for writing the memoir, including how he uses language and word choice to convey his message around identity and how he uses rhetorical strategies to engage readers. Essentially, rhetoric is "the study of language and the study of how to use it" (Selzer, 2003, p. 280). Typically, students study reading and writing rhetorically in the latter years of their secondary education. However, learning the skill of determining an author's rhetoric, looking closely at their language and word choice and the writing moves made, can and should happen in the earlier years. This focus can be a way to teach students how to read texts such as film or books from another lens as seen in the before reading activity.

Rhetorical Reading Activities

Lamb (2010) explained that rhetorical reading is a way for students to focus on the author's purpose and the text when reading nonfiction texts such as *All Boys Aren't Blue*. Teachers often have students read literature to focus on character development; however, rhetorical reading helps students to make the shift from *what* to looking at *how* the author is delivering their content (Lamb, 2010). This is not always an easy shift to make for students; yet it will foster students' ability to think deeply about how the writers are developing a topic. For example, when reading *All Boys Aren't Blue*, students can begin to think about how Johnson explores the essence of Black Queerness with family and society.

To help students with practicing this shift from reading for the "what" to more rhetorical reading of the "how" students can practice with the introduction of *All Boys Aren't Blue* using the Tone Discovery activity. Students read the introduction of the text and while reading, look closely at his words choice to determine the different tone(s) the writer creates and explore how the writer's diction supports such tone. With this activity, teachers may want to provide students with a mini-lesson on tone and diction with examples. For example, tone is a writer's attitude toward their subject matter revealed through the use of diction, figurative language, and organization. To identify the tone, the reader should think about how the piece would sound if read aloud. Examples of tone: playful, serious, formal, sarcastic. Yet the tone is determined by the author's diction (formal or informal), figurative language (metaphor, imagery), or organization of the text such as chronological or cause and effect. Since rhetorical reading is a different approach to reading nonfiction and analyzing text, these activities help students to transition to paying close attention to the "moves" the writer is making throughout the text. Double journaling (see figure 2.1) is a strategy that students could use to take notes about the tone(s) and explain how the tone is conveyed or shifting from one to another. To guide students' thinking, the teacher could ask, *what word choices does Johnson use to convey various tones throughout the text? How does Johnson's word choice convey different tones in chapter____? Is there a pattern or a shift with tones?* On the left side of the graphic organizer, students can determine the term and place the quotes from the text and on the right, students can construct their response to the selected quotation.

By working through this activity, students should be able to notice and express how the author evokes tone and how the tone could potentially shift throughout the piece of writing, or how the writer creates clear patterns for certain tones. For example, in *Act 2: Family*, in the chapter *Dear Little Brother*, Johnson writes a letter to his little brother (p. 123). In the beginning, he starts off with a happy tone discussing their positive childhood memories and then shifts to toward a serious tone as he discusses how he defended him as children. Two other chapters where students can determine tonal shifts are *Chapter 7: Nanny: The Caregiver, the Hustler, My Best Friends* (p. 128)

Tone: Serious	
"This book is an exploration of two of my identifies- Black and Queer- and how I became aware of their intersections within myself and in society. How I've learned that neither of those identities can be contained within a simple box; and that I enter the room as both of them despite spaces and environments I must navigate." (p. 5)	Johnson explains the intersectionality of Blackness and Queerness. By his use of diction formal diction with words such as intersections, society, identities, he supports the idea that Black Queer people walk into spaces as their whole identity and should be to be freely expressed.

Figure 2.1   Double Journaling Example.

and *Chapter 16: Don't Know Why I Didn't Call* (p. 277). Students should have the space to work on an activity like this one in a collaborative manner because they can discuss their findings and support each other. Rhetorical reading does not have to happen in isolation; instead, students can be thought partners with each other and determine different strategies that convey the author's purpose and intent. Lastly, the double journaling activity can assist students with note-taking when reading. As such, students will have a plethora of evidence and analysis to use in their constructed responses.

Says/Does Analysis

Another activity that students can participate in while rhetorical reading is called Says/Does Analysis. While reading, students are encouraged to read closely and think about what different lines or passages from the text *does* as well as what it *says*. This can help students think about the language and word choice of the writer. Focusing on the writer's rhetoric, students should know that *says* means to summarize the content of the text and *does* describes how the writer constructed or organized the writing. Figure 2.2 provides an example of how this activity could be used in classrooms.

Rhetorical Envelope

Rhetorical appeals are strategies that writers use to draw in their audience. Johnson uses these appeals to convey various examples of language used throughout the Black Queer community. First, students should become

Paragraph(s) from Text	What the Paragraph *Says*	What the Paragraph *Does*
Agency- a word I didn't know when I was that young- is a guiding principle that I wish we taught young kids more…. I would love for us to ask the deeper questions about who and what they are. (p. 49)	The writer is asking for people to allow children to explore their own identity outside of society's standards. They believe that children have the capacity of knowing themselves and their interest. In this example, he highlights clothing to express this idea. Therefore, we should give children the space to explore their identity.	In this paragraph, the author challenges adults by charging them to shift their thinking of heteronormative ways and give students the opportunity to be and dress how they feel.
The world gives you no breaks as a Black woman. I know it was likely even harder raising a Black queer kid in a society that already makes it difficult to raise a Black child without the additional marginalization. I know you knew from a very young age that I was going to be queer. From early on, you were putting the pieces in place to ensure that I had the community I would need when I got older. (p. 177)	The writer explores their appreciation for their mother and how crucial she was in creating a warm and accepting community for his as a Black queer kid. They believe that Black queer children need a support environment to flourish and come to terms with their identity.	The author implores that adults work hard to create safe spaces for Black queer children in their families and the community around them.

Figure 2.2   Say/Does Chart.

aware of the appeals: logos (logic-reasoning), ethos (character, ethics), and pathos (emotions). Learning and exploring rhetorical appeals can be a fun and engaging activity for students to determine the effect of language within literature. In groups, give students an envelope with various lines and passages from different places throughout the text. Students would read the line or passage and determine which rhetorical appeal matches and explain why. Have students consider the following question, *which rhetorical appeal is the writer using to convey his purpose?* Figure 2.3 offers rhetorical envelope examples.

Precis Paragraph

In English class, students should have multiple opportunities to engage in writing activities in response to literature. Students may be aware of constructing a summary paragraph with vivid details about the text. However, when looking at rhetoric, students construct precise paragraphs as summaries because they help students "read and listen" to what the author is saying but also this type of writing helps students "learn to read and listen to what others have to say with greater comprehension, to question and evaluate what they have read" (Lamb, 2010, p. 45). Students respond well to this type of writing because they can take their summary writing skills to another level. Through

Quote	Type of Appeal	Justification
I know as Black boys and men, we are not conditioned to share emotions in this way. So, for those who read this, I hope it will be an important display of love. (p. 123)	Pathos	Appeals to the readers emotions by discussing Black boys and men showing emotion within society.
My queer identity is a part of my Blackness, and you never made me separate the two. (p. 127)	Pathos	Appeals to readers emotions discussing Blackness and Queerness,
Although the national rate of homelessness for LGBTQIAP+ youth is near 40 percent the rate in my family has always been 0 percent. (p. 139)	Logos	Appeals to the readers logic using statistics such as 40%.
Secretly, I wanted to be like you... I was unsure if I was a boy or a girl or a science project, but I knew you existed, which meant that I, too, existed out there somewhere in whatever form that may be. (p. 165)	Ethos/Pathos	Appeals to either emotion or ethics as the writer talks about the feeling of being queer, learning and understanding their identity.

Figure 2.3   Rhetorical Envelope Examples.

Sentence 1: Name of author, genre, and title of work, date in parentheses; a rhetorically active verb (*such as claims, argues, asserts, defines, explores, or suggests*); and a "that" clause continuing the major assertion, main idea or thesis statement of work.

Ex: George Johnson, in their memoir "All Boys Aren't Blue" (2020) explores the intersections of race and gender identifies for Black Queer youth.

Sentence 2: An explanation of how the author develops and supports the thesis (i.e., evidence) usually in chronological order.

Ex: They supports their thesis by giving examples from their lived experiences as a Black Queer individual with family and friends.

Sentence 3: A statement of the author's apparent purpose, followed by an "in order to" phrase.

Ex: Johnson hopes to bring awareness to the Black Queer community in order to motivate others to appreciate and protect them.

Sentence 4: A description of the intended audience and/or the relationship the author establishes with the audience.

Ex: Their audience is the Queer community and other allies who wants to understand the intersections of race and gender.

Figure 2.4   Precise Paragraph Example (adapted from Lamb, 2010).

the use of this strategy, students are able to construct their writing around the writer's use of language. The first time trying this activity, students might struggle, but with multiple opportunities to practice and targeted feedback, students can excel in this type of writing. Have students select a chapter from the text to read and construct a precis paragraph to write about Johnson's intent or purpose. Figure 2.4 provides an example of what this precis paragraph might look like.

AFTER READING *ALL BOYS AREN'T BLUE*

Collaborative Rhetorical Analysis

Upon completion of the novel, it can be common practice for students to construct the standard five-paragraph essay where students are asked to respond to a question. While that form of foundational writing is essential, educators should rethink different writing tasks for students to engage in both independently and collaboratively.

At the close of the text, students can work on constructing a collaborative rhetorical analysis. An activity like this can help students apply all they have learned about rhetorical reading and rhetorical analysis. For example, the students can respond to this prompt, *write a response in which you analyze the rhetorical strategies George M Johnson uses to achieve his purpose for writing. Support your analysis with specific references to the text.* Together, students can work on constructing the introduction with a clear thesis describing three rhetorical strategies and the conclusion paragraphs. Individually, each student could construct a paragraph based on one of the rhetorical strategies. Questions for them to consider are *Consider how George uses language to describe himself throughout the novel and how that language changes. How do people use language to describe George throughout the novel? How does that change?* The collaborative rhetorical analysis challenges the standard five-paragraph essay narrative and focuses on targeted writing instruction for students. Furthermore, students are able to use any part of the memoir manifesto to write their responses.

BEYOND *ALL BOYS AREN'T BLUE*

In a pre-reading activity, students watched video clips of Black Queer representation on television and film before reading *All Boys Aren't Blue*. As a way to extend the learning of rhetorical reading and rhetorical analysis, students can read GLAAD's *Where Are We on TV Report* for the year 2020–2021 (Lasky, 2021). Throughout reading the document, students can select a show and then a character, watch clips or full episodes of the show and construct a rhetorical analysis.

To further develop the knowledge gained through the reading of Lasky's report, students can select and analyze a current film or television show with or about Black Queer characters. Have students watch the episode or film and construct a rhetorical analysis of the text. Students can compare and contrast the experiences of characters and language presented in the visual text to *All Boys Aren't Blue*.

CONCLUSION

As adolescent learners grow as critical thinkers and writers around the lives of Black Queer youth, it is important to provide authentic literature that speaks to the diverse experiences of these groups of people. Students should be afforded the opportunity to shift their thinking from *what* the text says to *how* the text conveys a message. Engaging students in rhetorical reading and writing using books such as *All Boys Aren't Blue* invites them to think about how an author uses language throughout their writing to send a message to readers. Also, this type of reading and writing prompts students to be reflective on how they use language in their own lives. *How do I support Black Queer students? What language am I using to affirm their lives? How do we create spaces for Black Queer students to live, speak and be free?*

REFERENCES

Arao, B., & Clemens, K. (2013). From safe spaces to brave spaces: A new way to frame dialogue around diversity and social justice. In L. M. Landreman (Ed.), *The art of effective facilitation: Reflections from social justice educators* (pp. 135–150). Stylus Publishing, LLC.

Bishop, R. S. (1990). Mirrors, windows, and sliding glass doors. *Perspectives, 6*(3), ix–xi.

Johnson, G. M. (2020). *All boys aren't blue.* Macmillan.

Lamb, M. R. (2010). Teaching nonfiction through rhetorical reading. *English Journal, 99*(4), 43–49.

Lasky, M. (2021). GLAAD'S where we are on TV 2020-2021 Report: Despite tumultuous year in television, LGBTQ representation holds steady. https://www .glaad.org/releases/glaads-where-we-are-tv-2020-2021-report-despite-tumultuous-year-television-lgbtq.

Reid, S. (2020). *There's more to our lives: Reflecting on the materials we select to "Culturally Relevantize" our curricula.* Green Schools National Network. https ://greenschoolsnationalnetwork.org/theres-more-to-our-lives-reflecting-on-the-ma terials-we-select-to-culturally-relevantize-our-curricula/.

Selzer, J. (2004). Rhetorical analysis: Understanding how texts persuade readers. In Charles Bazerman and Paul Prior (Eds.), *What writing does and how it does it: An introduction to analyzing texts and textual practices* (pp. 279–308). Routledge.

Chapter 3

Characterization and Symbolism in Superhero-Themed Graphic Novels with *You Brought Me the Ocean*

René M. Rodríguez-Astacio

The popularity of superhero stories has been on the rise during the last ten years due to the franchising of DC and Marvel's Cinematic Universes. Superhero-origin stories, in particular, open the grounds to explorations about identity, as they are often an allegory of going into a journey of finding oneself. These superheroes-origin stories are attractive to viewers, as it rouses cheers for a character in the margins of society to rise, save the day, and grow. For a person who identifies as a member of the LGBTQ community, this opportunity might present a mirror (Sims Bishop, 1990) in which they might apply a queer perspective and find queer kinship, similar to the scene in *Spider-Man: Into the Spiderverse* where all five Spider-people meet each other and happily exclaim, "You are like me!" (Kahn, 2018).

As such, texts featuring a teenage superhero's origin offer adolescent readers a bridge to critical and meaningful examinations of narratives of youths, such as navigating social expectations and their complexities, growing up and discovering their sense of self and desires, and becoming responsible and empathetic members of society. In the English Language Arts classroom, this lends itself to critical examinations of characterization, an important aspect of writing a superhero character. One such book, *You Brought Me the Ocean* (2020) by Alex Sánchez and illustrated by Julie Maroh, lends itself to the teaching of characterization and symbolism in the English Language Arts classroom as it humanizes Jake, also known as Aqualad in the DC Comics universe, whose hero's journey is tied to his developing identity as a gay African American teenager, and his relationship to his friends and family.

SUMMARY OF *YOU BROUGHT ME THE OCEAN*

You Brought Me the Ocean, written by Alex Sánchez and illustrated by Julie Maroh, is a graphic novel from DC's Ink imprint for young adult readers. It tells the story of Jake Hyde, known in the DC Universe as Aqualad, an African American high school senior from Truth or Consequences, New Mexico, who dreams to study oceanography. To do this, Jake applies to the University of Miami, a secret he keeps from his best friend and neighbor, Maria. Maria, who is a Mexican and Jake's classmate, wishes for them to apply to a university close to their hometown together. Jake's desire to leave the town and live close to the ocean also creates tension between him and his overprotective mother, as she too wishes Jake would attend college near his hometown because she fears bodies of water due to the drowning of Jake's father. As Jake keeps high hopes of being admitted to his dream university, he also keeps another secret from his mother and Maria: Jake is gay. One day, Jake notices one of his classmates, Kenny, who is a Chinese American and is part of the swimming team. During one of their classes, Zeke, a classmate, bullies Kenny for being gay. Kenny brushes off Zeke, as he is used to his sexuality as a point of conversation. Jake is fascinated by Kenny standing his ground and decides to approach him, planning a hike for them during the weekend to get to know each other. Jake keeps this information from Maria and lies that he will be spending the Saturday helping his mother at work.

During their hike, Jake asks Kenny how he found out he was gay, and Kenny shares his story with Jake. As the two boys talk about coming out and their families, Kenny asks why Jake always wears long-sleeved shirts. Jake explains that he wears them because he has birthmarks running along his arms that glow at the touch of water. At this, he adds that he has always felt different. Just then a sudden storm looms over the boys, flooding the valley they are in. As they struggle to reach a safe place away from the flood, Jake's powers awaken, and he can veer off the flood away from them. Kenny promises not to tell anyone about what he just witnessed. As the school year progresses, Jake falls in love with Kenny and has a falling out with his mom and Maria. Maria finds out Jake's secrets and is disillusioned that her best friend lied to her.

Similarly, Jake finds out the secret his mom has been keeping from him: his father never drowned, for he is Black Manta, who is now on the rise and possibly looking for Jake. Jake's mother panics and begins packing their car to run away. However, Jake is determined to face his problems and stop running from secrets. As such, Jake decides to come out to his mother, who accepts him unconditionally. Jake then sneaks out to see Kenny at the water grove but is found by the school bullies, who now know Jake is gay. Jake then summons his powers to defend himself and Kenny. Zeke takes a video of Jake and his powers before leaving and threatens to expose Jake to the entire world. Jake, however, declares he is ready to tackle whatever the world throws at him.

BEFORE READING *YOU BROUGHT ME THE OCEAN*

Superheroes in Popular Culture

With the current exposure of superhero cinematic universes, comics, trade paperbacks, manga, video games, and young adult novel adaptations, teachers can engage students in conversation about their understanding of what is a superhero before reading *You Brought Me the Ocean*. In doing so, students activate their schema about their exposure and conceptualization of superheroes and popular culture. For example, a student might bring up films like *Into The Spiderverse* or the recent cut of DC's *Justice League,* live-action and animated series, such as *WandaVision, Young Justice, Power Rangers, Raising Deon, Miraculous: Tales of Ladybug and Cat Noir*, and *Umbrella Academy*, the popular manga and its anime adaptation *My Hero Academia*, video games like *Marvel the Avengers* or *Marvel Ultimate Alliance 3*, comic book characters that are written with a young adult appeal, like *The Unbeatable Squirrel Girl* and *Moon Girl and the Devil Dinosaur*, and toys and collectibles such as Funko Pops, and even board games such as Thanos Rising and Marvel Villainous. There might even be students who write fanfiction or draw fanart. Inviting students to talk about their favorite superheroes or previous experiences when growing up not only allows students to examine the exposure of superheroes in popular media but taps into students' wealth of knowledge. This conversation can be complemented with the teacher bringing in clips of films or comics strips, or even task students.

Lastly, teachers can also work to conceptualize and humanize superheroes with their students. In many instances, superheroes are an allegory for social justice topics and their personal daily lives oftentimes reflect the human side of superheroes.

- What is a hero?
- What is a superhero? Do you think there is a difference between a hero and a superhero?
- What are the typical traits of a superhero?
- How do superheroes save the day?
- In which mediums can we see superheroes?
- Which superheroes do you know?
- Why are superheroes popular? Can you provide an example?
- Who gets to be a superhero?

Another aspect teachers can ask students to work on in preparation for reading the graphic novel is to research Jake Hyde and his journey as Aqualad. Jake is a fairly new character in the DC Universe, and he was first introduced in *Brightest Day* #4 in 2010, where Aquaman took Jake under his mantle. Prior to Jake, the title belonged to Garth, who later on became Tempest. With both Garth and Jake sharing the same alias yet having different backstories and power sets, students can track the difference between the two characters by creating character profiles. This is similar to both Miles Morales and Peter Parker being Spiderman in the Marvel universe. Moreover, Jake has appeared across different mediums, such as the TV show *Young Justice*, and most recently as part of the *Teen Titans* (2016). With the increased exposure of superheroes in the media, it is common to now find publishers like DC Comics and Marvel take interest in crossing over different mediums. Taking into consideration these publisher's ever-growing roster of teenaged superheroes, it makes sense to see superheroes entering the world of YA and graphic novels as these characters can be appealing to young adult readers. This opens the possibility for writers to expand on their stories, as is the case with Jake.

What is a Graphic Novel?

Teachers can engage students in conversation about their experiences or knowledge on reading graphic novels. In doing so, students share their familiarity with the history, production, and reading of comics and graphic novels. Thus, teachers can begin this conversation by posing some guiding discussion questions. Some example questions are:

- What is a graphic novel?
- What does the term graphic novel mean to you?
- How do you read a graphic novel?
- What do you read first in a graphic novel, the words or the pictures?
- What are some elements of a graphic novel?
- Is there a difference between comics and graphic novels?
- How are graphic novels different from comics? How are they similar?
- How are graphic novels produced?
- Have you read a graphic novel before? Would you like to share some examples?

Depending on students' responses, teachers can then decide whether to introduce students to the basics elements of comics and graphics, how are they produced, or how to read and decode the text and images being presented. In the following paragraphs, there will be suggestions of materials that teachers could use to develop students' schema.

One aspect that might be of interest for students is the history of comics and graphic novels, given how superheroes popularized comics as the medium that we have come to know and relate to superheroes. In recent years, many educators have favored the inclusion of comics books and graphic novels, recognizing the importance of visual literacy as a critical component of learning (National Council of Teachers of English, 2005). However, the inclusion of comic book and graphic novels in the ELA classroom have also met resistance, as it has been perceived as not real books, thus not counting as actual reading. The creation of the term "graphic novel" was coined because of this very reason. Looking to introduce American audiences to European comics, Richard Kyle coined the term in 1964 with the intent to distance said comics from their American counterpart (Gravett, 2005). American comics were perceived as a source of disposable entertainment, popularized by episodic stories about superheroes and printed periodically on cheap paper. Thus, the use of the term graphic novel was meant to elevate comics as a serious form of literature. Nowadays, the term graphic novel is used to refer to stand-alone stories published in volumes as opposed to the episodic nature of comic books. Nevertheless, both comics and graphic novels make use of sequential art as means of storytelling. This knowledge is important for teachers to discuss with students as a means to dispel any prevailing misconceptions about comics and graphic novels that may still be circulating. Visual literacy is an essential skill in today's world.

Another aspect teachers might also touch upon is the mechanics of reading a graphic novel, as students' abilities might range from beginner to accomplished (Boerman-Cornell & Kim, 2020). For example, students might wonder how to read from panel to panel, or whether to read the words of the pictures first (Boerman-Cornell & Kim, 2020). While reading comics and graphic novels might be perceived as a great way to appeal to reluctant readers, the reality is that decoding pictures and words might be challenging, as the pictures are not merely illustrating what is being told through words. Reading comics and graphic novels can be challenging due to how pictures and words work intrinsically together to create meaning. In the production of comics and graphic novels, artists make intentional use of pictorial elements to create the said meaning and establish synergy with the words. As such, it is important for students to build an understanding on how artists choose to create a story. One way to get started is by introducing students to vocabulary pertaining to the parts that make a graphic novel, such as panels, gutter, speech bubbles, sound effects, and narrative blocks. ReadWriteThink (2005) has a graphic organizer titled "Comic Book Primer" that can be used to introduce students to important terminology. Teachers can pair this resource with a primary text to identify comic book elements. For example, pages 9 and 10 from *You Brought Me the Ocean* feature all the elements mentioned in the

"Comic Book Primer." Teachers can provide students with sticky notes to annotate the elements presented in those two pages. Picture books that make use of elements from graphic novels might also work here, such as Santat's (2016) *Are We There Yet?* an inventive title that invites the reader to play with the book by turning it upside down, serving as an example that there is no one specific way to read graphic novels.

Teachers can also discuss how words and pictures interact together as a multimodal text. In his seminal piece, McCloud (1993) discussed seven different types of interactions that can be brought to students' attention during the reading of the graphic novel. Figure 3.1 includes these terms and examples from *You Brought Me the Ocean.*

By understanding how artists combine pictures and words, teachers can build student's ability to cite evidence from the text by explicitly stating the page they would like to address and explain what is occurring in the page or a sequence of panels. Moreover, this allows students to decode how pictures are created and combined with words to convene meaning. This allows for students to critically analyze story elements such as characterization and symbolism through the synergy of words and pictures. Similarly, teachers

Interaction	Definition	Example from *You Brought me the Ocean*
Word specific	The pictures illustrate what is being told through the words. A reader can read aloud or listen to someone read the words in each panel and still understand the story without any need to look at the pictures.	In the closing pages of the graphic novel, pages 182-183, Jake narrates the aftermath of the confrontation between Zeke and him. This is accompanied by a splash of Jake, as he unpacks his bags, while Kenny stares at him. The narrative block conveys the necessary information without the reader having to look at the illustration.
Picture specific	The sequence of pictures tells the story without any need for words. Oftentimes words are just sound effects to what is occurring in the pictures.	On page 54, during Jake's and Kenny's hike, we see a sequence of events in which the pouring rain floods the canyon, and the sudden rising tide threatens to drown both Jake and Kenny. The characters' speech bubbles contain grunts and oomph's as they struggle to run away to safety by climbing to higher ground.
Duo specific	The pictures and the words convey the same meaning and are not dependent on each other for the reader to understand a sequence of event or a single panel.	On page 65, Jake learns his application to attend University of Miami is denied. Both pictures and images show Jake's disappointment at the news, as the narrative blocks reveals his innermost thoughts while the pictures show Jake wallowing in his emotions.
Additive combination	In this sequence, two combinations can happen: a. the words elaborate or amplify what is being portrayed in a picture, or b. picture elaborates or amplifies what is being told through words	An example of how pictures can amplify what is being told by words can be found on page 50, during Jake's and Kenny's hike in the dessert. Jake shows his enthusiasm for oceanography by explaining to Kenny how the dessert was once covered by water, but now the water runs deep beneath them. The pictures show Jake and Kenny sitting in the ground at the top of the page. As the readers eye's travel down the splash page, reading the speech bubbles with Jake's explanation, we see a confluence of water pockets running underground. This image amplifies what the conversation between the two characters is really about: the confluence of Jake's identities, his secrets and intricacies.
Parallel combinations	The pictures and the words each tell different parts of the story without intersecting. The events or ideas might be connected but are not occurring in the panel at the same time.	On page 33, Jake tells Maria he wants to meet with his teacher for a letter of recommendation. However, in the next page, we see Jake follow Kenny to swimming practice, a narrative block accompanying the picture explaining how Jake had already asked his teacher for a letter of recommendation. In reality, Jake lied to Maria so that he could try to talk to Kenny.
Montage	A sequence in which the words in a panel become part of the pictures.	On pages 56-57, there is a spread of Jake with his arms raised, attempting to stop the crashing waves from drowning him and Kenny by redirecting the flow of water over them. The word "Fwoosh!" is used as onomatopoeia but is stylized in the same color and shape as the arcs of water going over both boys.
Interdependent	The most common combination of pictures and words found in graphic novels and comics. Both pictures and words work together in synergy to create meaning. A reader would not be able to rely on just the pictures or the words alone to understand what is being shown in a panel.	The opening pages of the graphic novels are an example of an interdependent combination. The pages contain narrative blocks that present Jake as the main character, while the pictures provide visual information to the reader, such as the setting, and Jake's race, age and gender.

Figure 3.1   The Seven Interactions between Pictures and Words according to McCloud (1993).

can read Kowalchuk, Kullber, and Peteranetz's (2017) piece, "Discovering Literacy through Comics," with students, as it offers a brief and succinct look at how the synergy between images and text work in a comic to create story elements. For example, it explains how from a single panel readers can decode story elements, like setting and characters. The article also introduces students to important elements and vocabulary, such as panels, gutters, speech bubbles, and captions. The article itself is in the form of a comic, which models the information being presented to students. This can be paired with the above-mentioned "Comic Book Primer" (ReadWriteThink, 2005).

Lastly, *Picture This: How Pictures Work* (2016) by Molly Bang is an excellent resource to build vocabulary on how to discuss how artists purposefully use visual elements to create images. The following lists summarize the said principles, but these are presented at large and with visual examples. As such, Bang's text is a great resource for students and teachers to visit. The principles are:

1. The use of smooth, flat, horizontal lines and shapes suggests a sense of stability and calm as these can be associated with the ground or floor.
2. The use of vertical lines and shapes are dynamic as they suggest energy and sense of gravity, especially if they extend from a horizontal stable surface, like trees and buildings.
3. The use of diagonal lines and shapes suggest motion, like cars driving on a highway. Diagonal lines can also be used to denote tension, like beams of wood that seem about to fall down or hills as surfaces that characters could climb. An artist could also use a sense of depth and colors to further achieve the sense of motion.
4. Objects placed on the top half of the page or panel provide a sense of happiness, accomplishment, and clarity, whereas objects place on the bottom half suggest sadness, failure, and gloom.
5. Objects placed at the center of a page or panel command attention, causing the reader to focus their attention on said object.
6. The use of light backgrounds creates a sense of safety, while darker backgrounds provide a sense of danger.
7. Rounded edges of objects feel safer than pointed edges. For example, most weapons, like swords and knives, feature piercing pointed edges that could threaten someone's life.
8. An object's size is associated with strength. For example, think of a character feeling nervous on their first day at a new school. An artist might choose to present this scene as a small person cowering in front of the looming large school building.
9. Association of objects is stronger through the use of color than by shapes. For example, think of a parent and their child wearing clothing of the same color on a day out.

10. Contrast within pictorial elements such as colors, shapes, and sizes allows the reader to notice patterns and create meaning.

Understanding these principles provide students another opportunity to exercise their critical thinking and visual literacy skills.

WHILE READING *YOU BROUGHT ME THE OCEAN*

Character Study

Graphic novels are a great medium for students to study characterization. Through visual depictions of body language, facial expressions, and actions, readers are able to gain insight into what characters do, say, and don't say. For example, in the third panel on page 40, Jake and Maria are sitting at a table having lunch and Jake has just lied to her about spending his Saturday helping his mother with work when in reality he will be spending his day hiking with Kenny. We gain insight into Kenny's thoughts on how he is feeling guilty about lying and his body language reflects it, as he is slouching and avoiding Maria's gaze, who in turn is looking at Jake with an expression of disappointment. Thus, this panel sets the stage for the theme of truth and consequences between Jake and Maria. As posed by Boerman-Cornell & Kim (2020), "as we understand the characters, we also have a window to the themes" (p.42). In the following paragraphs, an approach on how students can utilize to start a character study and continue gathering evidence as they read in order to identify themes in the story is shared.

One of the salient themes throughout the graphic novel is the consequences of our actions when the truth is concealed, which is referenced in the opening pages of the novel (p. 12) as Jake lives in Truth or Consequences, New Mexico. As such, students can work on a character study to examine Jake as they read through the novel. Teachers can introduce S.T.E.A.L. (Speak, Think, Effect on others, Actions, and Looks) as a strategy and a graphic organizer for students to jot down their observations as they read (ReadWriteThink, 2004; figure 3.2).

Close Reading of Text and Images

As previously mentioned, the multimodal nature of graphic novels invites readers to close readings. Interpreting the meaning created by both text and images not only invites readers to closely follow characterization, but also identifies emerging themes and the use of visual elements such as colors as symbolism. The following sections provide examples of close readings of text and images.

Element of characterization	Guiding Questions	Textual and Visual Evidence (dialogue, descriptions, body language, facial expressions, page number, etc.)
Speak	What does Jake say to others? How does Jake speak to others (Maria, his Mom, Kenny, Zeke, Mr. Mendez, etc.)? What does Jake do not say to others and keeps a secret? How does Jake communicate his feelings about his queerness? To who?	Pages 13-23 portrays Jake's and Maria's interactions. From Jake's perspective, they are best friends. In pages 24-26, we see how Jake struggles to hold a conversation with his mother, as it seems she is overprotective of him. They argue constantly. On page 77, Jake lies to Maria on how he spent his weekend.
Thoughts	What does Jake think, value or believe in? What motivates Jake? What does Jake leave unsaid? What is Jake afraid of? What does Jake want?	On pages 21-23, we hear Jake think to himself how he is appreciative of Maria's family and how he is lucky to have her as a friend. However, he has not told Maria he has already applied to the University of Miami as shown in the first panel of page 34. On page 136, he asks to himself "Will I be doomed to drift to life in a sea of secrets?"
Effect on Others	What kind of relationships does Jake have with others (Maria, his mom, Kenny, Zeke, Mr. Mendez, etc.)? How does Jake treat others (Maria, his mom, Kenny, Zeke, Mr. Mendez, etc.)? How do other characters and Maria reach when they learn Jake is gay? How do other characters react to Jake's powers? What are the ramifications of keeping secrets from friends and family?	Jake has been keeping secrets from Maria and his mother. On pages 112-115 we see how Maria feels betrayed by Jake by not telling her of his sexuality. She feels betrayed. She tells Jake, "Do you know me at all?" (p. 115)
Actions	How does Jake behave? How does Jake react to others? How do others react to Jake? What are the consequences? How does Jake come to term with his sexuality? How does Jake come to terms with his powers?	As the story progresses, Jake keeps himself to his thoughts and distances himself from his friends and family. On pages 135, he feels betrayed by his mother, who kept the identity of his father a secret. Through introspection, Jake understand he is doing the same to others around him.
Looks	Describe Jake's physical appearance (clothing, features, specific characteristics, visual characteristics related to superpowers). How does Jake feel about his look? Does the author use specific visual elements to portray Jake? What effect does the color blue has on the reader's understanding of Jake? What are the birthmarks that Jake has? Why does Jake hide his birthmarks?	Jake begins to wear blue colored clothing during his first hike with Kenny on pages 41-59. The use of this color codes Jake as queer when associated with Kenny's hair color, which is also blue. Jake's birthmarks light up when in contact with water (p.52). They are blue.

Figure 3.2   Sample Graphic Organizer for Character Study Using S.T.E.A.L.

Character Relationships

One of the most salient themes in the novels is the relationships Jake has with the people in his life. However, as Jake's inner conflict progresses, he begins to keep secrets and even lies to his mother and best friend, which puts a strain on their relationships. As such, teachers can introduce discussions questions to students in order to discuss how Jake's growth as a character affects his relationships with his friends and family. Students can use the evidence gathered in their S.T.E.A.L. chart to elaborate on these questions:

- What are the secrets Jake is keeping from his mother? Maria? Himself?
- Do you think it is appropriate for Jake to keep secrets?
- What is making Jake keep these many secrets and hide the truth?
- Is keeping secrets a learned behavior Jake picked up from another character?
- How do these secrets affect his relationship with his friends and family? His mom? Maria? Kenny?
- What are the consequences for Jake to keep these many secrets?

Students can cite evidence to discuss these discussion questions. For example, one of the most powerful scenes in the graphic novel is the day that Jake and Kenny go on a hike (pages 41–59). Jake wants to get to know Kenny, but does not want Maria to tag along for fear that she starts asking questions, especially about his sexuality. To avoid hanging out with Maria, Jake lies that he will be helping his mother with stuff from the clinic. When Saturday arrives, Jake leaves and meets Kenny at the canyon on the outskirts of town. As they trek into the road ahead, Jake asks Kenny how he knew about his sexuality. While this is a powerful scene where the reader gains insight into Jake's mind and his secrets, the exchange between Jake and Kenny is augmented thanks to the scenery in each panel, as the progression from sunny to stormy weather on pages 41–59 reflect Jake's inner turmoil, adding weight to the emotions coursing through Jake. This is an important element of the graphic novel that teachers can bring to student's attention.

On page 41, we see Jake and Kenny leaving town and heading into the canyon. Jake and Kenny are shown following a trail as they talk, their surroundings wide open. On the next page, as their conversation leads Kenny to ask whether Maria is Jake's boyfriend, we see a trench in the distance. In the next panel, a fallen tree trunk blocks their path. Just then Kenny asks Jake "Does she knows about you?" implying he knows that Jake is gay. Jake lingers in front of the fallen trunk while Kenny climbs on top of it, replying with "Um, know what about me?" "Relax, I am not going to out you" Kenny replies from atop, the last panel showing Kenny offering his hand to Jake so he can propel himself and climb over the tree. Although small, the action of Kenny in the last panel on page 42 indicates Kenny is an ally to Jake, helping him understand his situation as a knowing member from the LGBTQ community.

Personal Awakenings

Another instance in which close reading is beneficial is to discuss the theme of personal awakenings. On page 48, where the weather suddenly brews into a storm as Jake confesses his innermost secrets to Kenny. In this scene, the reader can observe "how the setting is rendered as an image on the page and how it reflects the mood" (p. 38). In the following panels, the storm intensifies as Jake shows Kenny the birthmark along his arms, the scene climaxing into heavy rain that almost drowns Jake and Kenny. This brings Jake's power to awaken, which also serves as an allegory of his awakening as Jake is beginning to make sense of his desires and what stands in his way. As such, a close reading of this scene can help students start contemplating the narrative parallels between Jake as an adolescent and Jake as a superhero. Teachers can prompt students with discussion questions such as:

• In which moment did Jake's powers awaken? Provide evidence.
• What prompted Jake's powers to manifest?

- Will Jake's powers offer him the ability to solve his own problems?
- How is Jake the teenager different or similar to Jake the superhero?

Symbolism

Throughout the graphic novel, there are instances in which symbolism is used to expand on the story, establish a mood, and direct the readers' attention to Jakes's growth as a character and relationships. This is an aspect the teacher can discuss with students in-depth. Due to its visual storytelling components, symbolism is a recurring story element in comics and graphic novels. Just as readers decode images and text in a graphic novel, graphic novels also require readers to decode ideas and themes through the synergy between pictures and words. As such, it is common for comics and graphic novels to introduce symbols, as these can be placed in a single image that the reader might pick up on at a glance. Oftentimes these symbols might even be subtle and might require readers to do a close reading of the text in order to decode ideas and meaning. As such, symbols are an integral part of visual storytelling in graphic novels, as these become a vehicle for the reader to connect and understand how ideas and story elements are realized throughout. Thus, it is important for teachers to discuss symbolism with students as a means for them to connect story ideas and make meaning. In the case of *You Brought Me the Ocean*, symbolism is a vehicle for readers to understand Jake's journey. Teachers can introduce discussion questions for students.

- What specific artistic choices are used by Maroh in the creation of pictures?
- Where can we find some of those visual elements? Can you provide examples?
- What do visual elements, such as shape and color, tell you about the characters? About the story?
- How do colors impact the story?
- How do colors influence the way we perceive the characters?
- How does Maroh depict the color blue? In which instances or objects is this color used and to what effect?
- Are there visual symbols that might have caught your attention as you read the graphic novel? Which ones?

As students discuss these questions, a connection between Jake's aquatic powers, the use of the color blue, and water as a symbol might arise. Teachers can then prompt students to find evidence and the effect that these visual elements have on the story and how we perceive Jake both as a teenager and a superhero. The following paragraphs provide some examples.

The use of the color blue. One example of symbolism is the use of the color blue by Maroh on page 41, where Jake and Kenny are forefronted in the illustrations through the use of the color blue; the scenery's colors are earthy and muted, while Jake's blue-green tracksuit and Kenny's blue hair. This establishes a visual association between Jake, who is curious about Kenny's experiences with his sexuality, and Kenny, who is openly gay and a hair color that is oftentimes worn by members of the LGBTQ community. We also start seeing Jake wear blue-colored tops of different hues, such as a button-up shirt and a hoodie toward the end of the novel (p. 73). Kenny also gifts Jake a turquoise stone as a romantic gesture (p. 98), as it reminds him of the ocean, and Jake by association (hence, *You Brought Me the Ocean*). Maroh also uses blue in other situations, such as the color of Jake's scars when they glow (p. 170) and the final emotional confrontation in which secrets come to light as means to convey mood. Lastly, throughout the novel, another element that is colored blue is water (p. 9), which is in itself another symbol.

Water as a symbol of nourishment, inner state, and narrative confluence. Throughout the novel, water in its different states is used to denote different meanings. For example, water is fluid, which resonates with the theme of sexual identity. Moreover, Jake's relationship with water is shown in two different forms: healing and nourishment, and as well as tempestuous to signify his inner state. For example, on pages 53–59, we see how a sudden flood in the canyon brought in as a storm might be representative of Jake's inner state, especially how all the secrets that he is keeping from others, like his desire to leave town and his sexuality are drowning him. On pages 101–105, we see Jake joining Kenny at the school pool, where he shares he never learned how to swim. Kenny offers to teach him and as the two boys interact, it becomes a moment of intimacy and respite for Jake. This also contrasts with the arid desert town of Truth or Consequences, New Mexico, and Jake's desire to study oceanography. Water is also used in the graphic novel to denote the confluence of Jake's personal life and his superhero awakening. On page 50, Jake explains to Kenny how once the desert was abundant with water, but it now lies in the ground beneath them. On the page, the illustrations zoom out and show a confluence of pockets of water underground each connected by thin water streams, to which Jake adds "A whole fluid world . . . bubbling up . . . and breaking through the surface" (p. 50). This image takes the entirety of the page, with two separate panels each zooming into Jake and Kenny's face to show their conversation around the image of the underground water pockets. This powerful image captures the essence of the novel, as it symbolizes not only the narrative parallels but also Jake's innermost desires that will, as he says, "[break] through the surface."

AFTER READING *YOU BROUGHT ME THE OCEAN*

Following the reading of *You Brought Me the Ocean*, ask students to complete their character study using S.T.E.A.L. Once finished, offer students an opportunity to share the evidence they have gathered. This provides the students a chance to share their notes, discuss their impressions of the text, and take an in-depth look at the novel and Jake as a character. Teachers can also choose to divide students into groups and have each discuss a specific aspect of Jake using S.T.E.A.L. to unpack and analyze thematic elements that surface as they discuss their findings. Similarly, students can be divided into teams. Then, the teacher can then assign each team to complete a second S.T.E.A.L. chart for another character, such as Kenny or Maria. Another suggestion is for students to complete a S.T.E.A.L. chart for Kenny and then ask them to compare and contrast both Jake and Kenny experiences as male queer teenagers of color. Both Jake and Kenny have different experiences when it comes to their identities as male gay teenagers of color. For example, Kenny has a conversation with his father about his queerness (pages 66–69). As such, students can discuss the following discussion question: How do Jake and Kenny view and experience their identity as queer people of color? Once students are finished, students can come back and debrief with the entire class. A teacher can ask students to create poster board versions of their S.T.E.A.L. chart for a presentation.

Discussing the Confluence of Coming Out and Superhero-Origin Narratives

As a superhero-origin story endowed with queer significance (Fawaz, 2016) and youth stories, Sánchez crafts a narrative confluence that invites for a superhero character study to examine Jake's intersecting identity, queerness, and the communities as the graphic novel centers immersive representation of people of color and their communities. Figure 3.3 presents some examples on how some symbols connect to the studying of characterization, symbolism, and queerness.

BEYOND *YOU BROUGHT ME THE OCEAN*

Exploring Other Superheroes

You Brought Me the Ocean is one of the many recent teenage superhero stories. In 2018, DC Entertainment announced the creation of two new imprints focused on original graphic novels. Each new imprint spotlights different

Symbols	Connection to queerness	Evidence
The dry New Mexico desert	Maroh's successful consonance between the text and illustrations purposefully utilize the setting of the dry New Mexico desert to augment the pressures of social expectations on adolescents by using water as an allegory to discuss gender, sexual fluidity, and healing versus the dry dessert backdrop that denotes inner conflict and friction between characters.	The sequence of events on pages 41-59. Third panel on page 31, when Mrs. Archer explains "Gender and sexuality are fluid, like water. Love can take many forms."
The color blue	Muted colors highlight the racial and sexual identities of the characters, like using blue to denote queerness through Jake's birthmarks and Kenny's hair against the pervasive earthy color palette. By using blue in this manner, Maroh establishes a visual association between Jake and Kenny as members of the LGBTQ community.	Jake's shirt and birthmarks (p. 73) Kenny's hair (p. 30)
Jakes powers	Jake's powers reflect his inner emotional state in terms of his queer identity.	Kenny testing his new found powers at home after coming out to Kenny on pages 70-71. Jake feeling tender and exposed as he shares his problems with Maria's father, who acts like a paternal figure to Jake, on page 140.

Figure 3.3   Examples of Symbols and Their Connection to Characterization, Symbolism, and Queerness.

readers, with DC Zoom aimed at content created for middle-grade readers, while DC Ink focuses on young adult readers. These new offerings are brought by an "All-Star Talent Line-up" (DC Comics, 2018), which includes well-known YA writers that have built a strong readership such as Marie Lu, Melissa de la Cruz, Mariko Tamaki, Jason Reynolds, and Gene Luen Yang. Some of these graphic novels feature well-known teenaged characters, such as Beast Boy, Raven, as well as teenage versions of older superheroes, such as Wonder Woman, and Batman. Marvel has published similar titles aimed at young adult readers in the form of collected volumes from recent teenage superheroes. However, these are published in the form of a graphic novel, a book proper, rather than the typical trade paperback in which volumes are collected. Some examples of these include *The Unstoppable Wasp*, *Mrs. Marvel*, *Miles Morales*, *Shuri*, and *Ironheart*. Some of these superhero offerings are not only available in the form of graphic novels, but also as young adult novels.

With this in mind, teachers can invite students to independently read their choice of superhero. Students can not only work on a character study but also use this project as means to also research social justice topics that the superhero believes in and stands for. For example, *Faith*, published by Valiant Comics, has been an advocate for positive body image. Similarly, La Borinqueña is a Puerto Rican superhero that advocates for the well-being of Puerto Ricans and promotes knowledge about the history of the island. Most recently, an anthology titled *Ricanstruction: Reminiscing & Rebuilding Puerto Rico* was published as an effort to raise funds for relief efforts toward the victims of Hurricane Maria in Puerto Rico. It features characters from the DC Universe working alongside La Borinqueña and Puerto Ricans in reconstructing the damages to the local flora and fauna of the island. Some of the pieces also touch upon the history of the island. As such, this could not only foster an inquiry toward social justice, but also work as a mirror, window, or sliding glass door (Sims Bishop, 1990) for students. Another example is Marvel's *The Unstoppable Wasp*, in which Nadia creates a team called G.I.R.L. composed of young women who are scientists. The book includes visibility of many intersectional identities, such as dis/abilities, nationality, language, gender, socioeconomic status, religion, sexuality, and race, and opens up conversations about the underrepresentation of women in the sciences. *Moon Girl and the Devil Dinosaur* also includes a superhero who is also the smartest character in the Marvel universe and tackles issues such as inequalities in education.

Create Your Own Superhero

Teachers can invite students to create their own superheroes. Having undergone a character study, students can use the S.T.E.A.L. graphic organizer in figure 3.1 to create and build the profile of their character. This is a project that teachers can assign in groups or individually. As part of the requirements of the activity, teachers can extend the graphic organizer by also adding additional requirements, such as superpowers, an origin story and, also an inquiry toward social justice topics that their superhero would stand for. This activity also has the potential for students to use multimedia to present their superhero. For example, students can write a comic script presenting the origin story of their superhero. Then, students could produce a comic book or a video trailer of their character by using stock pictures from the internet, using video tools from applications such as TikTok, or even claymation. Students can then present their projects to the class.

Further Reading

Once students have finished discussing their character study, teachers can refer students to *Teen Titans Vol 2: The Rise of Aqualad*, which collects issues 5–8 when the series was launched as part of the DC Universe Rebirth line. Students can read this volume as a means to compare and contrast two different versions of Jake as presented in graphic novel and comic book forms, respectively. Damian, the current incarnation of Robin, is now the new leader of the Teen Titans, composed of Raven, Beast Boy, Star Fire, and Kid Flash. Jake Hyde, from New Mexico, knows that he is different and longs to find his place in the world. This version of Jake has already come out to his mother and is also aware of his powers. However, he keeps this knowledge between him and his mother. Jake is also secretly dating Kenny, but their relationship is strained, as Jake wants him to come out to his father. In a last attempt to find a reason to stay, Jake reveals his superpowers to Kenny, who breaks up with him. At the same time, the news is broadcasting the current struggle the Teen Titans are involved in, a prison break of inmates that have aquatic powers. Jake feels he belongs in the Teen Titans and decides to set off and become part of the team. While the continuity is different, as the story was created by a different writer, students can take this opportunity to also discuss the possibilities for Jake outside of New Mexico after the ending in *You Brought Me the Ocean*. The story also opens a window to further exploration of his origin story, as his mother, Lucia, plays a much bigger role, and Jake's sexuality is not entirely weaved into his origin story and just happens to be gay.

Author Study

Teachers can also invite students to do an author study after they finish reading *You Brought Me the Ocean*. For example, teachers can assign Julie Maroh's graphic novel, *Blue is the Warmest Color*, and study Maroh's artistic choices, like the use of the color blue, for example. Similarly, teachers can invite students to read a novel from Alex Sánchez's oeuvre, as he is one of the most important LGBTQ voices in young adult literature. Students can read Sánchez's (2020) piece on the importance of LGBTQ representation across different genres, as well as the possibilities of the coming out story.

CONCLUSION

Coming-of-age stories in young adult literature capture the complexities, anxieties, and development of adolescent life and identity. The same can be said about superhero-origin stories, as these too capture the intricacies of identity and personal growth through parallels brought upon superheroes' experiences, especially young heroes in the midst of exploring their identity such as Jake/Aqualad. *You Brought Me the Ocean* is an excellent vehicle for exploring both of these aspects as it portrays not only the character's identity as a superhero but also exemplifies the coming to terms with his queer identity. As a multimodal text, the pictures and the text enhance the studying of characterization and symbolism. Similarly, its narrative confluence of coming of age, origin stories, and coming out allow for an in-depth examination of Jake's adolescent life and identity. With the current increase of superhero-themed graphic novels aimed at young adults, teachers can tap into these narratives to offer students not only the means to analyze books within this medium but also stories that they can identify with, even if they often present larger than life figures such as superheroes.

REFERENCES

Bang, M. (2016). *Picture this: How to read pictures*. Chronicle Books.

Boerman-Cornell, W., & Kim, J. (2020). *Using graphic novels in the English Language Arts Classroom*. Bloomsbury Academic.

DC Comics Official Press Release. DC reveals new young adult and middle grade imprints: DC Ink and DC Zoom. https://www.dccomics.com/blog/2018/02/05/dc-r eveals-new-young-adult-and-middle-grade-imprints-dc-ink-dc-zoom.

Fawaz, R. (2016). *The New Mutants: Superheroes and the radical imagination of American comics*. NYU Press.

Gravett, P. (2005). Things to hate about comics. *Graphic novels: Everything you need to know*. HarperCollins.

Kahn, A. (2018, December 31st). Spiderman is straight, but *Into the Spiderverse* is a coming out story. *The Washington Post*. https://www.washingtonpost.com.

Kowalchuk, I., Kullberg, A., & Peteranetz, J. (2017). Discovering literacy through comics. *Voices from the Middle*, 24(4), 9–14.

Maroh, J. (2013). *Blue is the warmest color*. Arsenal Pup Press.

McCloud, S. (1994). *Understanding comics*: *The invisible art*. William Morrow Paperbacks.

National Council of Teachers of English (2005). Multimodal Literacies. *National Council of Teachers of English*. https://ncte.org/statement/multimodalliteracies/

Percy, B., Khoi, P., von Grawbadger, W., Hester, P., Scott, J., & Mhan, P. (2018). *Teen Titans Vol. 2: The rise of Aqualad*. DC Comics.

ReadWriteThink. (2004). Defining characterization. *ReadWriteThink*. http://www .readwritethink.org/files/resources/lesson_images/lesson800/Characterization.pdf.

ReadWriteThink. (2005). Comic book primer. *ReadWriteThink*. https://www.readwrit ethink.org/resources/resource-print.html?id=30296.

Sánchez, A. (2020). The times they keep a-changin. *English Journal*, *110*(1), 20–24.

Sánchez, A., & Muroh, J. (2020). *You brought me the ocean*. DC Comics.

Santat, D. (2016). *Are we there yet?* Little Brown Books for Young Readers.

Sims Bishop, R. (1990). Mirrors, windows and sliding glass doors. *Perspectives: Choosing and Using Books for the Classroom*, *6*(3), ix–xi.

Chapter 4

Color Palettes and Peculiar Panels

Studying Narrative Structure in Tillie Walden's On a Sunbeam

Nicole Ann Amato and Jenna Spiering

Discussions of narrative structure—such as how a story begins, how time is managed, how different details are unveiled, and how characters are situated in those events—are always happening in English Language Arts (ELA) classrooms. Teachers often ask students to consider how an author's choices about text structure contribute to meaning, themes, and the literary and aesthetic impact of a work of literature. Books with nonlinear and complex narrative structures are fruitful for facilitating discussions that grapple with an author's choices. Contemporary young adult novels (e.g., *First Part Last* by Angela Johnson and *We Are Okay* by Nina LaCour) and often-taught classics in ELA classrooms (e.g., *The Handmaid's Tale* by Margaret Atwood and *Fahrenheit 451* by Ray Bradbury) employ these complex structures to build suspense, requiring readers to make active and recurring predictions and to consider biases and assumptions they may bring to their reading of the story. However, traditional discussions of narrative structure often ask students to complete a plot diagram, identifying elements such as exposition, inciting incidents, rising/falling actions, the climax, and a resolution. We think these discussions are limited in that they only ask students to retell the story in a linear fashion. We want to push ELA teachers to move beyond low-level assessments of reading comprehension with plot diagrams, and instead move toward more dynamic discussions of the relationship between narrative structures, character development, and themes.

Graphic novels and comics present narrative structures in unique ways with their ability to move between time frames through typography, the use of color, and different panel structures. As a result, reading graphic novels becomes a complex, multimodal act of literacy. Design elements—such as panels, gutters, lettering, shading, color choice, and sound effects—provide readers with a "complex environment for the negotiation of meaning" (Jacobs, 2007, p. 19). In this sense, reading comics is most like the way our students must read and navigate popular media. Tillie Walden's webcomic *On a Sunbeam* offers multiple opportunities for students to engage with this multimodality and the way it illuminates the nuances of narrative structure. In this chapter, we offer instructional approaches that ask students to consider how an author's choices regarding structural elements (i.e., color, panel structure, manipulation of time) within the graphic format develop complex characters and thematic understandings.

NOTE TO READERS

Tillie Walden's freely accessible webcomic *On a Sunbeam* has been characterized as a space opera, a subgenre of science fiction that centers on interplanetary warfare, melodramatic adventure, and chivalrous romance. The print edition of this book is 533 pages and is available in both hardback and paperback. Throughout the chapter, we will occasionally refer to page numbers from our print editions of the text. We will also always include chapter numbers for readers who are working from the web-based version of the text.

On a Sunbeam is an LGBTQIA+-inclusive text, featuring multiple queer romantic storylines, nonbinary characters, and nonnormative family structures. Walden's graphic novel also features a uniquely queer setting that is completely devoid of cisgender men and asks students to consider what family, friendship, and relationships look like in this reality. However, explicit discussions of gender and sexuality are, with the exception of two brief scenes, never the major conflict of the narrative arc.

SUMMARY OF ON A SUNBEAM BY TILLIE WALDEN

In two alternating time lines, the reader follows Mia as she navigates life as the newest crew member of a team traveling in a fish-shaped spaceship restoring ruins of historic structures. Weaved into this story are flashbacks of Mia's time at boarding school where she develops a budding romance with Grace, a new schoolmate who seems to disappear as quickly as she has arrived. Readers must navigate the dual time lines to figure out how Mia's work on the spaceship is tied to Grace's sudden departure from school. In addition to Mia and Grace's romance, the reader will meet and learn the backstories of Mia's crewmates and how they came to work on the ship.

BEFORE READING *ON A SUNBEAM*

Before reading *On a Sunbeam*, we encourage teachers to provide students with a variety of opportunities to notice and name techniques of narrative structure within the context of other visual media such as film, television, short webcomics, and children's picture books. Specifically, we ask students to look for examples of how creators indicate shifts in time and space through design choices such as color, text, and panel structure. This will prime students for noticing and naming the ways Walden navigates dual time lines within *On a Sunbeam*.

Noticing and Naming Narrative Structures

Ask students to brainstorm a list of popular stories, films, and television shows that utilize alternative time lines—any time line that deviates from chronological, sequential order of time. Some possible viewing suggestions include, but are not limited to, television shows like *Jane the Virgin*, *Anne with an E*, and *Orphan Black* or movies like *The Miseducation of Cameron Post*, *Into the Spiderverse*, *Inside Out*, and *If Beale Street Could Talk*. This list is not exhaustive, as students will be able to name even more options. A short class activity could be asking students to take notes while rewatching an episode/film of their choosing. Ask students to pay careful attention to shifts in time and to take notes on what the creators are doing to make these time shifts noticeable to the viewer. The following guiding questions can be posed to students:

1. How do you know when time passes or shifts in the story?
   1. What do you see, read, hear, and so on that indicates a shift in time?
   2. What effect, if any, does this have on your understanding of the story? What questions is it answering? What questions is it generating?
   3. How much time do you think has passed? What clues make you think this?
2. What clues/hints within the dialogue between characters cue to the audience that more information is coming? What effect does this have on your understanding of the story? What questions is it answering? What questions is it generating?

Put students in small groups and have them share their observations with each other. Create a crowdsourced list of techniques that can be posted in the classroom as a reference for when they read. For example, in the television series *Anne with an E*, flashbacks are cued to the viewer by a shift in color and tone. Scenes that look back on Anne's experience in the orphanage utilize dark, muted colors, echoing sounds, and a slower, more dramatic pace to underscore that Anne's memories of her time in the orphanage are marked by sadness, distance, and pain. In contrast, the television series *Jane the Virgin* utilizes an unnamed and unpictured narrator who more directly cues to the viewer shifts in time through voiceovers as well as text on the screen. Over time, the use of voiceovers and text creates a comedic relationship between the narrator and the viewer where context, clues, and commentary about the characters are offered.

Visualizing Time

After exploring shifts in time in popular film and/or television, have students practice this again using short webcomics. Freely accessible webcomics such as Jillian Tamaki's are one possible source. We are fond of the following: *Lane's Eyes, After We Broke Up, T-Fights, This Face,* and *Covid Hygiene.* Students should also be encouraged to explore resources such as Webtoons as well as print comics from local newspapers. We encourage teachers to make copies of the comics for students to cut up, separating the panels into singular units. Give students time to rearrange them in a variety of ways (sequential, vertical, horizontal, one page, two pages, etc.). Have students read their peers' rearrangements. Afterward, the following questions can be posed to students:

1. Where are the reader's eyes supposed to travel across the page? How do you know?
2. How does panel design and shape indicate movement and time?
3. Can you put the panels in a different order that still makes logical sense to you? Why or why not?
4. How is the reading experience impacted by the various rearrangements?

For example, in Jillian Tamaki's webcomic *Covid Hygiene,* there are twenty panels organized in ten rows of two columns that follow an unnamed character as they take off their clothes, burn them, wash their body, and then repeat the process again three days later. There is very little text, no dialogue, and only four colors used. *What features of the comic indicate shifts in time (pay attention to captions, the clock, and the background color)? What imagery helps them understand whether they should be reading the panels from left to right or from top to bottom (pay attention to the order the character removes their clothing)?* Ask students to cut apart each panel and rearrange them. Can the story be logically told in different arrangements (e.g., 1 single column of twenty panels *or* four columns of five rows of panels) *What is the effect on meaning if the frames are reorganized or if the time line changes?*

Similarly, Walden employs a combination of color shifts, panel organization, and text to indicate shifts in time. Working within a short comic, such as Jillian Tamaki's *Covid Hygiene,* will prime students for noticing these decisions as they read *On a Sunbeam.* Additionally, this will give teachers the opportunity to slowly begin introducing terminology specific to graphic novels such as panel, frame, color palette, caption, and emanata. Figure 4.1 offers terms and definitions that may be useful for teachers and students.

Reading Color

Picture-book artists and authors sometimes use color strategically to indicate shifts in time, mood, and theme. Read aloud excerpts from one of the following texts (using a document camera if possible or project a digital edition) and ask students to pay attention to the colors being used. Picture books are particularly helpful here since students are more than likely already familiar with the genre of picture books. Figure 4.2 offers a list of possible texts to use for this activity.

After reading aloud one of the texts above to students, pose the following questions: *What colors were repeatedly used? What might these colors indicate to the reader? How do you know?*

A quick note about color: we are intentionally selecting texts where authors are making color choices to communicate very specific features of the story.

Graphic Feature	Definition
Panel	A single frame or box that contains a sequence or segment of action.
Frame	A frame is the shape or organization of a series of panels.
Gutter	The space, usually white, between panels and frames.
Bleed	An image that extends beyond the edges of the panels, frames, or pages.
Splash Page	A full-page illustration in one frame.
Emanata	Lines that indication motion or movement, usually drawn around the object in motion.
Palette	The combination of colors used
Caption	Text that cues additional information to the reader such as narrative voiceovers, times, dates, and setting.
Speech Bubble	Indicate dialogue between characters. The shapes of these can change indicate tone, mood, and volume.

Figure 4.1 Technical Vocabulary for Reading Comics.

Picturebooks	Examples of Color Usage	What does this suggest to the reader?
They Say Blue by Jillian Tamaki	Primary colors (red, blue, yellow), as the story progresses the color palette expands into secondary and tertiary colors	The colors shift with the elements of nature being described, the imagery follows the changing seasons
Sidewalk Flowers by JonArno Lawson and Sydney Smith	Gray scale background/world with a young girl wearing a red coat holding yellow wildflowers	As the young girl picks wildflowers while walking her distracted dad, everything she notices and picks is a vibrant color against a grayscale world.
Leo: A Ghost Story by Mac Barnett and Christian Robinson	Shades of blue, black, and white	Leo is outlined in blue crayon to indicate he is a ghost, where other characters are shaded in a dark blue to illustrate they are alive

Figure 4.2   Picture Books for Analyzing Color.

However, not all comics and graphic novels use color with this level of intentionality. In fact, color and being able to reproduce color in additional prints can be influenced by financial and technological reasons at the publishing level. Color costs more money in both creation and reproduction and is not always a decision made by the artist.

Drawing Gender

The visual nature of picture books and graphic novels make them productive sites for exploring constructions of gender and sexuality. Students will come to these texts with assumptions and biases about how to identify a character's gender and sexuality. Kedley and Spiering (2017) suggested explicitly engaging students in queer, critical discussions about these assumptions as a way to disrupt oft-held myths about the relationship between gender and sexuality. The following discussion questions, culled from their article, can be applied to any of the starter texts we've suggested thus far, as well as Walden's novel:

1. How do you (as the reader) know each character's gender or sexuality? On what assumptions do you base your identification? On what assumptions do characters base their identifications?
2. In what ways does the character perform gender and/or sexuality differently throughout the text? How do other characters react to that in positive and negative ways?

3. How do we use text and the images in the graphic novel to understand our answers to these questions?

Further, children's books using animals as characters offer an opportunity for readers to engage with descriptions and displays of gender relative to characters that aren't so directly linked to society's traditional understandings of gender norms. We suggest asking students to briefly (90 seconds at most) draw a pair of characters in popular culture that exhibits binary views of gender, such as Batman and Batgirl, Micky and Minnie Mouse, or the bear family from the Charmin toilet paper commercials. *What did students draw, in that short of a time frame, to distinguish between genders?* Engaging in these activities and enquiry discussions will prepare students to engage with their assumptions and biases about the characters in Walden's story.

WHILE READING *ON A SUNBEAM*

While traditional literary elements can be explored within a graphic novel, we align with scholars who argue that graphic novels require a more specific vocabulary that attends to the artistic choices a cartoonist is making. The following activities ask readers to more closely explore those artistic choices in order to theorize about the impact of the complex narrative structure in Walden's *On a Sunbeam*. Please refer back to Table X.1 for definitions of specific terminology.

Annotating Graphic Novels

In order to get a full breadth of meaning in a graphic novel, one needs to be adept at understanding the relationship between form and content differently than they would need to be in a traditional prose novel. Elements such as color, use of panels, and gutter space, and typography are all important features that convey meaning in graphic formats. However, many of our readers often come to graphic novels with underdeveloped skills for them because they have not traditionally been prioritized in explicit reading instruction. For this reason, annotating features of graphic novels is an excellent way to scaffold for students how to navigate the relationship between form and content.

Annotating, referred to by some scholars as "noisy scribbles" (Narter, 2013), can be tedious and cumbersome for readers. Intended to support students in engaging metacognitively with their reading, annotating can unintentionally ruin the joy of reading, with some readers reporting it slows them down. However, slowing down is exactly what we want readers to do when engaging with graphic novels. We want students to linger in the panels. Here, we suggest a systematic way for readers to look through *On a Sunbeam*. This can take many forms and knowing that all classroom contexts are different (webcomic, text form, classrooms rich in technology), annotation can happen through various vehicles (e.g., Google Jamboard, where students add examples to several boards, post-it notes that are color-coded to track color usage, bookmarks, and Padlet walls). Below we offer four features to focus on and a suggested chart for students to track their observations (see figure 4.3).

1. Author's use of varying *color palettes* to indicate shifts in time between dual narratives, shifts in mood/setting
2. Author's use of varying *gutter* styles and *panel sizes* and shapes to convey action, movement, and passage of time
3. Author's use of *imagery* such as body language, facial expressions, and emanata (motion lines) to develop characters and their relationships
4. Author's use of *text* within speech and thought balloons to signal if a character is whispering, yelling, and so on.

Walden's text is long. The print version exceeds 500 pages. We do not suggest students do this for the entire book, but rather encourage students to engage in collaborative annotation or individually work on small sections of

Chapter & Page	Graphic Feature	Observation Notes	Effect of Feature
	Which graphic features are you describing? (panel, color, dialogue, imagery)	*Describe to the best of your ability what you see.*	*What is the effect of this feature on the reader? In other words, how does this feature contribute to a reader's meaning making?*
Ch 2, pp. 31-34	color	the pink palette becomes more vibrant when Char and Mia go deeper into the hidden rooms at the ruins, it feels almost fiery	Is the additional color in these moments building intensity and suspense because there is mystery surrounding these places?
Ch 15, pp. 363-364	Panel, imagery	9 stacked horizontal panels the width of the page, each one is slighter taller than the next, each row zooming in on natural elements (rivers, mountains, forest), the last panel on this page shows the crew arriving at their destination with nervous gazes	Indicating the passage of time as the crew travels through multiple terrains, building intensity as the group cautiously enters a new part of space

Figure 4.3   Sample Graphic Organizer for Tracking Graphic Features in *On a Sunbeam*.

illustrative chapters. By carefully dissecting one or two chapters, we believe students will be able to see more clearly the artistic choices Walden is making to tell this story. We have filled out the first couple of rows of the chart as a model.

Tracking Predictions

Walden's world-building creates a story that will leave students with more questions than answers at various parts of the text. Part of Walden's ability to sustain mystery and suspense is her dual narratives. The shifting time lines frequently pivot at critical moments. To cultivate students' curiosity and questioning, we suggest a chart where students can record what they don't know.

Collaborative Conversations about Comics

Although people often think of reading as a solitary and independent act, part of the joy of reading comes from engaging with peers about our reactions, questions, and theories. Since reading graphic novels critically might be new for many students and teachers, utilizing literature circles as a means for curious and collaborative discussions will encourage rereadings and lingering in panels to find and explore details that readers may have missed during initial reads.

In traditional literature circles, we might find roles such as the question generator, summarizer, word wizard, and visual artist. These roles tend to support students in comprehension of a text. However, literature circles are highly adaptable activities that can be customized to meet the needs of the students and the text. For example, some scholars suggest creating roles that encourage students to take critical stances toward the characters and themes by locating stereotypes, power hierarchies, and dominant discourses within multicultural and political texts (Thein, Guise & Sloan, 2011). However, the goal is to encourage students to think really carefully about how the author's choices with regards to form and structure are working to create a complex graphic narrative. In service of *On a Sunbeam*, we will draw from Low and Jacobs'(2018) literature circle roles for discussing graphica to craft text-specific questions about the artistic, linguistic, and aesthetic choices Walden makes throughout her novel.

Low and Jacobs suggested six roles (with cheeky and witty names!) for students to ask of a graphic text: Image Mage, Gutter Dweller, Text Maven, Palette Cleanser, Synergizer, and Superfan. Table 4.1 provides an example chart that outlines each role, its purpose, and questions specific to Walden's *On A Sunbeam*. While all six of the roles here as defined and discussed by

Table 4.1 Roles, Purpose, and Questions (adapted from Low & Jacobs, 2018)

Role	Purpose	Questions to Pose for Walden's On a Sunbeam
Image Mage	Considers how images, icons, and figures are represented within a graphic text (p. 323).	How does Walden use body language, facial expressions, and emanata (motion lines) to convey character traits, emotions, and actions? How do these images also help to establish the relationships between the characters?
Gutter Dweller	Considers the layout of the pages within a graphic text, panels, and blank spaces between them (p. 323).	Walden uses a number of splash pages (full page panels) throughout the text. What do you notice about these panels? Where are they most often located? What function do they serve in terms of the narrative structure? In other words, what are they signifying to the reader? What effect does this have on the mood of the story? Find a scene where Walden uses a nontraditional panel arrangement. What is happening in these panels? What directions do your eyes need to travel to read the story? How do you know? Find a scene where Walden does not use straight lines to break up panels. What is happening in these panels? Why might Walden be breaking from the straight lines?
Text Maven	Considers all linguistic/semiotic elements and their role in contributing to the meaning of the graphic text (p. 328).	Pay attention to Walden's use of speech and thought bubbles? How do you as the reader know who is speaking? In what tone? How does Walden differentiate between a character whispering or yelling? In what other instances, beyond speech between characters, do you see text? What purpose does this text serve? Find a scene (or chapter) that has no dialogue. What does the absence of speech indicate to the reader about the story? mood? characters?
Palette Cleanser	Considers the role that color and grayscale play in conveying narrative tone and characters' state of mind (p. 328).	What color palette does Walden use in each time line? How do these colors change over the course of the novel? What colors are added? What patterns do you notice about when new colors are introduced to earlier palettes?

Synergizer	Considers relationships among images, words, and other elements in contributing to the meaning of a graphic text (p. 328).	How does Walden's use of color and panel structure help the reader understand shifts in time? What effect does this have on the mood of the story? Find a moment in the text where Walden is shifting between time within a single page. How does a reader make sense of the story in these moments? Why might Walden be doing this in these particular moments? How do these moments help us understand the characters?
Superfan	Connects the graphic text to larger contexts such as reviews, critics, author interviews, adaptations, historical and contemporary events (p. 330).	Tillie Walden wrote this story while living in Japan. In what moments can you see the influence of Manga on her own work? If you've never read any Manga, browse a few books and then come back to Walden's work. Listen to Belle and Sebastian's song *Asleep on a Sunbeam*. Tillie Walden said so. What do you think? When will your joy be complete? Of *OAS*, Tillie Walden writes, "I know nothing about either the genre of science fiction or the actual mechanics of existing in space. I always got crummy grades in science, too" but she goes on to say that her hope for *OAS* was to "create a version of outer space that I would want to live in." What do you think of the world she created? Does the "science" have to work for her story to work? Read excerpts from Tillie Walden's other works, such as *I Love this Part, Are You Listening?* or *Spinning*. Or find her Tarot Deck! What stylistic choices and thematic elements do you see across Walden's work? How is Walden's novel disrupting dominant narratives about topics such as family, romance, adolescence, migration, colonization, and so on? What historical and/or current events can you draw from to support this argument?

Low are Jacobs are included, the Synergizer and Superfan roles should be reserved for after reading discussions, since they support students in moving from identifying and naming elements of graphic forms to analyzing and synthesizing their impact on the story as a whole.

AFTER READING *ON A SUNBEAM*

Despite some naysayer's views that graphic novels are neither literary nor rigorous reading material, *On a Sunbeam* lends itself to complex discussions about its themes for adolescents in our classrooms. Up to this point in our chapter, we have asked readers to analyze the nuts and bolts of graphic storytelling, breaking it down into its parts. Now we want readers to grapple with how these artistic choices develop Walden's themes of queerness, kinship, found families, gender, and coming of age. In other words, how would telling this story in chronological order (or in Black and white, or with uniform paneling) impact our understanding of Walden's world and characters? What would be gained or lost by telling this story differently?

Thematic Analysis and Discussion

"My initial goal with Sunbeam was to create a version of outer space that I would want to live in. So of course that includes tons of queer people, no men (did you notice?), trees, old buildings, and endless constellations." (Walden, 2018)

Queer YAL "can offer readers alternative, unexpected, surprising methods and models of thinking through the maybe, the perhaps, the uncertain, and the yet-to-arrive" (Matos & Wargo, 2019, p. 10). Walden's use of dual time lines and flashbacks coupled with characters who are rebuilding ruins of a historical past offers readers "queer alternatives for livability, for being" (p. 10). *On a Sunbeam* reimagines boarding school stories but in a wholesome, near utopic, and galactic genderqueer world. With the exception of a male-coded cat named Paul, Walden creates a futuristic reality devoid of cisgender men. Walden expects her readers to quickly "get on board" (bad space pun!), offering very little exposition that confirms her characters' gender and sexuality. For us, these choices are radical and offer readers queer stories that disrupt LGBTQ narratives that link coming out with coming of age (Thein & Kedley, 2015). Walden pushes readers to consider how queerness, gender, and sexuality can be central to a story without being the conflict of the story.

For example, the book opens in a boarding school. A reader could assume that this is an all-girls boarding school. Later in the narrative, the reader will recognize several queer romantic relationships between schoolmates (p.

18) as well as Char and Alma, crew leaders of the reconstruction ship (pp. 167–168). As the reader learns each character's backstories they see that Mia has two moms and later, that Grace has three sisters and a mom (pp. 198–207). Walden spends no time explaining the queerness of her world to a heteronormative gaze. Instead, she intentionally creates a story where this is not explained, allowing the reader to grapple with their own assumptions and understandings of gender and sexuality. For example, *does the reader find it unexpected that athletic events are so important at a boarding school? Are they surprised that a group of women are traveling around doing construction work? Are they surprised that women hold all leadership roles in the book?*

Students understanding of gender and sexuality will inform how they read characters and relationships in this book. *For example, are readers viewing Char and Alma as parental figures to Jules, El, and Mia? Are Mia's classmates picking on her and Grace because they are queer or a reaction to Grace's perceived class privilege (i.e., she has her own single room and X snatches her necklace)? Why does Jule's mockingly address Char as Charlotte but then later passionately defends El when they are misgendered by the new captain?*

Students should be encouraged to engage in these discussions by going back into the text (and their annotations) to find visual and textual moments that support their responses. Figure 4.4 offers a list of themes and possible discussion questions.

Developing Digital Theme Boards

Using Google Jamboard, Google Slides, Prezi, or another collaborative web-based platform, have students create digital collages or boards that trace one

Themes	Discussion Questions
Gender	How does Walden disrupt traditional gender expectations?
Sexuality	What assumptions about sexuality are you making because of the way characters are gendered?
Family	How does Walden develop and portray familial dynamics on the crewship? How does this disrupt heteronormative understandings of family?
History	What is the significance of the ruins? What does it reveal about the values of the crew members?
Coming of Age	How does Mia's character come of age in both timelines?

Figure 4.4   Themes and Discussion Questions.

of Walden's themes across the text. Using the screen capture function with the digital edition of the webcomic, have students cut and paste 3–5 key scenes or moments from across the text that illuminate one of the themes. For example, a student who chooses to trace Mia's coming-of-age may decide to pull images that illustrate how Mia's body language, posture, facial expressions, mood, clothing, and hair change throughout the course of the story as she becomes more confident in herself, her work on the spaceship, and her relationships. A student interested in tracing how Alma and Char cultivate familial kinship with Jules, El, and Mia might draw attention to scenes where they are drawn in traditional family imagery (e.g., family meals, game nights, arguments about protecting the younger crewmembers, retiring, and building a home together). Possible themes for students to trace throughout the story include gender, sexuality, queerness, kinship, family, romance, coming of age, utopia, colonization, technology, environmentalism, history, and school.

Extended Discussion: Examining the Role of Color in Establishing Racialized Characters

Walden never names the race or ethnicity of any of her characters, but at times is using color and imagery to cue diversity and difference among them. Together as a class, read Ronald Wimberly's (2015) graphic essay *Lighten Up.* After reading the graphic essay, use the following questions to facilitate a discussion about the relationship between color and skin tone in visual mediums:

- What is Wimberly's argument about the impact of art on our collective memory?
- Discuss the dual meanings of the phrase *lighten up.*
- How does Wimberly's anecdote about the Hulk underscore his message?
- What is the effect of telling this story in comic form versus traditional essay?
  - In other words, what would be lost if Wimberly wrote, say, an op-ed or long-form essay about this incident with his editor? How does his form bolster his content?
- Wimberly writes of color, "What purpose does it serve?" Connecting to *On a Sunbeam,* what sense do you make of Walden's purpose in shading characters like Char and Grace differently from other characters? What other visual cues does Walden employ that might indicate a racial and ethnic difference in the characters?

Although we are not asking students to complete any writing or projects in response to this discussion, we think it is important for teachers and students to explore the ways race and racism show up in spaces and moments we do not often consider, such as color usage in comics. Additionally, we think this is an opportunity for teachers to consider the benefits and limitations of the #ownvoices movement when curating classroom materials. Walden is a white, queer woman. Her novel is and is not, at times, an example of an #ownvoices text. The absence of named racial and ethnic identities in this book also means readers will bring their own frames and biases to the story. A *superfan* (Low & Jacobs, 2018) might know that Walden created this comic while living in Japan; *are the spaceships drawn as koi fish as a nod to this? Is Mia Japanese?* We don't know what the racial and ethnic dynamics are, but we can say for certain that Walden is drawing and coloring characters differently. *What does it suggest to readers that Walden's characters from the Staircase are colored more darkly?* We believe this additional reading and discussion offers teachers an entry point into unpacking how race manifests in graphic novels even when the content of the story is not explicitly about race.

BEYOND *ON A SUNBEAM*

In the following extension activities, we want to encourage teachers to provide opportunities for students to engage in additional forms of multimodal literary responses to multimodal texts. We believe that using graphic novels in the classroom only to reproduce traditional forms of assessment undercuts the multimodal potential of comics in the classroom.

Creating Audiobook Adaptations

At the core of adaptation, work is accessibility: whose body and mind can access stories in what forms? This is, unfortunately, often where we find comics used in classrooms: as a bridge between a reader and a challenging text (Crawford, 2004; Edwards, 2009; Gavigan, 2011). We want to offer an alternative way of conceptualizing comics' place in classrooms: *how are these works actually limiting access to some readers and how can students work toward making them more accessible?* As a visual medium, graphic novels are generally inaccessible to readers with visual impairments. However, there have been recent examples of this work being done with success. For example, Noelle Stevenson's *Nimona* was adapted into an audiocomic that included a full ensemble cast to perform the narrative. In a very different style of translation, Chad Allen's *Seen* was adapted to an audiocomic, a form of audiobook that describes each panel and takes a listener through what they would see on the original print pages. *Seen* is available for free to stream online and we recommend listening to a few minutes of it to get a sense of what Chad Allen is doing in his adaptation.

In small groups, have students select a small portion of the text. Perhaps a chapter, or maybe a crucial scene within a chapter. Students can create a script for their audiobook adaptation in the style they choose: ensemble cast or audiocomic. Another possibility would be for everyone to complete the same chapter or scene and to compare and contrast how each group interpreted and performed the same moments differently. This activity will push students to grapple with how to translate shifts in time and space that Walden marks with paneling and color palettes for a reader who can only hear the story, rather than see the story. We believe this process and work attends to content as well as element mastery.

Creating a Class Podcast Series

Podcasts are another multimodal practice that students could use to synthesize their learning. Ask students to spend some time researching podcasts. How are they structured? How long are episodes? How many speakers are generally featured in a single podcast episode? How do creators organize topics in a series? What are the threads or through lines that tie a podcast series together? For example, *Dissect*, hosted by Cole Cuchna, is a serialized music podcast that examines a single album of music per season, one song per episode. After having students explore the types and styles of podcasts that exist, brainstorm a structure for a series based on Walden's *On A Sunbeam* (or on comics broadly!) where small groups of students each own a single episode. As a class, they could collaborate on their theme, structure, and focus of each episode. Each small group could then develop the content for each episode.

CONCLUSION

As a former secondary ELA teacher (Nicole) and a former middle school librarian, (Jenna), we came to graphic novel advocacy through different experiences. While Nicole battled with colleagues and department heads to make space in curriculum for graphic novels, Jenna was witness to the frequency and fervor with which youth checked these materials out of the library. One of the most common responses we get from undergraduates studying to become ELA teachers is that graphic novels are great for students' independent reading. Rarely do they see the potential of these texts to rigorously and adequately address ELA standards. We believe this is because teachers do not always know how to engage with graphic novels in ways that attend to the rigor of its form. We feel strongly that graphic novels like Tillie Walden's

On a Sunbeam offer teachers rich opportunities to facilitate highly engaging and intellectually stimulating conversations about the relationships between content and form. Just as graphic novels engage with complex, multiple literacies, the activities we have outlined in this chapter offer teachers a variety of ways to leverage students' multiple literacies as a response to reading. As a queer graphic novel, *On a Sunbeam* provides ELA teachers with a model for how queer content and graphic forms are not at odds with ELA standards and instruction.

REFERENCES

Crawford, P. (2004). A novel approach: Using graphic novels to attract reluctant readers and promote literacy. *Library Media Connection, 22*(5), 26–28.

Edwards, B. (2009). Motivating middle school readers: The graphic novel link. *School Library Media Activities Monthly, 25*(8), 56–58.

Gavigan, K. (2011). More powerful than a locomotive: Using graphic novels to motivate struggling male adolescent readers. *The Journal of Research on Libraries and Young Adults, 1*(3), 7–8.

Jacobs, D. (2007). More than words: Comics as a means of teaching multiple literacies. *English Journal, 96*(3), 19–24.

Kedley, K. E., & Spiering, J. (2017). Using LGBTQ graphic novels to dispel myths about gender and sexuality in ELA classrooms. *English Journal, 107*(1), 54–60.

Low, D. E., & Jacobs, K. B. (2018). Literature circle roles for discussing graphica in language arts classrooms. *Language Arts, 95*(5), 322–331.

Matos, A. D., & Wargo, J. M. (2019). Editors' introduction: Queer futurities in youth literature, media, and culture. *Research on Diversity in Youth Literature, 2*(1), 1.

Narter, D. (2013). Pencils down: Is mimicking the behaviors of "Good Readers" bad for good readers? *The English Journal, 102*(5), 63–68.

Thein, A. H., Guise, M., & Sloan, D. A. L. (2011). Problematizing literature circles as forums for discussion of multicultural and political texts. *Journal of Adolescent & Adult Literacy: A Journal from the International Reading Association, 55*(1), 15–24.

Thein, A. H., & Kedley, K. E. (2015). Out of the closet and all grown up: Problematizing normative narratives of coming-out and coming-of-age in young adult literature. In Darla Linville and David Lee Carlson (Eds.), *Beyond borders: Queer eros and ethos (ethics) in LGBTQ young adult literature* (pp. 3–20). Peter Lang.

Walden, T. (2018). *About on a sunbeam.* https://www.onasunbeam.com/about.

Walden, T. (2018). *On a sunbeam.* https://www.onasunbeam.com/.

Wimberly, R. (2015). Lighten up. *The Nib.* https://thenib.com/lighten-up-4f7f96ca8a 7e/.

Chapter 5

"About Being Free"

Exploring Identity, Queerness, and Radical Possibility through Verse in The Black Flamingo

shea wesley martin

"Queerness is not yet here," José Esteban Muñoz writes on the first page of his groundbreaking 2009 text, *Cruising Utopia* (2009, p. 1). Thus, queerness (or queer pedagogy) is a powerful foundation for examining literature and its connections to the world around us in our high school English/Language Arts classes full of messy, beautiful, and brilliant "not yet heres." Dean Atta's *The Black Flamingo* is a masterclass in queering form, structure, and narrative through verse. His attention to space and word provides readers with permission to unpack what exists on the page, but also imagine and wonder beyond it. Atta tells us that being a Black drag artist is "about being free" and the freedom Michael experiences as a drag artist echoes throughout Atta's use of poetic devices, conflict, and structure to tell the story (Atta, 2020, p. 379).

In his journey to self-discovery, Michael navigates relationships with a blended family and an assortment of friends, bullies, and strangers. Through his poetry, friendships, and performance, Michael learns what it truly means to be free. This young adult text illuminates the journey of a boy learning to strut his truth while also reconciling with his inability (or refusal) to adhere to prescribed norms. This novel in verse is for the kids (and adults) who might need a little nudge to let their fierceness shine.

The Black Flamingo makes readers smile, cry, and want to start a revolution in the streets. Today's secondary students are boundless in their critical analysis, self-discovery, and advocacy. In between homework and extracurricular activities, they are leading movements in their communities and around the world to demand equality, justice, and freedom. Thus, reading texts where protagonists grapple with identity and question the world can help students further develop their curiosity, critical analysis skills, and leadership. The best books open up possibilities to readers. Let Atta's words and these strategies be your guide to queering literacy instruction and unapologetically asking "what if?"

SUMMARY OF *THE BLACK FLAMINGO*

Set in the modern-day United Kingdom, *The Black Flamingo* details the growing up and coming out journey of mixed-race Greek-Cypriot and Jamaican protagonist, Michael. Through Michael's narration and written poetry, we witness his reckoning with complex identities and relationships along with cultural and societal norms. In Atta's verse, readers witness Michael's journey from child to college student and find joy (and hope) in his transformation from a young boy to a fierce drag queen who embraces both his masculine and feminine identities. By exploring the intersections of gender, sexuality, and race, *The Black Flamingo* offers a glimpse into modern-day British LGBTQ culture and schooling.

BEFORE READING *THE BLACK FLAMINGO*

Note to Teachers

Dean Atta's *The Black Flamingo* explores the nuances of identity through striking verse that compels readers to reflect upon their own identity markers and how they show in the world. As such, teachers should take great care when designing the container for using this text as a whole-class novel or independent reading. Establishing a "brave" classroom culture should be prioritized before digging into this dynamic text (Arao & Clemons, 2013). As Arao and Clemons outlined in their chapter, "From Safe Spaces to Brave Spaces," brave spaces differ from safe spaces in that they ask participants to critically engage in ideas surrounding "braveness" in discussion, embrace the discomfort that accompanies unpacking identity and structural inequities in society, and commit to a culture of continued learning and discussion (pp. 139–140). While laying foundational work may take additional instructional time, students will benefit from norms for discussion, reflection, and reading that center growth, listening, and accountability.

Dean Atta holds little back in this text. He writes about Blackness, queerness, and gender fluidity in its truest and rawest forms. Given this truth, teachers should be aware and prepared to address sensitive topics discussed in the text including, but not limited to, date rape, child assault, race (racial profiling, colorism, policing), homophobia, bullying, sex, and recreational drug use. Many of the aforementioned sensitive topics are not focal points of the novel. However, teachers may want to consult guidance counselors, local LGBTQ community organizations, and/or advisors of your school's LGBTQ affinity club for support and resources.

Unpacking Identity through Dotted Lines

A core theme of Dean Atta's novel is identity development with close attention given to the ways Michael navigates the world given his identity as a Black biracial, gay boy growing up in London. Thus, a discussion of intersectionality, or "the social, economic and political ways in which identity-based systems of oppression and privilege connect, overlap and influence one another," may be helpful in preparing students to engage with the text (Bell, 2016; Crenshaw, 1987). When preparing to discuss identity, power, and privilege with students, be mindful of the container in which conversations will exist as well as the diverse knowledge-set and experiences of learners. The following activity (unknown origin) is a foundational diversity and equity exercise aimed at helping participants unpack identity, consider how privilege and oppression impact their daily life, and make connections between their experiences and those of others. It has been adapted for secondary classrooms and designed to be completed in 1–2 classroom sessions to help teachers begin and/or continue conversations about how social identity markers affect individuals' experiences of the world.

Preparation. To begin, provide students a social identity wheel and/or organizer with an overview of the following identity markers: race, ethnicity, socioeconomic status, religion, native language, gender identity, sexual orientation, family structure, ability, and age. Have students complete some sort of reflection in which they identify and reflect upon their own identity markers. Encourage students to share their experiences with a partner. When done, review the following definitions for the following words with students: privilege, social power, oppression, agent/privileged identity, target/ oppressed identity, prejudice, and intersectionality. When reviewing terms with students, consider using definitions provided by Adams, Bell, and Griffin in *Teaching for Diversity and Social Justice* (1997). These definitions are widely accepted and used by diversity, equity, and inclusion practitioners and thus are easily accessible online for educator use. Encourage students to do their own meaning-making and discuss these terms before engaging further in the activity.

Execution. This begins as a silent activity requiring student reflection and movement. Around your classroom, place ten posters each with an identity marker listed at the top and a horizontal line in the middle. At one left end of the line, write T/O or "target/oppressed." At the right end, A/NO or "agent/

not oppressed." Each student should be provided ten stickers (or a marker) to complete the activity. Students should take time to reflect upon their identity in society along with social power and privilege as they walk around to each poster and place a sticker representing their identity along the identity line (see Figure 5.1).

When done, teachers may choose to have students reflect independently or facilitate a conversation about trends, questions, and reflections on the visuals around the room using the following discussion format. To begin, have students move to the identity marker posters using the following prompts as directives: identity that you are proudest of, identity you think about most often, identity you think about least often, identity you like to learn more about. Following each prompt, consider asking students to discuss their reflections with others at the same posters or with students at neighboring posters. In order to help students make connections and begin thinking about collective identity and diversity in your classroom space, prompt students by asking "what do you notice about the dot placements on the posters around our classroom? What might this reveal about our community dynamics and experiences?" As students share, consider asking them to make connections to

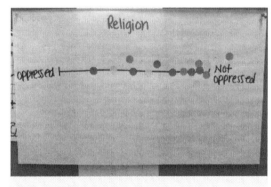

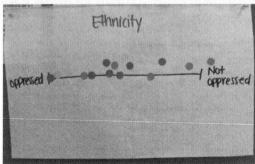

Figure 5.1   Identity Dot-Line Charts (Classroom example published with permission from Daniella Suárez Boyd, High School Math Teacher, Florida).

their own lived experiences and use "I" statements to avoid making assumptions about the experiences of others (example: according to the "class" chart, it seems like many of us have privilege when it comes to class or money. I don't necessarily feel that way because my family is working class so I feel like that might impact how I interact with others when we discuss issues of class or resources).

This discussion might be difficult for students as it may reveal disparities, tensions, and conflicting ideas about privilege/oppression. Because of this, it is helpful to set solid norms for engagement with students and allow space for engaging in multiple ways. You know your students best so prepare engagement and discussion strategies that work best for your group dynamics. At the end of the exercise, it is helpful to have students reflect on the activity as a whole along with spending some time to process their thinking and emotions. End the exercise by thanking students for sharing their truths and participating in a tough conversation. Name and acknowledge that this is a never-ending conversation, particularly given the central theme of identity in *The Black Flamingo*. Before transitioning to another activity, allow space and time for students to independently reflect on the following prompts.

- What questions and/or reflections did you have when completing the Identity Dot Line?
- How might your social identity markers afford you certain privilege in society? How might you experience oppression and/or prejudice given your social identity markers?

Reading Poetry: Making Connections Between Form and Meaning

The novel's verse structure begs a brief review on structure, form, and integral terms such as stanzas, line (breaks), and poetic devices used to convey meaning to readers and audiences. This pre-reading activity also presents teachers the opportunity to highlight other LGBTQ poets, makes connections to community and world, as well as begins conversations about themes of identity development, finding your voice, and overcoming barriers. Instead of reviewing devices and structure in isolation, select a few poems to use in your review. Given the performance nature of poetry (and its importance in the novel), consider including spoken word poetry or poetry that has both audio and written formats available for analysis.

Table 5.1 provides a list of suggested poems written by LGBTQ poets for teachers to consider as they prepare to read *The Black Flamingo* with students.

Table 5.1 Paired LGBTQ Authored Poems for *The Black Flamingo*

Suggested Texts	⟵→ *to* The Black Flamingo	Discussion Prompts
"Accents" by Denice Frohman	Frohman's poem addresses sentiments of home and family while also capitalizing on the performance aspect of spoken word poetry. Frohman's focus on language and family invites a conversation about identity related to language, ethnicity, family histories—three topics extensively addressed in Atta's text.	How does Frohman's performance engage the audience in dialogue and understanding of community? Consider your own caregivers and/or parents. What words, phrases, and imagery might you use to describe their presence in your life?
"Heartbeats" by Melvin Dixon	A heart-wrenching poem that details living with an HIV/AIDs, "Heartbeats" allows for expanded conversations about the virus, intimacy, and gay histories. The structure of the poem provides a platform to discuss how poetic structure and intentionality affect storytelling and themes.	Consider the structure of "Heartbeats." How does Dixon's couplet structure (and word choice) serve his purpose and messaging?
"dear white America" by Danez Smith	Smith's scathing address is a rage-filled, honest indictment of the United States' history of violence against Black folks. With both a written and live performance available, this poem invites discussions and analysis related to Blackness, anger/rage, performance, and use of form/structure which may provide a natural link to Atta's gripping verse.	After watching the live performance and reading the poem, how does Smith's presentation and/or form impact how you receive and interpret the poem? Smith addresses the poem to "white America." What are the benefits/limitations of this choice in getting his main ideas about race, violence, and pain across to the audience?
"Of Dark Love: I" by Francisco X. Alarcón	Alarcón writes about a forbidden love (and desire to love out loud) in this poem which connects well to Atta's characterization of Michael's relationships with coming out and finding love as a gay Black boy. Consider also revisiting the poem while reading *The Black Flamingo*.	How does the structure of the poem contribute (or not contribute to) a sense of resolution in the last stanza? How does Alarcón's use of imagery impact our understanding of the speaker's love and desire?

"One Geography of Belonging" by Kayleb Rae Candrilli	Candrilli's poem is an ode to their trans body, a declaration of honor, beauty, and truth within the geography of their being. Addressed to their mother, this poem can be used to discuss themes of parent-child relationships (and transition) as well as body image and gender also included in *The Black Flamingo*.	How does Candrilli's use of geographic imagery and language help readers understand their sentiments about their body and relationship to their mother?
"Twerk Villanelle" by Porsha Olayiwola	An ode to her lover, Olayiwola's poem offers a glimpse into queer adoration, joy, and performance—a wonderful introduction to Atta's use of verse to queer structure, language, and narrative.	Olayiwola pairs strict villanelle structure with hip hop dance and queer love in this poem. What does the contrast offer to readers in forms of understanding queerness, joy, and love?

WHILE READING *THE BLACK FLAMINGO*

Dean Atta's verse is a gift that affords deep analysis and rich discussion when reading. From his masterful use of space and line breaks, to his poems within poems, to the intricate development of Michael's character and relationships, this text provides readers with the opportunity to grapple, question, reflect, and imagine in ways that are revolutionary.

As students read the book, encourage them to be attuned to how Atta uses structure and form to convey the intricacies of identity and relationships, particularly Michael's relationship with his mom ("Barbies and Belonging"), friends ("Drag"), and love interests ("Just Be a Man"). Queering literacy allows educators to use literacy as a framework to examine gender, sexuality, and societal norms through using a critical lens that invites students to make connections between texts, their own experiences, and the world around them (Blackburn, 2002; Miller, 2015). When we do so, we must consider how we might center the affirmation and celebration of nuance, how we might reckon with how queerness is not only an infinite space of possibility, but also a revolution against what has previously been defined. In that, review the strategies below, but also dream beyond what you are used to doing in your literacy spaces and try something new. Ask kids how they might want to engage with the text. Give them options. Release control and sit in potentiality. It's worth it.

Tracking Identity Development: Exploring the Development of Intersectional Identity

An organizer can be a great tool for tracking how Atta illustrates Michael's identity development throughout the novel. Building on the theme of intersectionality (and the pre-reading activity), the "Tracking Identity Development"

Page Number (and/or excerpt)	Identity Markers Explored (circle)	What's happening?	How does this affect Michael's development and understanding of his own identity?
Example: pp. 57 - 58 "Unlikely gladiators, / a crowd gathers, pushing us closer: / 'Fight! Fight! Fight!' / A familiar chorus around here / but not one I've ever chosen to sing."	Race Ethnicity (Gender) Ability (Sexuality) Native Language Socioeconomic Status / Class Religion Family Structure Age	In this scene, boys from Michael's school demand Michael and Alistair, another choir boy, fight outside of school. Michael beats up Alistair and when asked to continue he refuses and runs away.	The bullying Michael experiences confirms assumptions and messaging about what boys "should" do and how they should act. He asks to change schools because he doesn't feel comfortable at that school doing something he loves (singing).

Figure 5.2 Tracking Identity Development Organizer (created specifically for this chapter by shea martin, 2021).

organizer can help students unpack scenes and lines in the text while also giving them concrete examples of how identity interacts with societal norms and structures to influence a person's trajectory. While the example in table 5.2 centers Michael's development, it could also be used to analyze the development of Daisy or Lennie.

Unpacking gender norms in Michael's life. In the first few sections, Atta portrays Michael's exploration of gender through his interactions with family, friends, and classmates. As students read "Barbies and Belonging" (pp. 9–34), "Sandcastles" (pp. 35–48), and "Music and Stars" (pp. 49–100), have them complete a chart that chronicles how Michael's exploration of gender is impacted by events at home and school. Grounding the chart in setting and character interactions allows for further discussion on the differences between Michael's home and school life. For example, Michael struggles with acceptance and safety at school as a boy. We are introduced to this dichotomy in "Barbies and Belonging" in which Michael's mother supports his desire to explore the feminine by gifting him a Barbie doll. On the other hand, However, Atta juxtaposes this safety and acceptance at home with depictions of Michael's difficult schooling experience. In "Music and Stars," Michael is bullied into fighting another classmate because of perceptions about sexuality. These differences not only offer space for students to analyze how setting and relationships impact Michael's journey toward self-acceptance, but also may create space for further dialogue about safety, acceptance, and identity development in your own school environment.

Unpacking the Connection through Literature Circles

In *The Black Flamingo*, there is a bold confluence of form/structure and character development and connections to current events, history, and activism. Having students unpack the connections between Atta's structure and narrative both independently and in small-group settings offers them an opportunity to analyze how Atta uses poetic devices, structure, and tone to portray the complexities of identity and relationships.

Literature circles are a staple of English/Language Arts classrooms. While the strategy allows students to unpack and discuss texts in small groups, it is easy to use the group as a strategy meant to police student engagement (and provide a concreteness that is antithetical to the fluidity of queerness and queer pedagogy). While roles are mostly designed to help students focus and remain accountable to their own analysis, it often becomes an obligatory function of discussion which might detract from a true grappling with the complexities of literature.

Propose a literature circle activity that is rooted in fostering a love of reading (and rereading), making connections, reflection, imagination, and rich

Table 5.2   Reimagining Literature Circle: Roles and Examples

Role	Description	Examples (Music and Stars)
The Architect	A large part of one's analysis of *The Black Flamingo* is paying great attention to how Atta's structure and form exists in service of plot, themes, and character development. The Architect is obsessed with *structure and form*—line breaks, space, and poetic devices with special attention to how the author utilizes form and structure to emphasize and present the narrative.	While most of the text is right-aligned in this section, Atta shifts the alignment on page 62 in which he writes about flamingos fighting (or kissing). The text is written in the shape of a heart which seems to soften the tense moment between Michael and his mother on his birthday. Although Michael has just been forced to fight Alstair, the heart-shaped verse in which Atta writes, "Flamingos fighting/can look just like kissing," evokes empathy from readers given Michael's struggle and development with sexuality, gender, and self-acceptance (Atta, 2019, 62).
The Web Designer	Relationships are a key component of Atta's novel. The complexities of Michael's relationships with friends, family, and strangers guide his understanding of himself in the world. The Web Designer is a "relationship expert." They study the section focusing on an examination of the *relationship dynamics* (and the impact of those relationships on Michael's trajectory).	Michael experiences many conflicts and shifts in this section. Two schools, bullying, new friends, and a birthday. While his school life is difficult (with classmates' bullying him for being a choir boy and changing schools), he finds safety in Uncle B, his mom, and new friend Daisy which allow him space to grow, explore his interests, and be held accountable for his actions.
The ID Expert	Given the integral theme of identity development, students should always be attuned to how Atta's verse is complicating *understandings of identity* (and how it affects one's relationship to the systems, structures, and people).	In this section, Michael experiences prejudice related to his sexuality. At one school, he is forced to fight another classmate, while at another school, he is ridiculed and judged for his sexuality based on religion. Through the depiction of the bullying (and how Michael responds to it), Atta illuminates the messaging Michael receives from society about expectations related to gender and sexuality. These experiences only seem to build on top of his experiences as a younger child.

The Connector	The Connector: Michael's journey is chock full of connections to current events, history, geography, and the journeys of all students. In the literature circle, the Connector's role is to analyze the text specifically looking for connections to self, the world, and other parts of the text.	Interestingly enough, Michael's difficulty with the boys at his first middle school seem to connect to his difficulty with his first boyfriend, Callum ("Barbies and Belonging"). Callum likes Michael but already knows and messages that Michael's interests in Barbies and the color pink are deemed inappropriate by society. I think both incidents (Callum's dismissal and the forced fight) impact Michael's journey of self-acceptance. I wonder what messages we've been given as youth that impact our own journeys and understanding of identity. For example, we definitely hear messages about what is appropriate for different genders and certain age groups.
The Dreamer	Authors make choices about which narratives are centered, what happens in a text, and how the text is structured. The Dreamer's job in this literature circle activity is to interrogate the author's choices and wonder "what if?" Imagination is such an integral piece of queer pedagogy and abolitionist teaching. Don't be afraid to encourage students to dream beyond the text, to put themselves in the pilot's seat and position themselves as worthy of creating.	I know Michael meets Daisy at his new school, but what if Michael hadn't let the bullies at his first school deprive him of his creativity and love for music? I imagine Michael continues to sing and allows that to inspire a musical act or band called *The Black Flamingo*. What if Michael became a star instead of just looking at them? I wonder what would have happened if Atta chose to depict the fight as actual flamingos fighting instead of including the verse on page 62. How might that have changed how we viewed the sad scene between Michael and Alistair?

discussion. As students analyze, discuss, and create deliverables related to selected portions of the texts, teachers should circulate and be mindful of tensions and breaches that may arise due to discussions of sensitive topics. Thein, Guise, & Sloan (2011) noted that literature circles can foster student-student dialogue, curiosity, and criticality but teachers should be acutely present and available to help ensure the braveness of spaces. Remind students of norms you have co-created and established as they begin to engage. For this activity, encourage students to read the assigned section at least three times: once for enjoyment, a second time with all roles in mind, and a third time with their specific assignment in mind (to prepare for the discussion and/or collaboration).

Many literature circles happen in isolation with students discussing in small groups and providing a record and/or accountability sheet to the teachers. Many times this prioritizes assessment over creativity, conversation, and analysis. Instead, have students create a representation of their discussion (think JamBoard/Slide/Poster), present their discussion to others (perhaps a six-word recap or presenting a dramatic rendering of an "aha" moment), or reflect individually about it. Figure 5.3 offers examples of visual recaps of Literature Circle discussions from students in the Love and LiteraTea 2020–2021 cohort.

Both proposed activities examine how Dean Atta addresses nuance, fluidity, and abundance of identity through narrative, form, and structure. In many ways, Atta's verse is the quintessential mentor text for queering narrative. As students read, consider explicitly naming the "queering" of storying. *Think and Pose: How is Atta using form, characterization, and tone to talk back to Eurocentric, cishet ways of storying? What can we learn about the expansiveness and malleability of queerness through Atta's verse?*

When engaging students in the above guiding questions, you may want to scaffold your questioning by using the following prompts:

- What do you consider to be a "normal" structure for a book? How is this book different? What does the difference afford the reader in experiencing the narrative?
- Consider which identities are considered most "normal" in society. Why are those identities considered normal while others aren't?
- Given the two questions together, what might Atta be trying to say about normalcy and possibility within queerness and verse narrative?

AFTER READING *THE BLACK FLAMINGO*

While there are a multitude of strategies, one might use to engage student thinking and creativity after finishing the novel, teachers should choose

Figure 5.3   Black Flamingo Literature Circle Boards (Love & LiteraTea, 2021).

activities and prompts that offer students an opportunity to go beyond traditional writing tasks such as essays or short writing prompts. Extending assignments beyond traditional writing tasks is also part of queering literacy practices.

"Doing The Most" One Pager

For many English/Language Arts teachers, the one-pager has become as much of a staple in the literacy classroom as written essays. However, like essays, many teachers rely on strict guidelines, detailed rubrics, and concise directions for the one-pager thus stifling creativity and stripping students of autonomy and space to imagine. The "Doing the Most" one-pager challenges the rigidity of the assignment and allows students more space to be creative.

Just as with traditional one-pagers, teachers should provide students with basic guidelines. Consider providing students with guidelines on what areas they should focus on, textual citation requirements, and any other essential requirements. Tell students they'll be assessed on their analysis, creativity, and audacity. If this makes you uncomfortable, embrace it. Your students who have mastered the art of "doing well in school," might also be uncomfortable: "what do you mean audacity? I'm not creative!" The point of "doing the most" is to give all students the space to discover and dig into how they best process and create. I do suggest limiting the size of the "page," but remind students that the page can be virtual or physical, 2-D or 3-D, and

include directions to continue beyond the page (think links, attachments, and/
or how the page is presented). Encourage students to go over the top with
their assignments and give them the time to do (and present) it. Prepare to
offer students examples and tools for engagement (think: glitter, magazines,
printer, coloring materials, access to technology, music). "The Most" can
include any type of intentional references and/or offshoots from the text such
as quotes, pictures, lyrics, models, current event references, pop culture notes,
maps, original art/poetry, etc. Let the students shine and encourage them to
go beyond!

"Flip It and Reverse It": A Verse Challenge

In honor of Missy Elliot's (2002) iconic song, "Work It," this poetry challenge asks students to choose a section of the book, "flip it and reverse
it." Atta's first-person narrative and creative use of poetic structure allows
infinite opportunities for inferring, dreaming, discussing "what ifs?" related
to structure, form, and plot. When students flip and reverse it, they begin
by analyzing the structure, form, devices, and content of the section of
poetry. Ideally, students should choose (or be assigned) a selection rich in
character emotion and actions. As students analyze, consider providing a
graphic organizer where they can make notes on structure, form, devices,
and what's happening in the text. When done, ask students to speculate on
Atta's decisions regarding perspective, structure, form, and details of the
scene.

As students "flip it and reverse it" (Elliott, 2022), their task is to rewrite
the verse making significant shifts to at least two of the following: narrator/
perspective, structure, poetic devices used, resolution. Allowing students to
change how the scene resolves encourages imagination and creativity. Invite
students to recite their flipped and reversed revisions aloud and/or post them
to a class blog. When presenting, students should read/display the original
text, explain their unpacking of the author's choices, present their own, and
provide a brief explanation of their decisions behind their flipping and revers-
ing of the scene. Suggested excerpts for the "Flip it and Reverse It" Verse
Challenge:

1. Michael's Barbie Christmas (pp. 18–19)
2. Queerdo and Weirdo (pp. 81–82)
3. "Men Who are Not my Dad" (pp. 142)
4. Michael in heels (pp. 274–275)
5. Lennie's Speech (pp. 298–299)
6. "What It's Like to Be a Draft Artist" (pp. 371–372)
7. Stretch: Jack and Michael (pp. 385–387, 391–394)

BEYOND *THE BLACK FLAMINGO*

Comparing *The Black Flamingo* and *Batty Boy*: Close Analysis and Discussion

Like *The Black Flamingo*, *Batty Boy* by Dior Clarke and Blaine Ho-Shing explored the nuances of Blackness, gender, and sexuality through a Jamaican-British lens. The coming out narrative and childhood/adulthood snapshots allow for a wonderful pairing with Atta's portrayal of Michael's journey. After reading *The Black Flamingo*, consider showing *Batty Boy* and pairing it with four distinct scenes in the novel:

1. The Batty Bwoy taunts + Coming Out (pp. 124–127)
2. The fight with Alistair (pp. 56–58)
3. The Black gay club experience (pp. 333–343)

Questions to consider:

- How does the film's narrative compare and/or contrast with Atta's depiction of similar experiences in Michael's journey?
- What is lost and gained through the choice of mediums (verse and film)?
- If you were to portray these events, what might you want to include and/or omit for audiences?

The Mixtape

Throughout *The Black Flamingo*, Dean Atta makes multiple references to historical and contemporary music and pop culture. Students could examine and discuss the relevance of references such as *Kinky Boots* (pp. 173, 229), Beyoncé (pp. 84, 127, 216, 232, 275, 317, 320, 339, 380), and Bob Marley (pp. 84, 96, 98, 142, 151, 216, 287, 305). Have students create a mixtape with songs by artists referenced, as well as songs they think would also fit in with the text. Encourage students to build their mixtapes in a streaming service to share with others. In addition to mixtapes, students could complete an artist statement in which they explain their reasoning for the inclusion, placement, and meaning for each song. If you want to really let kids shine, let them create cover art, come up with their "producer" name and suggest they do short promos for their *Black Flamingo* mixtape.

Show Out with Spoken Word!

From singing to drag performance, Michael's journey of self-discovery is full of performance, creativity, and poetry about his experiences. Plan your own in-class open mic for students. Spend some time watching and discussing spoken word poetry about identity and growth. Have students write and perform their own poems.

CONCLUSION

In the introduction to his story, Michael tells readers the story is a fairy tale, that he—our often prehensive and sometimes fierce narrator—is "the fairy/finding [his] own magic" (Atta, 2020, p. 3). What is most true, however, is that this book, Michael's story and Atta's verse, is *the magic*. Like LGBTQ folks, just the existence of this narrative in the world is a gift. The strategies and ideas presented provide you some tools to make the magic come alive in your own learning spaces. May it unearth fierceness, joy, criticality, and revolution when read, taught, and discussed.

REFERENCES

Arao, B., & Clemons, K. (2013). From safe to brave spaces. In L. M. Landreman (Ed.), *The art of effective facilitation: Reflections from social justice educators* (pp. 135–150). Stylus Publishing, LLC.

Atta, D. (2020). *The black flamingo*. Balzer + Bray.

Blackburn, M. (2002). Disrupting the (hetero)normative: Exploring literacy performances and identity work with queer youth. *Journal of Adolescent & Adult Literacy, 46*(4), 312–324.

Bell, M. K. (2016). Teaching at the intersections. *Teaching Tolerance*. https://www.learningforjustice.org/magazine/summer-2016/teaching-at-the-intersections.

Crenshaw, K. (1989). Demarginalizing the intersection of race and sex: A black feminist critique of antidiscrimination doctrine, feminist theory and antiracist Politics. *University of Chicago Legal Forum*. Vol. 1989, Article 8.

Miller, S. J. (2015). A queer literacy framework promoting (a)gender and (a)sexuality self-determination and justice. *The English Journal, 104*(5), 37–44.

Missy Elliot. (2002). Work it. Tim "Timbaland" Mosley.

Muñoz, J. E. (2009). *Cruising utopia: The then and there of queer futurity*. New York University Press.

Thein, A. H., Guise, M. and Sloan, D. L. (2011). Problematizing literature circles as forums for discussion of multicultural and political texts. *Journal of Adolescent & Adult Literature, 55*(1), 15–24.

Chapter 6

"To Go Somewhere I Knew Someone Would See Me"

Narrative Structure, Flashbacks, and Social Worlds in Candice Iloh's Every Body Looking

Ryan Burns

Historically, storytelling has privileged a clear sequence and structure of beginning, middle, and end. Yet recent developments in adolescent literature, including popular media texts, challenge these dominant forms of narrative with an abundance of novels composed in verse, like snapshots or vignettes, and texts that filter through a kaleidoscope of narrative events in a nonlinear fashion. As an example for examining narrative structure that resists this predictable pattern, Candice Iloh's *Every Body Looking* (2020), written in verse and composed of 336 individual poems, breaks from the linear unfolding of narratives so often seen in literature. Instead, Iloh, a Black, queer, nonbinary author, carefully threads narrative strands from different time periods and social worlds, including elementary school, middle school, high school, and college. In this way, like a life story stitched together with flashbacks, Iloh invites readers to examine the narrative structure and to consider the development of meaning in the protagonist's struggles and triumphs. In this context, structure can best be understood by the ways in which authors and creators "marry the various . . . parts together harmoniously and aesthetically," even when those parts are not bound to a chronological timeline (Prather, 2019, p. 102).

As teachers of secondary literacy, we know that with writing, especially, narrative forms of composition, "there is no box, no precut pieces, and only the foggiest of pictures. You're cutting the pieces to make them fit a picture you're not even able to visualize yet" (Prather, 2019, p. 101). Using Candice Iloh's *Every Body Looking* in the secondary English Language Arts classroom with a focus on examining structure helps to achieve a goal of developing student experimentation with and understanding of "how arrangement contributes to meaning" (Prather, 2019, p. 103). This chapter offers opportunities to consider the ways in which Iloh utilizes different poetic techniques and strategies by writing in verse to build a narrative structure that engages the reader in meaning making. More specifically, the learning experiences that follow will focus on how structure is used to develop the individual poems and larger narrative, and thus, the arc of the protagonist's personal story through her narration of life in various social worlds in which she participates and occupies.

SUMMARY OF *EVERY BODY LOOKING* BY CANDICE ILOH

"Here's the scene: I'm seventeen and graduating" (p. 4). In *Every Body Looking*, Ada, the daughter of Nigerian immigrants and a recent high school graduate, begins her first year at a Historically Black College. For the first time in her life, she is away from her family and attempting to construct and define her life on her own terms. With this exciting personal freedom comes opportunities to learn and grow through new friendships, dating, social events, and her love of dance. As a dancer, Ada continues to move with her body and develops newfound self-awareness and confidence as she discovers aspects of herself that were otherwise off limits at home. The dance studio soon becomes a new home as she sees potential in herself with the help of fellow dancer, Kendra. From the first day they meet on campus, Kendra challenges Ada to spread her wings and follow her passions. As the two dancers spend more time together, their friendship grows more intimate, stirring feelings in Ada to explore the possibilities of her sexuality beyond the limitations of heterosexuality that her parents expect of her.

Despite the thrill of the present moment, memories linger from Ada's childhood and adolescence, including family strife from her erratic mother's battle with addiction, the demanding expectations of her religious father, and the trauma of sexual abuse. As flashbacks ebb and flow, Ada reaches emotional extremes as she grapples with college life, trying to fit in, and carrying the heaviness of questioning and exploring the possibilities of her own queerness. These moments, both past and present, cause her to wrestle with how she sees herself as a young Black woman, her body, and the eventuality of finding a path toward healing, liberation, and joy.

BEFORE READING *EVERY BODY LOOKING*

Guiding and Essential Questions: Focus on Narrative Structure

In addition to using student questions and curiosities that frame specific topics or lessons, there are several teacher generated prompts that can be used to anchor the reading and teaching of *Every Body Looking* with a particular focus on structure: *How might writing in verse impact telling a story? What choices in craft does Iloh make to structure the narrative? How might Iloh's choices inform how readers generate meaning about the novel? In what ways does the structure of the novel help the reader to understand the protagonist and their story? How might Iloh's choices inform the aesthetic impact of the novel? How might a story in verse impact the reader differently than a story written in prose?* These questions will help to move classroom discourse from a focus on the *what* of the text and toward a closer examination of the *how* of the text or the structure that Iloh develops in writing of the novel. By slowly integrating questions on text arrangement and inner structure, students will develop an awareness and language that connects structure to meaning in this and other mentor texts, including student-selected texts. In addition to the guiding prompts on structure, thematic questions can also be used to situate conversations on coming of age, empowerment, and growing up, as well as critical conversations on race, religion, and gender. Ultimately, as students navigate the text in consideration of arrangement, they will be able to put questions of structure side by side with questions of meaning and how one set informs the other.

Brainstorming Narratives

In reading and writing, "almost nothing in a story is neutral, since almost everything in a story contributes to the context in which the story's audience finds meaning" (Salesses, 2020, p. 94). This is especially so with narrative plot lines and structures that are not organized in a linear way. To this end, as a beginning step in reading *Every Body Looking*, invite students to brainstorm familiar texts (books, films, television shows or series, video games, etc.) that use nonlinear storytelling techniques, such as those that jump between moments in time, past and present. To model this kind of thinking, offer students a sample text or series of texts and collaborate as a class to see how and why these conclusions are drawn. Programs like *13 Reasons Why, Euphoria, Stranger Things* and *The Walking Dead* utilize flashbacks, jumps in time and plot, and other techniques that structure the visual text and impact how the reader or audience experiences the narrative. For example, in *Stranger Things*, such devices help to generate suspense through pacing and dangerous action. At other times, like in *The Walking Dead*, flashbacks have been used to focus on characterization and the development of character origins and histories. Through this exercise in brainstorming narratives, looking at *how* an episode is structured or arranged can reveal great insight into *what* is depicted or represented.

After naming titles and texts as part of a whole class share-out, elicit responses from students about what patterns or themes they notice between the texts. *How are the texts similar? How are they different? What observations can be made about the genres, formats, or other stylistic conventions or structures?*

Using Structure to Think About Our Social Worlds

Salesses (2020) and Muhammad (2020) encouraged a critical approach to how we support readers and writers, and this is especially important in their exploration and understanding of content, text structure and the impact on meaning, and the realities of their own lives. Throughout the narrative, Iloh uses flashbacks to reveal how Ada participates in different social worlds at different times, including school, home, church, and dance, to name a few. Before reading, and in advance of the after reading experience that follows, prepare students to work with the concept of narrative structure through social worlds by modeling and describing the spaces and communities in which you participate. In table 6.1, I model some of my social worlds across six different categories. Each category reflects a different sphere of my life, bringing with it unique practices, languages, rules, and ways of being.

Additional social world categories, both in person and from a distance, might include other activity groups such as sports, non-sport groups or communities, music-based groups, online networks, etc. Alternatively, this segment of the lesson can also be accomplished using a fictional character or another individual familiar to students.

Table 6.1 Sample Graphic Organizer—Using Structure to Think About Our Social Worlds

Family: Son, grandson, brother	*Social Networking:* Frequent Twitter user with other educators	*Hobbies and Interests*: Writing group, LGBTQ book club, training at gym
Career: High school English teacher; advisor to Gender-Sexuality Alliance, college adjunct instructor	*Geography/Location:* United States, New England, Rhode Island, Providence	*Education:* Doctoral candidate—online/distance cohort

Following, invite students to reflect on and identify some of their own social worlds and the roles that they take on in those spaces. This can include their roles at home and school, as well as sports and music, among other interests and hobbies. Students can also consider activities, communities and other affinity-based groups, alongside any involvement in advocacy and activism. To expand on their reflection, visual enhancements such as images, drawings, and clipart, can also be used to reinforce student understanding of their social worlds. For example, a student athlete might select an image or logo from their team or sport, while a member of the Environmental Club or the Gender-Sexuality Alliance might display a significant image or symbol that reflects their participation in that group.

As part of Ada's journey, we witness some of the personal, cultural, and social consequences that she experiences as a result of not always knowing or following the rules at different times, including when she attends church with her father (pp. 47–57). As a next step in this critical learning experience, invite students to list some of the ways that make their selected social worlds particularly unique. The following focus questions can be used to help students make observations about their social worlds or even pose questions to make connections with each other: *What do you notice about the rules (spoken and/or unspoken) in this social world? What does it look and feel like for an insider in this social world? For someone that might be an outsider? Do any of your social worlds or groups conflict or collide? If so, how do you handle that?* Because our social worlds can be very personal and sometimes private, it is important to take necessary steps in supporting the class community. If sharing or reporting out is not common practice, consider inviting students to create pairs or groups with close classmates. This informal opportunity to connect and talk can build a larger class conversation where students are held with care as they share personal writing.

WHILE READING *EVERY BODY LOOKING*

Following Ada's Journey: Building a Timeline

The learning experiences during reading in this chapter challenge students to think about the novel in nonlinear ways because of its nonlinear composition. As a whole class, use the collaborative timeline feature on Padlet (or another preferred digital platform or paper-based method) to give space for students to simultaneously read the novel and process and develop the narrative events according to the major sections: "Elementary Schools" (First and Second Grade), "Middle School" (Sixth and Seventh Grade), "High School," and "College." These sections will later be used in subsequent learning experiences as students consider text structure and the impact it has on narrative events and sequencing. It is important to note that while no specific dates are used in the novel, Iloh utilizes moments in Ada's life according to school-year signposts. These bands of time will help students to collectively consider what they are reading as they encounter it, while also reorganizing it into the Padlet timeline by the level of schooling.

Exploring Structure by Questioning

Reading this novel in verse encourages students to consider Ada's journey across different social settings from a young child to a college-aged adult. It also asks readers to consider the nonlinear composition of the narrative as a result of her personal becoming through reflection on critical events that have happened in the past and are simultaneously organized in between current moments in her present life. While reading *Every Body Looking*, we can model and guide students in generating questions and following their own queries of *why* and *how* around the structure of the narrative and the implications of Iloh moving from one time period and moment to another.

Prather (2019) offered general questions to help unpack thinking about text structure. Several modified prompts to address Iloh and her decision-making processes as the author include: *Why does this section follow that section in the novel? How does Iloh take the reader along in this reading experience? How does Iloh use transitions within the narrative to create both cohesion and tension? Why might Iloh use those transitions between those sections?* These suggested prompts, at a minimum, can move students to reflect on the choices that Iloh has made in the development of the individual poems that make up each section as well as the larger novel itself.

To illustrate this point of the activity, consider the "College" section (pp.133–142) where Ada has her first gynecologist appointment at the clinic on campus. These excerpts find Ada anxious as she begins living her life as an adult away from home: "I heard/you're supposed to go/when you turn eighteen or/or when you've stopped being/a good girl" (p.136). Upon arrival, she soon answers health questions about her experiences and partners as she observes the sights, sounds, and smells of the examination room. Ada shares: "she tells me/we are going to do this/my body, having heard this demand before/begins to kick from its bottom/begins its convulsions/begins its rituals" (p.138). Ada, in the present moment, feels the sensations of the past and the unrelenting trauma that has stayed with her. Still in the present, Iloh concludes this section with a personal testimony from Ada titled "Down there": "a place you don't touch/is a place he touched anyway/is a place I could not talk about/is a private thing/is a secret/is unknown" (p.142). This moment transitions to a section on "First Grade" that directly responds to the trauma of sexual abuse Ada experiences as a child. In such an arrangement of the text, Iloh juxtaposes snapshots from the present with the past in order to show the reader how the protagonist still feels these painful memories in and through her body. Thus, the poems in one section help us to understand the poems in another section and from another time.

This learning experience around writer choices on text structure and arrangement can also be scaffolded with whole-class modeling of other queer affirming adolescent titles or verse texts of choice, such as *The Black Flamingo* (Atta, 2020), *Chlorine Sky* (Browne, 2021), or *Clap When You Land* (Acevedo, 2020). As a mentor text, *Every Body Looking* also welcomes the possibilities of recent poetry from living poets. Some collections that fit thematically and structurally include *Love from the Vortex* (Sealey-Ruiz, 2020), *Autopsy* (Collins, 2017), *My Mother was a Freedom Fighter* (Monet, 2017), *Black Girl Magic: The BreakBeat Poets, Volume 2* (Brown, Simmonds & Woods, 2018), and *LatiNext: The BreakBeat Poets, Volume 4* (Chavez, Olivarez & Perdomo, 2020). Beyond verse novels and poetry, Trung Le Nguyen's (2020) Young Adult graphic novel, *The Magic Fish*, also serves as a mentor text for examining text structure in addition to its thematic focus on coming out, stories and fairy tales, and the love of family and friends. In addition to literary text, informational and nonfiction selections can also be used to support student understanding of internal and external structure, what signposts and elements to look for, and the *how* and *why* behind these decisions and choices of structure. Sample LGBTQ informational texts for an adolescent audience include *Beyond the Gender Binary* (Vaid-Menon, 2020), *Stonewall Riots: Coming Out in the Streets* (Pitman, 2019), and *A Quick and Easy Guide to They/Them Pronouns* (Bongiovanni & Jimerson, 2018).

Exploring Structure by Listing

In an interview on Books Are Magic (2020) with Jason Reynolds, Candice Iloh explained the vision for using verse to develop the structure of the novel. As readers "dance" through each chapter or poem, they witness the protagonist in

> different scenes, different time periods, between families, trying to please mom, trying to please dad, trying to please boys, trying to please themselves, trying to please their new roommate . . . doing this dance with life . . . and maneuvering . . . and having to dodge things, steps over things, go under things.

These choices in craft, like configuring a puzzle, help to "visually illustrate what the main character is really having to deal with her whole entire life" (2020). With this vision, another learning experience to incorporate while reading *Every Body Looking* includes listing the techniques and choices of craft that Iloh uses through writing in verse, in addition to the corresponding moments in Ada's life journey. As students continue to interact with the narrative and structure, generating a list can help readers to develop an awareness of "how the writer is piecing together the different elements" of the narrative (Prather, 2019, p. 105). Building on elements of the class timeline on Padlet, an optional graphic organizer can be a useful device to work through the list as the items relate to the structure of the text and the narrative itself, specifically Ada's navigation of her different social worlds. Table 6.2 includes four major time periods to frame text structure, defining moments, and open responses.

Following their individual or collaborative listing, invite students to reflect on what they notice, wonder, and questions about their findings. While facilitating, ask students: *What choices in structure might you make with this text? What are some of the possible implications on the narrative because of your choices? How would the story be different? What else would change because of the change in structure?*

Practicing with Verse: When I'm . . . Poem

As Ada navigates her different social worlds, and curates the snapshots and vignettes of her life, she finds herself in unique roles in each situation. This is an opportunity for students to analyze what the protagonist thinks and the feelings that she embodies as she narrates through these flashbacks, in addition to identifying her actions and the subsequent implications of these behaviors.

Below is the skeleton for a verse poem that will help students to explore the different roles that Ada plays in the novel. When working with the text, encourage students to think about what they read within and across the sections of the novel and what is revealed or can be inferred about Ada because of how the reading is structured. With this practice in writing in verse, the sentence stems can be revised and rearranged to fit the creative decisions of the student writer. In table 6.3, direct quotes from the text have been used to build a poem that reflects Ada's point of view across time periods.

Additionally, the skeleton can also be used for students to flip the focus from the character(s) in the novel to themselves by considering their own lives, past and present. Guide students to refer back to their documents for the before reading activity, "Using Structure to Think About Our Social Worlds," as this will help to scaffold and potentially inspire new thinking about some of their selected social worlds and their corresponding feelings, thoughts, actions, and behaviors in these situations.

Table 6.2 Sample Graphic Organizer—Exploring Structure by Listing

	Iloh's Techniques to Build and Develop Structure	Defining Moments in Ada's Personal Journey	Thoughts, Observations, Connections, Questions
Elementary School	Some of the poems in these sections have extra spacing between words and lines, while others emphasize structure through columns	Sleepovers at Granny's house (pp. 145–148); sexual abuse (pp. 148–150); misses her mother and visit to Dr. Matthew (pp. 155–170)	The more vulnerable and personal the poem, the greater the shift in structure compared to other poems that do not reflect such vulnerability or trauma
Middle School	Some poems/chapters integrate italics and forward slashes between words and phrases; focus of poem reflected in the shape of the poem (curved, pointing, widening)	Going between mom and dad's house (pp. 197–202); third new church in three weeks (p. 47); beginning to think about and question religion (pp. 50–57); drawing the dancers at church (p. 57–68); spending time with mom (pp. 264–277); aunty visit (pp. 94–112, 327–330)	Ada shifts from one setting with one parent to another and this highlights the differences in her relationships with mom, dad, and aunty; confessional tone in some of the poems/chapters dealing with religion
High School	Structurally, poems about Ada's family or from the parent perspective are longer and fuller	Dad discovers sketches of "Magic," the dancer (pp. 287–293); high school graduation, work and dance classes, and changes with mom (pp. 4–32)	Emphasis on dialogue between Ada and her parents and directives and demands from her parents
College	Poems in these sections are frequently juxtaposed with poems in sections from earlier times in Ada's life; some poems without any punctuation, just stream of consciousness writing; frequent use of words and phrases in block letters; emphasis on certain phrases through extra spacing	Beginning at HBCU (pp. 71–79); getting a new job and dating Derek (pp. 176–186); meeting Kendra and returning to the dance studio (pp. 207–212)	The more time Ada spends at college, the more she seems to be growing up and stepping into her most authentic self; earlier poems in this section frequently refer to her father while later poems refer less to her family and more to her current situations on campus

Table 6.3 Sample When I'm . . . Poem: Practicing with Verse

When I'm with my friends . . .	"It's hard to close out the world/when a whole new one/is sitting there/smiling up at you/waiting at your doorstep" (p. 308)
When I'm with my parent(s), family, guardians . . .	"There's no way I can tell him . . ." (p. 25)
When I'm with my partner . . .	"That what's/in my heart/feels/like too much/feels/so good/it's got/to be wrong" (p. 363)
When I'm with an older relative . . .	"Wanting to slap the smirk/off her face and wanting to/ease the burn behind my eyelids" (p. 112)
When I'm with strangers or meeting people for the first time . . .	"Five seconds/is all it really takes/to blow a first impression/to remember a face" (p. 131)
When I'm at home . . .	"In this house/I've learned that children/do no raise their voices to adults/do not accuse adults of being wrong" (p. 115)
When I'm at school . . .	"I was the funny black girl/my voice an instant punch line/my body an awkwardly shaped and useful pile of flesh/my hair styled too many years back" (p. 117)
When I'm at a party . . .	"She opens her eyes/only for a second/coyly smiles with them/using them/to invite me over/at first I think/to say no/then let my body/take me" (p. 314)
When I'm playing a sport or other activity/hobby . . .	"I look/to my left/and look/to my right/to see who/I dance with/and see/their bodies/in ready position/ then feel the memory/of the steps return" (p. 339)
When I'm by myself . . .	"I don't/have to be//anything//but this//I don't have to explain//everything I hear//everything I feel// everything I am//is mine" (p. 395)

Beyond the Boundaries: How Ada Envisions Freedom and Healing for Herself

Throughout the novel, Ada navigates moments of personal freedom and healing with moments in the narrative where she is seemingly limited and imprisoned either by the oppressive expectations of others or by the grip from memories of the past. Her story is one of coming to know herself and better equipping herself to embrace those people and ideas that heal and support her in moving closer to personal freedom, while releasing and moving forward from those that do not. For example, early in the novel, Ada reflects on how much she enjoys dancing as a child: "At age four dance hadn't been free/ but it was a cheaper way for Dad/to teach me about where we came from/ barefoot we danced bellies out wrapped in/colorful fabric skirts and dresses/ made in our home country" (p.29). Dance helps Ada not only to see her social worlds in different ways, but through this physical movement of her body, she discovers possibilities in responding to and questioning those social worlds and the people in them. Other reference points for this focus include Ada in middle school questioning the things she hears in her father's new church (pp. 50–55). While in college, Ada processes past sexual trauma (pp. 140–143), discovers what it means to dance for herself and be in possession of her own body (pp. 368–374), and offers a declaration of self-acceptance and empowerment (p.395).

With these starting points in mind, invite students to small group seminars to discuss and consider Ada's experiences through the frame of personal freedom and imprisonment. Using the text evidence and resources from before and during reading, elicit student discussion for the following: *What does Ada learn about herself? What are some ways in which others (individuals/structures/systems) limit Ada? What are some ways in which Ada limits herself through self-talk or decisions and choices? What are some ways in which Ada creates more space for herself as she grows as a character? What are some of the ways in which others support and nourish Ada in her quest for self-development on her path toward personal freedom?* (See table 6.4)

Upon completion of the small group seminars, invite students to use their findings and discussion points to construct a visual representation of what Ada has learned about herself as a way to share out and showcase. Encourage students to consider images, graphics, words, quotes, symbols, or other significant items that might reflect their findings from the novel.

AFTER READING *EVERY BODY LOOKING*

Mapping to Trace Narrative Strands in the Text

Ada's experiences in her past play a role in how she looks back on her life since graduating high school and beginning her first year of college. Those memories from childhood and growing up with her religious father and distant mother have helped her to develop new strategies, skills, and ways of being. After reading *Every Body Looking*, invite student pairs or teams to return to the text and their Padlet timelines to visually trace and investigate specific narrative points and the links or transitions that Iloh uses to join them together. To accomplish this task, organize small collaborative groups either physically in person or via a shared document if working in hybrid or virtual settings (Jamboard or Padlet would also be appropriate). In their teams, ask students to follow and discuss how the writer composed the strand of a single narrative line in the novel, selecting from "First Grade" (pp. 145–151, 197–203), "Second Grade" (pp. 155–170, 217–226, 237–248), "Sixth Grade" (pp. 83–118, 263–277), "Seventh Grade" (pp. 327–330), "Middle School" (pp.

Table 6.4   Sample Graphic Organizer: Beyond the Boundaries—How Ada Envisions Freedom and Healing for Herself

What Does Ada Learn About Herself?			
⇒ *Limiting* ⇐		⇐ *Expanding* ⇒	
How Do Others (Individuals/ Structures/Systems) Limit Ada?	*How Does Ada Limit Herself?*	*How Does Ada Create More Space for Herself?*	*How Do Others Support and Nourish Ada?*
Messaging from religious institutions: "Words are powerful/unless they're not biblical/unless they're not written by men/unless they're unlike/ Jesus's spit itself/ why can't I pray outside of his name?/why is my name not enough?" (p.53)	Toxic relationship: "where I don't/tell him/that he needs/ to go so I can be/ alone/. . . I let him touch me/. . . says that/I just need to let him/take my mind/off all of this/ says *ain't no way you could like girls when you can have this*" (pp. 389–390)	Empowerment from dance: "When I forget about/the fear/of pain/ of something coming/soon/ to hurt me/I am in possession/ of my whole body/my spirit runneth over" (p. 373)	Dance coach asking questions of Ada: "You/ who are you dancing for?/ he slows pace/stopping right/in front of me/*I'm talking/to you, sis/who are you dancing for?/he pushes, waiting/for me to answer.*

47–68), "High School" (pp. 3–44, 287–293), and "College" (pp.71–79, 121–142, 173–193, 207–213, 229–234, 253–260, 281–284, 297–323, 333–403).

Once each team has picked a section, guide students to reread just their selections in the order that they appear. Working within this range, students will move to identifying Ada's defining moments as part of their mapping of the narrative according to the time markers to see how this shifts their reading of the story and how they generate meaning. As students work closely with the text in consideration of the structure, these "external signposting(s) will help students to see the internal structure" and eventually "the units that make up the whole" (Prather, 2019, p. 105). Alongside or in between the defining moments, students can discuss and label emerging questions or salient points based on their reading and mapping of the narrative (see table 6.5). Using any preferred method, including the draw function in a Google Doc, each team can select a different way to visually represent their narrative strand.

To further investigate how the structure impacts what we read, invite members from each group representing different time periods or social worlds to convene and discuss their findings. When reporting out from the groups, elicit student responses to the following reflective prompts: *What happens when we visually chart or map the different sections of the narrative? What patterns or themes emerge? How might we understand Ada's emotions and feelings within this strand?*

Things Better Left Unsaid: Making Inferences

Though novels in verse may have fewer words on any given page than a novel written in prose, these dynamic texts are no less rich, complex, or worthy of investigation. Just as students would make inferences while reading a novel in prose, it is important to further develop these reading skills in texts with varying structures. Using table 6.6 as an example, invite students to return to specific parts of the novel, such as the ambiguous queerness at the conclusion, as a way to make inferences individually, as part of a small group, or together as a whole class. Ask students to consider: *What has Iloh left unsaid in this section? Why might she do that here? What impact does it have on the narrative and our reading of it? Would you draw the same conclusions if the story were written in prose?*

Character Life in Verse

Like Ada's flashbacks from her childhood, memories have ways of impacting and informing our present lives, including how we feel and the decisions that we make. Sometimes, these memories can even reflect how we see the world and how we respond to it, if we choose. *Every Body Looking* is just as much a story about looking forward and asking "Who am I?" as it is one about looking back and asking "Who was I?" Ada exemplifies these messages early in the novel: "when you start growing/further away from/what used to be home/you go looking for/somewhere/that lets you be/what's inside your head" (p.30). Articulating different parts of one's life story gives space for students to move beyond working with the text and pivoting to reflecting more intimately around the implications of these questions and issues in their own lives.

During this invitation to compose and create, encourage students to write in verse or experiment with shifting the point of view, as a way to reflect and practice the author's craft. As students curate these defining moments, just as Iloh has done for Ada's journey, students can refer back to their reading activity, "Practicing with Verse: When I'm . . . Poem" to guide them through further experimentation and other creative decision-making options. This task is flexible enough to meet any curricular requirements for writing assessments, and is customizable for building visualizations such as identity webs (Ahmed, 2018) or maps of writing territories (Atwell, 2002). Such enhancements for multimodal design and composition can also be

Table 6.5 Sample Graphic Organizer—Things Better Left Unsaid: Making Inferences

Section: "Seventh Grade"—Page 327–330

Sequence: This section (the only one under "Seventh Grade") follows and proceeds sections from "College" that explore Ada's emerging relationship with Kendra and her return to dance

#1 Ada reveals layers to her relationship with Aunty at the Nigerian parties in this section:

Defining Moment: "like clockwork all the women/responsible for the massive spread of jollof rice stews and fufu/emerge from the kitchen/marching clapping/shaking their shoulders/winding their hips/move from all sides.../ All the women dancing toward and around each other/rhythm of their bodies/moving as one" (p.327)

Thoughts/Questions: Much of Ada's connection to dance comes back to family and cultural significance. I wonder why she feels like she is not ready to join the women at this time.

#2 As Ada feels the energy of the women in dancing in the rented hall, she questions herself and her role:

Defining Moment: "Aunty extends a hand/stretched with a wave in my direction/an invitation to join her and the other women/. . . as if they all know how and what/they come from beyond names and roles/they've been given/witness something bigger/course through their veins/sense a confidence I don't yet think/I can call mine" (p.328)

Thoughts/Questions: When will Ada experience her moment of feeling "something bigger"? Of embodying the confidence of the women dancing here?

#3 Ada prepares for Aunt to return home to Nigeria after having spent a year in the United States:

Defining Moment: ". . . I like seeing her smile more like that/tell me stories of when she was a girl/how she *wasn't looking good for no man*/Listened as her voice began softening the more/time we spent together alone after the first time/I discovered blood in my panties/a time when she was the only person around who I could tell" (p.329)

Thoughts/Questions: I wonder if the love and softness that Ada sees in Aunty in this flashback is the love and softness that she is hoping for in the present moment for herself or for herself with Kendra.

#4 As a seventh grader, Ada reflects on the lessons that she had learned with and because of Aunty:

Defining Moment: "Aunty always . . . was teaching/me about/my feelings/and moving/me to say/what was/on my mind/Aunty/always a reminder/of fight/of pride" (p.330).

Thoughts/Questions: Given their previously challenging relationship (Section "Sixth Grade"), I wonder what Aunty has learned from Ada in the year that she has visited family.

integrated in digital ways with the use of video and other visual elements to expand further consideration of genre, format, and audience like Iloh does with the poems in the novel. During an optional share-out, writing celebration, or classroom publication, teachers can elicit responses from volunteers, or share their own composition to begin. Some follow-up questions might

Table 6.6 Sample Graphic Organizer—Things Better Left Unsaid: Making Inferences

What is Said	What is Unsaid
"Instead I stand still/ask him to listen/tell him/something's changed/tell myself/to breathe" (p. 403)	While Iloh does not reveal how Ada's father responds to his daughter's declaration, the absence of his reaction speaks to the new confidence that Ada embraces by the end of the novel and the ways in which she is speaking up for herself.
"When Kendra walks into the studio/clearly surprised to find me here/...walks over to sit down next to me/asks me what I'm doing here/*what I want/finally*"	Though never recognized in her younger years, the possibilities of queerness show up indirectly when Ada is in college as she listens to the voice of her desires and attractions in ways that she could not do while at home. While her relationship with Kendra is left open, Ada is better positioned to follow her heart now than ever before.

include: *How did you go about writing in verse? What choices did you have to make? In what ways did writing in verse change your thinking and writing processes?*

BEYOND *EVERY BODY LOOKING*

My Life in Verse

For this learning experience at the completion of reading, invite students to curate definitive moments from their lives across different time periods and social worlds. They can select moments that they are comfortable cultivating from their lives before elementary school (four years old and younger), elementary school (5–10 years old), middle school (11–13 years old), and high school (14–18 years old). Since personal histories can sometimes stir unwanted feelings and emotions, proceed with care and remind students that they are not expected to sit with or work with any moments or memories that they want to leave behind.

Sometimes pictures and other objects help us to remember certain moments in our lives. Encourage students to explore the items and artifacts that they have access to, including those on digital spaces. To further support their thinking, have students reflect on what happened to them or what was happening around them during these moments. *What did they feel in those moments? What did they smell, taste, touch, hear? How did this moment (or moments) change their thinking, perspectives, or future experiences?* Such opportunities to think and write freely help student writers to "retain their own authority, integrity, and personal artistic preferences throughout the creative writing process without fear of free-reigning bigotry" or other judgment from classmates or teachers (Chavez, 2021, p. 23).

As Marchetti and O'Dell (2018) note, "writers don't always have a structure when they start" (p. 89). Throughout their iterative writing process, support students in their handling of structure and how they decide to organize their ideas within the text, and more importantly, encourage them to revisit or reorganize their text as needed. This is also an appropriate time to refer back to the central text as well as any other mentor texts or student-selected texts used during this unit of study to help in the development of their conceptual and practical understandings around structure.

Exploring and Sharing Student-Selected Texts

How a text and its features are arranged can be incredibly complex. The ways in which a writer or creator structures a text can challenge even the most careful or confident reader. Thus, more experience with and exposure to a variety of texts across situations, including nonprint and multimodal, will better serve students as they approach similarly complex readings and invitations to write and compose in and out of academic spaces. As an extension to the before reading activity in which students brainstorm narratives that challenge text structure, and as a way to move beyond *Every Body Looking*, invite students to select and explore a text of choice from their own lives for further exploration.

Students can refer back to any writing or brainstorm material from before or during reading, in addition to reflecting on their own interests and social worlds. To this end, remind students that *texts* are many and varied, and that their selection should be something that engages them energetically and creatively or reflects their interests and lives outside of school, including but not limited to film, television, commercials, comics, novels, laws, buildings, billboards, art, performances, and so on. As students reflect on their selected texts and how it challenges notions of structure and arrangement, return to the opening questions that were used for Iloh's novel: *How might writing or composing in this way impact the text? What choices in craft does the writer or creator make to structure the text? How might these choices inform how readers or viewers generate meaning around the text? How might these choices inform the aesthetic impact of the text?* To conclude, make space for students to share their selected texts and findings, such as an in-person or virtual gallery or a recorded video on Flipgrid. However formal or informal, this opportunity should allow for students to see and respond to how their peers are thinking about and challenging text structure.

CONCLUSION

Candice Iloh is an emergent and dynamic voice in adolescent literature and *Every Body Looking* invites pedagogical possibilities and learning opportunities that move English Language Arts curriculum from routine to relevant and responsive, centering and amplifying the joy and liberation of the protagonist with each step she takes in discovering herself and becoming her most honest and authentic self. The poems are intimate, personal, vulnerable and can stand alone as singular texts, or as part of the whole novel. Using Iloh's writing in the secondary English classroom will no doubt support teachers in expanding the notions of narrative structure and author's craft and technique while also providing a mirror and window (Bishop, 1990) for students to see and experience Ada's multidimensional journey as they reflect on and narrate their own stories through memory and imagination.

REFERENCES

Acevedo, E. (2020). *Clap when you land.* Quill Tree Books.

Ahmed, S. (2018). *Being the change: Lessons and strategies to teach social comprehension.* Heinemann.

Atta, D. (2020). *The black flamingo.* Balzar + Bray.

Atwell, N. (2002). *Lessons that change writers.* Heinemann.

Bishop, R. S. (1990). Mirrors, windows, and sliding glass doors. *Perspectives: Choosing and Using Books for the Classroom, 6*(3), ix–xi.

Bongiovanni, A., & Jimerson, T. (2018). Limerence.

Books Are Magic. (2020). Every body looking - Candice Iloh and Jason Reynolds. [Video] YouTube. https://www.youtube.com/watchv=01kvLpNJDMk&t=1734s.

Browne, M. (2021). *Chlorine sky.* Crown Books.

Browne, M., Simmonds, I., & Woods, J. (2018). *Black girl magic: The breakbeat poets*, volume 2. Haymarket Books.

Chavez, F. R. (2021). *The anti-racist writing workshop: How to decolonize the creative classroom.* Haymarket Books.

Chavez, F., Olivarez, J., Perdomo, W. (2020). *LatiNext: The breakbeat poets*, volume 4. Haymarket Books.

Collins, D. (2017). *Autopsy.* Minneapolis, MN: Button Poetry.

Iloh, C. (2020). *Every body looking.* Dutton Books.

Marchetti, A., & O'Dell, R. (2018). *Beyond literary analysis: Teaching students to write with passion and authority about any text.* Heinemann.

Monet, A. (2017). *My mother was a freedom fighter.* Haymarket Books.

Muhammad, G. (2020). *Cultivating genius: An equity framework for culturally and historically responsive literacy.* Scholastic.

Nguyen, T. L. (2020). *The magic fish.* RH Graphic.

Pitman, G. (2019). *The stonewall riots: Coming out in the streets.* Abrams Books for Young Readers.

Prather, L. (2019). *Story matters: Teaching teens to use the tools of narrative to argue and inform.* Heinemann.

Salesses, M. (2021). *Craft in the real world: Rethinking fiction writing and workshopping.* Catapult.

Sealey-Ruiz, Y. (2020). *Love from the vortex & other poems.* Kaleidoscope Vibrations LLC.

Vaid-Menon, A. (2020). *Beyond the gender binary.* Penguin Workshop.

Chapter 7

Exploring *The Prom* as
Texts and Symbol

Terri Suico

The high school prom often looms large in adolescents' lives. Prom's pomp and circumstance have long been the subject of popular culture, and even before prom became part of the high school experience, dancing itself played a significant role in the lives of teenagers. However, this cultural institution has also been a perpetuator of harm against LGBTQ people with LGBTQ couples and people facing discrimination when trying to attend.

Both the excitement of prom and the discrimination that can come with it are at hand in *The Prom* (Mitchell et al., 2019), the young adult novelization of the Broadway musical. The story offers an approachable and humorous look at what this night can mean to students while also providing opportunities for rich literary study, such as an introduction to or reinforcement of skills like analyzing point of view, characters, and symbols. Written by a lesbian author, *The Prom* features two lesbian protagonists who come into their own by challenging and changing the mindset of their small town and getting to throw and attend an inclusive prom with each other. *The Prom*'s happy ending shows a narrative often not told in LGBTQ young adult literature since research shows that lesbian protagonists having a happy ending are not often part of LGBTQ young adult literature (Jimenez, 2015). Furthermore, Emma achieves her happy ending in her small, rural, working-class town, thus portraying that LGBTQ people in rural areas not only exist but can find happiness without escaping. While Emma is offered several opportunities to leave Edgewater, she recognizes that, "If every gay kid in Indiana leaves, then that means every gay kid in Indiana has to do this alone" (p. 156).

Another feature that makes *The Prom* well suited for the classroom is that the novel is just one version of the property. The story started as a stage musical, and the script for the libretto as well as the original cast recording are readily available. In 2020, the musical was adapted into a Netflix movie.

91

These forms make *The Prom* ideal for examining how a text changes as it is adapted for different mediums and the decisions the authors and directors make in terms of elements such as perspective and structure.

SUMMARY OF *THE PROM* BY SAUNDRA MITCHELL WITH BOB MARTIN, CHAD BEGUELIN, AND MATTHEW SKLAR

Set in the fictional, yet realistic, rural town of Edgewater, Indiana, in the present day, *The Prom* shares the story of Emma Nolan, a high school senior who knows firsthand the challenges of being gay in a small town. As the only out student at James Madison High School, she must contend with bullying schoolmates, an angry PTA president, and Alyssa Greene, her closeted girlfriend who is the daughter of the aforementioned PTA president. Emma just wants to go to prom with Alyssa, but Mrs. Greene and the PTA will not allow same-sex couples to attend. The public declaration that "tickets will only be sold to boy/girl couples" (p. 28) leads to increased bullying on Emma. When two narcissistic Broadway actors, Barry Glickman and Dee Dee Allen, arrive to champion Emma's cause in an attempt to get some positive press, the plot thickens. Told from Emma's and Alyssa's alternating perspective, the book deftly shows the prejudice that can be inflicted upon gay and lesbian teens in a realistic way, the importance of challenging stereotypes, and what it means to be truly inclusive.

BEFORE READING *THE PROM*

Interrogating the Prom

One of *The Prom*'s strengths is its relevance to many students' lives. Given the presence of the prom in popular culture and schools, students will likely have heard about the event and seen various depictions of it on social media and in movies and television. This background knowledge and the prom's prominence in the novel make it a viable way to introduce or review symbolism in literature. Additionally, the topic offers the chance to think about how symbolism functions outside of the classroom, which can make the content and skills more memorable.

Before reading, teachers can prepare students to consider the prom as a symbol by inviting students to consider what they know about the prom and what prom might stand for in regards to American high school experiences. Students can revisit these initial findings as they read the book. To begin, students could identify what they associate with prom. Through individual brainstorming as well as small-group and whole-class discussion, students might consider the following prompts: *Explain and describe prom to someone who is unfamiliar with it. What traditions, actions, or objects are often associated with prom? Why might some consider prom a major event in American high school experiences?*

After exploring the questions and identifying trends in student responses, students could examine how prom is depicted in popular culture. Using clips from television shows like *Riverdale, Dawson's Creek, and Glee*, movies like *To All the Boys I've Loved: Always and Forever*, documentaries such as *Hard Times at Douglass High*, and online magazines such as *Teen Vogue*, which feature articles on styling ideas for prom, and news articles from sources such as Money.com (Glum, 2016) that describe the cost of prom preparations, have students answer the three questions above using only the information they find. Once they have answered the questions, the class can then compare their findings with each other as well as what they identified during the initial discussion. The purpose of this is to help students begin to conceptualize how prom is depicted and what it might signify beyond a dance. This exploration can also provide the opportunity for students to examine the assumptions that are embedded in coverage and stories about prom. For instance, many of the television, film, and documentary clips presume that teens and their families have expendable income for an extravagant evening. Furthermore, many of the media portrayals of prom, particularly ones prior to the 2010s, often presume an overwhelmingly white event with a focus on heteronormativity, with an emphasis on male and female romantic entanglements and gendered clothing such as the boys wearing tuxedoes and the girls wearing gowns. Acknowledging these shortcomings allows students to see the restrictiveness of the portrayals and also sets the stage for the events in *The Prom*.

After this, students could ask the three questions listed above to people outside of the class. Ideally, students could ask people from different age groups in order to get a variety of perspectives. The next day, once students have shared the responses they gathered, the class's attention can shift from prom's more tangible elements to what the event signifies in relation to the high school experience and growing up. This focus lets students start to think of prom as a symbol in addition to being a literal event. The teacher can then introduce or remind students of the literary definition for symbolism and ask students what the prom might symbolize.

Entering the Text with Essential Questions

Essential questions serve as a way to extend the concepts to the world beyond the classroom. This can pique students' interest before they enter the text. *The Prom* lends itself to numerous lines of inquiry that prompt students to interrogate the story's content, style, and medium. For instance, the question *What does it mean to be inclusive?* is at the heart of the plot. The most obvious instance of this issue comes when Mrs. Greene and the PTA throw two proms, one prom that is only for Emma and another prom that all of the other students attend. However, other examples, such as the requirements that must be met to attend prom (pp. 28–29), also illustrate how exclusivity and inclusivity are at work in the story. These requirements stress a heteronormative worldview, such as "Gentlemen are expected to wear a suit and tie. Ladies are expected to wear modest evening attire, with dresses no shorter than knee length . . . Tickets will only be sold to boy/girl couples" (pp. 28–29).

Content and style are at the heart of another essential question, *How are opinions, perspectives, and beliefs formed, and what can cause them to change?* Having the novel alternate between Emma's and Alyssa's perspectives provides readers with a sense not just what these characters think but also why they have these points of view. While there is less insight into Dee Dee's and Barry's perspectives, the story depicts them going from having self-serving motivations to wanting to champion a cause for the right reasons. Tertiary characters, such as Shelby, Kevin, and Mrs. Greene, show signs of being more accepting of Emma and her sexuality, and students can consider what prompts these characters to have this change of heart.

Finally, given *The Prom*'s transformation from stage musical to young adult novel to movie musical, having the essential question, *How does the medium affect the way a story is told and received?* encourages students to think about the story's journey and the necessary changes that come with each transformation. Comparing the different versions and delving into not just the modifications made to the story but also how and why the medium requires or allows for these differences can enrich students' understanding of the story and how medium and format matter. Before reading, the teacher can introduce students to the questions and offer different ways for students to engage with them. For instance, in guiding students through question one, a teacher could ask students to consider the ways in which proms are currently inclusive or exclusive. One way to accomplish this is through an examination of current prom policies in their school and other schools in the community. Beyond the local, teachers can also guide students in investigating the history of discrimination same-sex couples have faced when trying to attend prom and the legal ramifications of this discrimination (Lambda Legal, nd).

With question three, the goal is to have students consider how the medium used to tell a story changes the way a message is told and received. To do this, teachers can have students examine different forms of media, such as a news article, an Instagram post by a celebrity or internet personality, and an advertisement, that share a common theme but convey the message in different ways. For instance, the teacher might have students read a news story about prom costs, examine an infographic that provides statistics on how much people spend on prom on average, see Pinterest boards dedicated to prom planning, and watch a teen-created YouTube video with ideas on how to prepare for prom on a budget. As they read, watch, and listen, students should consider the following questions: *What message is each text trying to convey? How is the message presented—what senses does it appeal to? How is a language used to portray the message? Who might be the target audience be for this text? How is this message conveyed to this audience? What are the strengths and weaknesses of the text's message branding?*

After they have had the chance to think about their answers, students can engage in a whole-class discussion where they share their answers and eventually transition to a comparison of how each medium handles the message. The teacher can use this time to introduce students to the idea that, when thinking about adaptations, "no one mode is inherently good at doing one thing and not another; but each has at its disposal different means of expression—media and genres—and so can aim at and achieve certain things better than others" (Hutcheon & O'Flynn, 2013, p. 24). The class should revisit this concept throughout the unit, and introducing it before reading gives students the chance to engage with the idea before applying it to the novel and the different adaptations.

Examining Rurality in Setting

A key element of *The Prom* is the story's rural, working-class setting. Besides creating a fish-out-of-water situation once Barry and Dee Dee arrive (a situation more pronounced in the stage musical and film), placing the story in a small, country town also has implications on Emma's and Alyssa's characters and on the plot. While the town of Edgewater, Indiana, is fictional, it nevertheless reflects the realities of small-town life, such as teenagers socializing in a Walmart parking lot for lack of other options. The rural setting means that something like the prom would be the major social event of the year for the teens. This increases what is at stake and makes the furor over the prom, who gets to attend, and if it happens at all more understandable. Additionally, the small-town setting makes it plausible that Emma is the only openly LGBTQ student at her school and that the bullying and discrimination occur in such an overt way. According to an executive summary by the Movement Advancement Project (MAP) (2019), "the social and political landscape of rural areas makes LGBT people more vulnerable to discrimination. Public opinion in rural areas is generally less supportive . . . and rural states are significantly less likely to have vital nondiscrimination laws" (p. 3).

Activities that introduce students to the setting and its implications are vital, regardless of whether the students live in a rural, urban, or suburban area, since they might not have considered the challenges small, rural towns present to people who are LGBTQ. One activity is identifying characteristics, stereotypes, and tropes for rural America. To begin, the teacher can ask students to find school-appropriate memes about small-town and rural life. Each student should find at least two memes and be prepared to discuss why they selected these memes. As students share their memes with the entire class, the teacher should ask students to identify categories for the memes, such as "small-town relations" and "rural social life"; once the memes have been shared and the list of categories has been cultivated, students should then be invited to consider what theses memes and these categories mean in terms of small towns. In other words, according to what they have found, what are small towns truly like? The class discussion on this should focus on small-town life and what the students think is true, what is an exaggeration, what is a stereotype, and who is shaping these stereotypes. To combat stereotypes, the teacher can then have students learn more about living in a small town by watching YouTube videos on living in small towns, such as Abby Grace's (2019) video on living in a small town in Indiana, and reading news articles about rural life. Texts highlighting LGBTQ people living their life and experiencing joy in small towns should be addressed to complicate limiting views of rural spaces. After this, students can compare the characteristics and memes they initially identified with what they have just seen and read.

Students should also think about the implications presented by the small-town setting. The teacher might ask students how the small-town setting will affect the story and what this setting might mean for the characters and their outlooks, which connects with essential question two, "How are opinions, perspectives, and beliefs formed, and what can cause them to change?" Students could read the synopsis for *The Prom* and then consider how a story about a high school girl who wants to take her girlfriend to their school prom might be complicated by the rural setting. Having students learn more about the challenges that individuals who are LGBTQ might face in rural areas by reading parts of the MAP (2019) Executive Summary and find news stories about Indiana's Religious Freedom Restoration Act (RFRA) can offer further insight.

WHILE READING *THE PROM*

Tracing Characters

At the heart of *The Prom* are the characters of Emma and Alyssa. With the majority of the story told from either Emma's or Alyssa's perspective, the story offers an opportunity to explore these characters and their development as they confront the homophobia prevalent in their community and school. Besides character growth, *The Prom* allows for the introduction or reinforcement of related literary elements, including point of view and tone. The characters' different values, outlooks, and responses to situations become clear early in the book. In the first few chapters, readers see Emma's and Alyssa's contrasting views regarding Indiana and their very different views and experiences in their small-town high school. To take advantage of this, the teacher can periodically have students consider not just the content but how the character who is sharing the information shapes the story. For example, Emma's first thoughts are "Note to self: don't be gay in Indiana. Actually, that's a note for everybody else. I'm already gay in Indiana, and spoiler alert, it sucks" (p. 1). Emma then recounts how she declared herself as gay on her YouTube channel and the fallout from that action, including being evicted from her house by her parents. The chapter ends with her repeating her advice not to be gay in Indiana because "there's nothing here for you but heartbreak" (p. 6). In contrast, the next chapter, which is from Alyssa's point of view, opens with, "You've probably never been here, so let me tell you, Indiana is a beautiful place" (p. 7). She goes on to describe her view of what Indiana is like before explaining her relationship with her mother and how it hampers her ability to express herself freely.

From these two chapters, students get a sense of the characters and their perspectives, voices, and tones. After reading the chapters, students can be assigned a particular character to focus on for a character sketch. For these sketches, students or student teams identify both factual information, such as the characters' home lives and hobbies, and less tangible aspects about the character, such as the relationships and support systems they have in place. Specific prompts students can explore in small groups include creating a basic outline of their character, describing their character's tone and perspective, and hypothesizing what has influenced their character's perspective or outlook. Besides writing down their initial impressions, students can also incorporate visual elements by answering the prompts through a Pinterest board or Miro board for their character. Students can also use an online tool like Creately to create their sketches; besides letting them incorporate text with multimedia, these tools can also help students note the characters' progression and journeys throughout the story. Once the sketches are completed, students can share their visuals and graphics with the entire class. For example, when considering chapter one and readers' initial impressions on Emma's, students might link to news stories about Indiana's religious freedom law that allowed businesses in Indiana to discriminate against people who identify as LGBTQ and to pictures of a girl being isolated and ostracized by family and peers. Alyssa's visuals might include picturesque photographs of Indiana as well as depictions of a stereotypical straight-A, overachieving student. After the presentations, the class can engage in whole-class discussion to note comparisons between characters and the causes for the differences. For instance, the teacher can ask students to compare Emma's and Alyssa's perspectives and have them hypothesize what might account for these differences. Additionally, students can consider how the setting of small-town, working-class Edgewater, Indiana, affects the characters' views and experiences regarding their sexuality.

As the class gets further in the book, students can add to and amend their character sketches and as they continue to study the characters' perspectives and growth. For example, after reading chapter six (p. 43), students have additional information regarding how Emma and Alyssa are treated at school and how they react to this treatment and can update their character sketches. Studying the characters of Emma and Alyssa also connects with essential question two, *How are opinions, perspectives, and beliefs formed? What can cause them to change?* since the characters' experiences, such as Emma's estrangement from her family, have influenced their worldviews.

Students can also evaluate secondary characters Dee Dee Allen and Barry Glickman, the two actors who come to Edgewater ostensibly to help Emma but really want to rehabilitate their public image by taking up her cause. Although the information on these characters is limited, they present another chance to study character growth. Furthermore, considering how Dee Dee and Barry are portrayed in the novel prepares students to compare their depiction in the stage musical and movie. Specific questions to consider with these characters include their motivations for helping Emma, the relationships they have with each other as well as the other characters, and how they evolve during the course of the story. For instance, one of the readers' early impressions of Barry and Dee Dee comes when they attend a school town hall about the prom controversy; there, the characters display preconceived notions regarding the sophistication of Edgewater's citizens as well as motives beyond wanting to help Emma. When talking about Emma, Barry tells the angry locals, "Look at this poor creature! Wasting away under your judgment! Your criticism! Your off-the-rack offerings!" (p. 65) and "This is about you and prying open your tiny little minds" (p. 66). After reading Barry's introduction, the teacher might ask questions such as, "What is Barry criticizing when he addresses the town's citizens? How do these criticisms align with what we've discussed and explored when it comes to small-town life?" Dee Dee's first appearance is even more dramatic. After saying, "We didn't come here to make a scene!" (p. 66), she immediately instructs a teenager who is filming everything that is happening on a cell phone, "Darling, if you're going to take pictures, making sure you hashtag, 'broadway crashes the prom,' hashtag 'dee dee allen'" (p. 66). Here, students might be asked, "What is motivating Dee Dee to get involved? Is she trying wanting to avoid a scene?" Later, after it becomes clear at the separate prom for Emma that Barry and Dee Dee have ulterior motives, they stop pushing their own agenda and start being more genuinely supportive of Emma. Students have the chance to engage with essential question two as they analyze Barry and Dee Dee. Specifically, students can determine what has caused Barry and Dee Dee's change of heart.

The Prom as Symbol

As the students explored before starting the novel, prom can signify more than just a school dance. While they read, students have the chance to use the ideas from the prereading exploration of prom and consider how these ideas translate into the story. Since the meaning of prom in *The Prom* goes beyond the actual event, the novel lends itself to studying symbolism and how something can be both literal and figurative. Literally, the fight for prom and who can attend is central to the story. Figuratively, prom and the ability to attend it with one's significant other, regardless of gender or sexuality, represents the acceptance and support Emma and Alyssa long to find in their conservative, rural community and with their family.

To help them consider what prom might symbolize, students might track the ways that different characters describe and conceive of the prom. For instance, Alyssa states that this senior prom "is our last chance . . . I want to wrap my arms around her and let the whole world slip away" (p. 9). Emma later echoes this sentiment as she describes prom as "one night that's just ours, without hiding and sneaking" (p. 17). Other characters' perceptions of the prom reinforce the idea that it is about more than a dance. From the promposal, Emma and Alyssa witness (pp. 13–16) to the email the PTA and Mrs. Greene send emphasizing that "attendance at prom is a privilege, not a right" (p. 27) and stressing the heteronormativity of the event, what prom obviously carries weight beyond a school event (see figure 7.1).

Emma's shifting attitude toward the prom also emphasizes the idea that it carries significant weight. Emma initially says, "I just want to dance with [Alyssa]" (p. 17). Even after Principal Hawkins tells Emma that the ACLU is prepared to get involved and that "This [prom] is a big deal . . . For you . . . [and] all the kids just like you" (p. 49), Emma asserts that "I didn't ask for [Mrs. Greene] to turn this into a referendum on my personhood" (p. 87). However, after her experience with the separate prom and support from her grandmother, Barry, and Dee Dee, Emma accepts what an inclusive prom could symbolize. As she plans to share her story, she says, "I'm going to do my thing . . . and maybe next year, there will be a kickass prom in Edgewater, Indiana, for everybody . . . no matter who they love" (p. 158). She solidifies her new view on the importance of prom by asking Barry to be her date because "this will be a prom for every kid who never got theirs, and that

Scene Description and Page Number	Questions for Students to Consider
Nick's promposal to Kaylee at school pp. 13 – 15)	• Why does Nick choose such a public way of asking his girlfriend to attend prom? • Promposals call to mind public marriage proposals. What might this indicate about the significance of prom to the teens who are planning to attend? • Alyssa asks Emma if Emma is sorry that the two of them can't do a public promposal. What is preventing them from doing this? Do you believe Emma's assertion that she doesn't care? Why or why not? • After looking up examples of real-life promposals and the history of promposals, students can debate on whether or not they think that a public promposal is a good idea.
The PTA email regarding the prom and Emma's reaction (pp. 27 – 33)	• What are the requirements that the PTA has for students who want to attend prom? What stands out to you about these rules? • What sort of worldview and expectations are these rules reinforcing? • How does Emma respond to the rules? What allies and support does she have in combating this? • Given the setting, why would cancelling the prom be a major blow to students? • Connecting back to essential question 1, how inclusive are the PTA's rules?
The email announcing that prom is moving forward (pp. 82-23)	• Who celebrates with Emma when she finds out that the prom is going to happen? What are the motivations for these different stakeholders (Emma, Barry, Dee Dee, etc.) celebrating?
Alyssa's prom preparations (pp. 97 – 106)	• What do Alyssa's preparations for prom include? Who is the person driving these preparations? • Why is prom so important to Alyssa's mother? How does this compare to Alyssa's view on prom?
Emma's plan for an inclusive prom (pp. 158 – 160) and song about prom (pp. 163 – 164)	• How does Emma describe the sort of prom that she would like to see in Edgewater? • What is the significance of Emma asking Barry to be her date to an inclusive prom? • Consider the lyrics to Emma's song. Why does she want to attend prom with her girlfriend? • What might an inclusive prom in rural Edgewater, Indiana signify to people in and outside of the community? • Connecting back to essential question 1, how does the prom that Emma describes compare to the proms that were held by the PTA? Which prom is more inclusive?

Figure 7.1   Character's Views of Prom.

includes" (p. 159) Barry, who confessed to her that he was too scared to attend his high school prom.

Furthermore, students could examine the three different proms that occur. The first two, which happen on the same night (pp. 116–132), stand in direct contrast to the prom that closes the story (pp. 194–198, 203–207). As they read about the proms, which include the main prom that was attended by most of the students, the individual prom held on the same night that the PTA holds for Emma to appease the calls for equality, and the final inclusive prom, students could consider the purpose of each prom and what these events might signify to the characters of the story. Students can compare their insights on each event, which connects to essential question one, *What does it mean to be inclusive?*

AFTER READING *THE PROM*

Changing Perspectives

The choice to write the novel so that it tells the story primarily from Emma's and Alyssa's perspectives, rather than from a third-person omniscient perspective that is used in the stage musical and the movie, invites readers to consider how a story changes based on who tells it. The teacher can have students review the different types of points of view, identify which type is used in the YA novelization of *The Prom*, and explain how this point of view influenced the way the story was told by the authors and received by the audience. After establishing this, students can then explore how the story might change if told from a different perspective or point of view and what this change might mean for them as readers. For instance, how would the story look if it was narrated from Barry's perspective or if it was told from a third-person omniscient point of view with a more equal focus on Barry and Dee Dee in addition to Alyssa and Emma? The teacher can have students examine pages 75–81, which recounts Emma's first direct interactions with Dee Dee and Barry. In small groups, students should take note of what happens in this section, paying special attention to what they learn about Barry and Dee Dee. The groups will then be assigned to write the same scene from a different point of view, namely third-person omniscient, first-person from Barry's perspective, and first-person from Dee Dee's. After writing these, each group should share their writing with the class and explain why they made the choices they did. As they share and discuss their writing, the teacher should ask them how the story changes when told from a different point of view and what that might mean for the audience. For instance, how does the same story told from Barry's perspective change the focus and tone? Would this story be as interesting or relevant to a teen audience? Why or why not?

Exploring Mediums

After retelling parts of the story from different perspectives and considering the implications of changing perspectives the teacher can use back matter from *The Prom* (Mitchell et al., 2019), such as "Notes from Co-Writer Bob Martin on *The Prom*: the musical" and the interview excerpts as well as articles from sources such as *EntertainmentWeekly.com* (Canfield, 2019; Stack, 2019) to share information on *The Prom*'s journey from stage musical to young adult novel to movie musical. With these different forms, students can predict how the story might stay the same and might change with each iteration. During this, the teacher can guide students to think about the differences that the forms present in terms of audience (who a young adult novel is targeted toward versus who a stage musical, particularly one on Broadway, is geared toward) and authorship (who gets a say in how a story is told in a novel versus in a stage musical versus in a film) which connects to essential question three. To further illustrate the changes that come with different mediums, students can engage with the different adaptations of *The Prom*, such as reading scenes from the libretto (Beguelin et al., 2019), watching clips from the Broadway musical (available on various YouTube channels) and the movie (Murphy, 2020), and listening to selections from the original cast recording (Sklar & Beguelin, 2018), comparing the different versions with the novel.

One of the most significant differences between the novel and the other versions of the property is the focus. While the novel centers on Emma and Alyssa and tells the story from their points of view, the stage musical and movie also include Barry and Dee Dee as main characters. A way of illustrating this is by providing students with a list of the songs from the stage show and movie (see figure 7.2) along with the characters that perform them. After students examine the list, the teacher can lead a discussion on what the students notice about the characters' roles, what surprises them, and what predictions they can make regarding the differences between the novel and the other versions of *The Prom*. For instance, Dee Dee and Barry's appearances on the original cast recording signify that their roles there are much larger than their presence in the novel. Students might notice that they are featured in more songs than Alyssa and have a similar number of songs as Emma. Additionally, students might also note the characters of Angie and Trent, two

Song Title	Main Characters Involved
Act I	
Changing Lives	Dee Dee, Barry, Ensemble
Changing Lives (Reprise)	Dee Dee, Barry, Angie, Trent
Just Breathe	Emma
It's Not About Me	Dee Dee, Barry, Angie, Trent, Ensemble
Dance with You	Emma, Alyssa
The Acceptance Song	Trent, Dee Dee, Barry, Angie, Ensemble
You Happened	Kevin, Nick, Emma, Alyssa, Ensemble
We Look to You	Principal Hawkins
Tonight Belongs to You	Barry, Emma, Mrs. Greene, Kaylee, Shelby, Ensemble
Act II	
Zazz	Angie, Emma
The Lady's Improving	Dee Dee
Love Thy Neighbor	Trent, Ensemble
Alyssa Greene	Alyssa
Barry Is Going to Prom	Barry
Unruly Heart	Emma, Ensemble
It's Time to Dance	Emma, Alyssa, Barry, Dee Dee, Ensemble

Figure 7.2   *The Prom* Song List.

other attention-seeking Broadway actors who accompany Dee Dee and Barry and who are not included in the YA novel. The teacher might ask students how having additional adult characters and expanding their roles changes the story's dynamic.

Another instance that shows how the book diverges from the stage show and movie occurs near the end of the story. In the novel, Alyssa instigates the planning for the inclusive prom and gets some of the other students, including those who previously bullied Emma, to help (pp. 166–168, 175–198). In the stage show and film, Barry takes the lead, with assistance from Principal Hawkins and Dee Dee, Angie, and Trent (Beguelin et al., 2019, pp. 109–121). After having students review this section of the novel and then watch the associated scene in the film (Ryan, 2020, 1:43:43–1:53:45) or read the associated scene in the libretto, the teacher can ask students to identify and evaluate the changes and hypothesize why the changes were made. In partners or small groups, students can compare these changes and determine which version, to them, is the most effective (see figure 7.3). The students will then debate with other groups which version they found most effective. During the discussion, the teacher should remind students of the target audience for each property

Scene Description	Stage/Libretto (Beguelin et al, 2019, pp. 109–121)	Novel (Mitchell et al, 2019, pp. 166-168, 175-198)	Screen (Ryan , 2020, 1:43:43-1:53:45)
Planning the inclusive prom	Barry is the one who instigates funding and planning for the prom, with Principal Hawkins, Angie, Trent, and Sheldon also agreeing to put in money to help throw the prom. After some prodding, Dee Dee agrees to let them use her credit card that does not have a spending limit. After the actors do another reprise of the song "Changing Lives," the scene changes to intercuts between Alyssa and her mother and the gym, where Emma, the actors, and Principal Hawkins are decorating the gym. Mrs. Greene arrives and wants to put an end to the inclusive prom. However, other students and Alyssa stand up to her, and Alyssa comes out to her mother, which stops Mrs. Greene's protests. Alyssa and Emma reunite, and the prom comes together.	The scene alternates between Alyssa's and Emma's perspectives. Alyssa is the one who starts planning the prom by going to Principal Hawkins to reserve the gym and by creating a presentation to convince the adults and students to get behind her plan. Barry, Principal Hawkins, and a reluctant Dee Dee agree to fund the prom. Mrs. Greene interrupts the meeting to stop the planning, but Alyssa comes out to her and reveals that she loves Emma, and Mrs. Greene eventually relents. Emma and Alyssa reunite, with Alyssa taking an active role in the prom preparations.	The scene is very similar to what happens in the stage show, though there is less humor (for instance, Barry's line about decorating the gym with their blood and hair if necessary is cut). The scene also omits the reprise of "Changing Lives" in favor of having Barry reunite with his estranged mother, which does not occur in either the stage show or the novel.

What changes do you think improved the scene? What changes detracted from it?
I liked how the young adult novel let us see more of the preparations that went into the prom. In the show and movie, it just seemed like the prom happened without a lot of hard work, but the novel showed some of the additional work that went into it. Also, the novel mentioned that a lot of the students helped put together the prom, which shows that they are more accepting of Emma.

I didn't like the scene that the movie included with Barry and his mother. It seemed unnecessary and a little unrealistic given that we also see Mrs. Greene come around to Alyssa's sexuality.

Which version do you find the most compelling? Why?
I found the novel to be the most compelling because it blended elements of the stage show/movie while also putting Alyssa at the center of the action. Alyssa needed to do something to show Emma how much she cared about her and that she wasn't ashamed of their relationship, and the prom gave her the perfect opportunity to do this.

Figure 7.3   Comparing Stage, Novel, and Screen Versions of *The Prom* Example.

and why a particular target audience might want to see certain characters have more agency. The young adult novel is marketed toward an adolescent audience, and teen readers would likely want to see a teen character take the lead. However, a Broadway musical has to also appeal to adults as well as teens because it is not as easy for an exclusively teen audience to access due to location (New York City) and ticket cost. While the movie musical did enjoy wider distribution than a stage musical could, as an adaptation of the stage show, it maintains the show's structure and focus and therefore its targeted audience. The goal of this is not to deem one version superior to the other, but to help students grasp how and why adaptations diverge from their source material.

BEYOND *THE PROM*

Multi-genre Writing Project

The structure of YA adaptation of *The Prom* as well as the stage, screen, and cast recording iterations makes it well suited to a multi-genre writing project. Multi-genre writing offers a creative way for students to demonstrate their knowledge on content and skills, explore topics and elements such as theme, perspective, and character, and practice different forms of writing. Using different genres of writing and text, ranging from poetry and prose to social media posts and drawings, students combine these pieces to "re-create part of the *factual* world of [their topic] but also the *imaginative* world of dramatic scenes and characters' emotions" (Romano, 2000, p. 4, emphasis in the original).

While the majority of *The Prom* is told in first-person narrative prose, with the chapters alternating between Emma's and Alyssa's perspectives, the novel includes examples of other genres and references others. For example, excerpts of interviews done by Dee Dee and Barry bookend the story, and the book also includes an excerpt from a negative review of Dee Dee and Barry's new show. Besides this, the book refers to Emma's YouTube channel where she posts videos that allow her true self to come through and help her find "like-minded, queer friends" (p. 6) that she does not have at her school or in her town and incorporates other genres, such as the email sent by Mrs. Greene and the PTA regarding the same-sex restrictions for the prom (p. 27) and lyrics to the song Emma wrote for Alyssa and performed on YouTube (p. 163). The characters also mention, but do not show, forms of writing like prom tickets (p. 9), Instagram posts (p. 125), and Twitter posts (p. 132).

Given the different forms and the previous study, students have engaged in before, during, and after reading, having students create a multi-genre paper that demonstrates their understanding of the characters, the story, and perspective is a natural fit. Doing this can also provide opportunities for reinforcement and further analysis of topics students have previously encountered in the unit. For example, students can chart the continued references to Emma's YouTube channel to consider several of the essential questions as well as the story's setting. While Emma has few friends at school, she notes that the comments from her YouTube subscribers "feel like friends" (p. 6). After Emma posts a video about the separate prom that the PTA provided for her rather than let her attend prom with the rest of the students (pp. 131–132), she gets comments from teenagers "all over Indiana . . . [and] all over the country" (p. 142) who have experienced discrimination because of their sexual orientation. Even the students at Edgewater's high school take note of the video; Alyssa says "all of them are obsessed with the number of views she's getting and the semi-famous people who've shared the link" (p. 132) and some of the students feel guilty about what happened. Emma's feeling of community that she gets from the encouraging comments contrasts with the lack of support she gets in her physical community of rural Edgewater, Indiana, for most of the story. Students can compare the online setting and medium with Emma's experience in Edgewater, and using what they learned earlier about the challenges that LGBTQ individuals face in rural communities, they can offer ideas as to the importance an online community can have in these situations. Additionally, students can propose other ways that Emma or others like her can reach out to supportive communities, determine the inclusivity of these communities (essential question one), and explain how these different platforms and mediums might influence the way a story is told and received (essential question three).

This assignment can take different forms; one possibility is having students create a multi-genre paper focused on and from the particular perspective of one character, including secondary characters like Dee Dee, Barry, Shelby, or Principal Hawkins. Alternatively, students might retell *The Prom*'s plot using different genres as well as a variety of perspectives. For instance, as an alternative to Alyssa's account of the teenagers' interactions with Barry in the Walmart parking lot (p. 135), students might write an account of what happened from the perspective of another character or using a genre like an article for the school newspaper or a social media post. Another option would be for students to fill in the blanks of the story using different genres. For instance, they could choose to create an invitation and overview of expectations for the inclusive prom held at the book's conclusion. After revisiting parts of the story such as the PTA email that lists the requirements for James Madison's prom and Emma's criticism of these requirements (pp. 27–30), students might determine the inclusivity of these requirements and create expectations that demonstrate a more inclusive environment (essential question one). To encourage further thought and exploration about the role of different genres and mediums (essential question three), students might opt to share these expectations in a different form than what the PTA uses. For example, rather than an email, they might use an infographic, YouTube channel, or message board such as Discord to share this information. Students should be prepared to share their writing and explain the reasoning behind their choices.

Creating Their Own Adaptations

An obvious extension is giving students the opportunity to create their own adaptation of the story. This lends itself to multiple possibilities, which can support students' interests and abilities, and it also offers an authentic way for students to demonstrate what they have learned about point of view, character, perspective, symbolism, and medium. Adaptation options could include having students reconceptualize the novel, create a reader's theater script integrating the novel with parts of the original cast recording, or develop a proposal for a television or social media-based adaptation of *The Prom*. In addition to creating these adaptations, students should share their projects, thus allowing them to practice their communication skills and providing them with an audience to keep in mind when writing and performing. Besides presenting their ideas in class, students can also create videos of their projects, which can let their ideas be shared outside of the classroom with members of the school community. Sharing the projects with those planning the school's prom could be especially powerful in encouraging these decision-makers to ensure that prom is supportive and inclusive.

For the reconceptualized young adult novel, students can think of how to retell the novel using a point of view, perspective, and/or form. This could be a continuation of what they explored in the multi-genre writing project, but as an extension activity, this assignment would need to expand on what they initially did. One possibility could be reimagining *The Prom* entirely as a verse novel, with various poetic forms incorporated, or a choose-your-own-adventure story. To help further connect this to what students have learned, students should submit a justification of their choices grounded in literary concepts and the novel's content.

A second option for adaptation is giving students the chance to develop a proposal for adapting the story into another medium. This might mean reconceptualizing the story as a television series or a series of short videos using a social media platform like TikTok or YouTube. Another possibility would be to think about remaking the movie with a different cast or even a different tone. In any case, students will need to think about the benefits and limitations of the medium, the audience they would want to target and market this adaptation to, and the changes they would need to make. For example, if creating a series, students need to decide how the story would unfold and the changes that would need to be made to the plot to make it viable as a series. In this proposal, students would need to explain the premise and justifies the choices made.

CONCLUSION

Prom often occupies a significant place in many adolescents' imaginations and lives, and *The Prom* by Mitchell et al. (2019) honors its importance. By teaching students about the ways prom has traditionally excluded LGBTQ students while introducing or reinforcing devices like symbolism and perspective and offering chances to consider how adapting a text into different forms can shape the story, *The Prom* provides a plethora of rich and relevant opportunities for the ELA classroom. Beyond the curriculum, *The Prom* can serve as a starting point for readers to consider what inclusivity means and how to make it a reality.

REFERENCES

Beguelin, C., Martin, B., & Sklar, M. (2019). *The prom* [Libretto]. Theatrical Rights Worldwide.

Canfield, D. (2019, April 22). Breakout queer Broadway musical *The Prom* to get YA novel adaptation. *Entertainment Weekly*. https://ew.com/books/2019/04/22/the-prom-broadway-novel-adaptation/.

Glum, J. (2018). Teens are spending way more on prom than their parents did. Here's where the money goes. *Money.Com*. https://money.com/teens-are-spending-way-more-on-prom-than-their-parents-did-heres-where-the-money-goes/#:~:text=According%20to%20a%202015%20survey,cost%20of%20prom%20being%20%241%2C139.&text=A%20major%20factor%20for%20any,down%20to%20one%20word%3A%20fabulosity.

Grace, A. (2019). The reality of living in a small town in Indiana. *YouTube*. https://www.youtube.com/watch?v=QlQ-AQiVvb8.

Hutcheon, L., & O'Flynn, S. (2012). *A theory of adaptation* (2nd ed.). Routledge.

Jimenez, L. M. (2015). Representations in award-winning LGBTQ young adult literature from 2000–2013. *Journal of Lesbian Studies*, *19*(4), 406–422.

Lambda Legal. (n.d.). Same-sex dates and school dances. *Lambda Legal*. https://www.lambdalegal.org/know-your-rights/article/youth-dances.

Mitchell, S., Martin, B., Beguelin, C., & Sklar, M. (2019). *The prom*. Viking.

Movement Advancement Project. (2019). *Where we call home: LGBT people in rural America*. https://www.lgbtmap.org/file/lgbt-rural-executive-summary.pdf.

Murphy, R. (2020). *The prom* [Musical]. Netflix.

Romano, T. (2000). *Blending genre, altering style: Writing multigenre papers.* Heinemann.

Sklar, M. (Composer), & Beguelin, C. (Lyricist) (2018). *The prom* (original Broadway cast recording) [MP3 File]. Masterworks Broadway.

Stack, T. (2019, April 9). Ryan Murphy to adapt Broadway musical *The Prom* as Netflix movie. *Entertainment Weekly*. https://ew.com/movies/2019/04/09/ryan-murphy-the-prom-netflix-movie/.

Chapter 8

Focusing on Marginalized Identities through Imagery

A Fairy Tale Retelling and Remix with Dark and Deepest Red

Summer Melody Pennell

Fairy tales are not just for young children. Teaching a fairy tale, or a retelling of one, can guide students through complex ideas while examining genre and author's craft. These stories are engaging and familiar, and when students are less focused on what the plot is and more focused on what the plot *means*, deep critical thinking can occur. Studying fairy tales can also serve as "a vehicle for conveying . . . historical and cultural lessons" (Chapman, 2018, p. 29). For those worried about fitting fairy tales into a standards-driven curriculum, activities such as investigating different versions of a story (across time, locations, and media) easily meet several learning standards (Cavender, 2019). Fairy tales, like any texts, are appropriate for a variety of pedagogical goals. Their advantage is their familiarity, which can bring delight to students as they learn to examine childhood favorites in newer, more sophisticated ways. Even if students have not read the fairy tale you plan to examine in class, they are likely familiar with many of the archetypes such as the damsel in distress.

Fairy tales are not without problems, however. For example, the majority of fairy tales showcase strict gender roles and heteronormativity (Seifert, 2015). Examining fairy tales in classrooms can offer students opportunities to notice topics "that younger audiences do not, or should not, understand" such as the policing of women's bodies and sexual expressions (Cavender, 2019, para. 12). While fairy tales can be critiqued in light of this tendency, retellings can offer counters to these restrictive tales of princesses needing rescuing. They can also provide more racially and ethnically inclusive representation than the white princesses favored in popular culture, which can negatively affect the self-image of children of Color (Hurley, 2005).

One author whose fairy tale retellings include diversity in gender, sexuality, race, and ethnicity is Anna-Marie McLemore (they/them pronouns). McLemore is "a queer, trans, mixed-race Latinx author, and . . . writes main characters of color, queer and trans and nonbinary characters, who live, and win" (McLemore, 2021, para. 5). *Dark and Deepest Red* (McLemore, 2020) provides students opportunities to examine how the author uses imagery to create rich settings and complex, intersectional (Crenshaw, 1990) characters.

In this magical realism, fairy tale retelling, and historical fiction genre-bender, teens navigate magic (both real and perceived) coupled with the struggles of their cultures not being accepted by the mainstream societies of their communities. This novel also highlights not only the mere existence or survival of marginalized people, but their triumphs. Examining McLemore's layered text allows students to critically read and analyze how literary devices create narrative meaning, and how they are used to showcase the stories of people often left out of popular, European fairy tales. It can also be used in genre studies of fairy tales, magical realism, and historical fiction. The story is told in alternating perspectives and fluctuates between two time periods. Exquisitely crafted, this novel offers many avenues of analysis, multiple research topics, and a chance for Latinx, Romani, queer, and transgender students to have a mirror for their experiences while students of majority identity groups gain a sliding glass door (Sims Bishop, 1990). Using McLemore's text in a critical and anti-racist classroom space can allow teachers to "address historic violence and the erasure of marginalized communities, resulting in a pathway toward healing for all students" (Ebarvia, Germán, Parker, & Torres, 2020, p. 100).

SUMMARY OF *DARK AND DEEPEST RED* BY ANNA-MARIE MCLEMORE

In Strasbourg, in 1518, Lavinia (known as Lala to her family) works to keep her Romani family and her transgender love Alifair from harm by hiding their true selves as a dancing fever takes over the women of the town. Rosella and Emil live in the present day, in Briar Meadow, where every fall the "glimmer" arrives, and magic seizes the town. This year red shoes like the ones Rosella's family make mysteriously appear in Briar Meadow homes and are worn by the women and girls, making them bolder and more passionate. But in Rosella's case, the shoes compel her to dance, tying the present to the dancing fever in 1518 Strasbourg. As the story progresses Emil and Rosella (in the present time) learn to embrace their Romani and Mexican heritage, respectively, instead of repressing them for the comfort of others. Lala, Alifair, and others who do not fit in with the Catholic, white, heterosexual, and cisgender mainstream (in 1518) also find peace.

BEFORE READING *DARK AND DEEPEST RED*

To prepare students to read *Dark and Deepest Red,* they will need a working knowledge of transgender identities so that they can discuss them respectfully. Prepping students to discuss transgender identities is relatively easy, as long as teachers are willing to consistently correct students who may use the wrong terms. Teachers must ensure that they are familiar with the terminology and concepts surrounding transgender identities as well and are enthusiastically committed to affirming transgender identities. Background knowledge on the historical and cultural references will also help, as well as an understanding of the fairy tale "The Red Shoes." This fairy tale, written by Hans Christian Andersen, is a cautionary tale against vanity where a girl wears red shoes that compel her to dance (Andersen, n.d.). For historical and cultural references, the most prevalent in the narrative are references to Romani culture, and this exploration can continue during reading. Similarly, while students can spend a class period learning about "The Red Shoes," it should be referred to throughout their reading. What follows are suggestions for preparing students to read by learning about these topics and how they can continue exploring them while reading the novel.

Transgender Identities

While McLemore clearly explains that Alifair is a boy and alters his physical appearance to correspond to this identity, students may need a review of how to discuss transgender people respectfully. Explain to students that transgender is a term that refers to anyone whose gender identity (meaning the way they feel about their gender) does not match with their gender assigned at birth (meaning the gender declared by a medical professional at birth, usually decided by their genitals). This means that someone may be called a boy when they are born, but later they realize they are a girl, or nonbinary (meaning they do not identify as either boy or girl), or gender fluid (meaning their gender identity may fluctuate on a gender spectrum), or some other identity that is not "boy." In the novel, Alifair "worked so hard to hide that he was given a girl's name at birth . . . [such as] learning to bind himself beneath his shirts, [and] settling his voice as low as the other boys" (p. 15). However, it is important to stress to students that transgender people do not have to do anything to alter their appearance to be transgender: they just have to identify that way.

While Alifair chooses to make changes to his appearance and keep the fact that he is transgender a secret in order to survive, those changes may not be something all transgender people want to do. Some transgender people want to keep their identity private, some are "out" to everyone, and levels of outness can vary according to the circumstance, everyone's individual choices are valid and should be respected. Take the lead from transgender people and use the words they use to talk about themselves, and ask respectively if you are not sure. In the novel, students can notice how Alifair and others describe his identity and body, and discuss the implications of these descriptions.

To assist students with these terms, teachers can conduct a gallery walk where different terms related to gender are written on chart paper and placed around the room (suggested words and definitions in table 8.1). Teachers can point out which words are used in Anna-Marie McLemore's biography on their website, and talk through those words as a starting point if students are hesitant. Students can work in small groups to write what they think the words mean as well as any questions they have. After students have considered each word, a discussion can ensue clarifying what the terms mean. However, note that these terms change as people come up with new ways to describe their identity, so it is important to keep an open mind if you are later corrected about your use of a term.

Another activity to demonstrate how gender is socially constructed is a gender spectrum activity (Pennell, 2017). Students create three lists about what expectations society has for each group: men, women, and everyone regardless of gender. These lists are shared and placed in three different spots in the room, and students are asked to stand inside the triangle according to how they fit the different lists. No one is allowed to stand at one list unless they fit every descriptor on it, and no descriptors on other lists. This means that everyone is somewhere in the middle, visually illustrating how gender is not an inherent binary. If a student does not feel they fit anywhere within this system (e.g., a student who identifies as a gender), they can stand outside of the triangle created by the three lists. Teachers can facilitate a discussion about societal gender expectations, and how those might change over time, or between cultures. A simple example to illustrate this point is that in the 1800s in the United States, women were expected to wear dresses, and a woman wearing pants would be taboo. Now, women wearing pants is seen as normal and not as a gender transgression. Teachers could also facilitate this activity again after students begin reading, to see how their perception of their gender might change if compared to the gender norms present in 1518 Strasbourg.

Table 8.1 Gender words and definitions (from LGBTQ Vocabulary Glossary of Terms, The Safe Zone Project, n.d.)

Term	Definition
Agender	*Adj.*: A person with no (or very little) connection to the traditional system of gender, no personal alignment with the concepts of either man or woman, and/or someone who sees themselves as existing without gender.
Cisgender	A gender description for when someone's sex assigned at birth and gender identity correspond in the expected way (e.g., someone who was assigned male at birth, and identifies as a man). A simple way to think about it is if a person is not transgender, they are cisgender. The word cisgender can also be shortened to "cis."
Gender binary	*Noun*: The idea that there are only two genders and that every person is one of those two.
Gender expression	*Noun* : The external display of one's gender, through a combination of clothing, grooming, demeanor, social behavior, and other factors, generally made sense of on scales of masculinity and femininity. Also referred to as "gender presentation."
Gender fluid	*Adj.*: A gender identity best described as a dynamic mix of boy and girl. A person who is gender fluid may always feel like a mix of the two traditional genders, but may feel more men some days, and more women on other days.
Gender identity –	*Noun*: The internal perception of one's gender, and how.
Genderqueer	**1** *Adj.*: A gender identity label often used by people who do not identify with the binary of man/woman. **2** *adj.*: An umbrella term for many gender non-conforming or non-binary identities (e.g., agender, bigender, gender fluid).
Sex assigned at birth (SAAB)	*Abbr.*: A phrase used to intentionally recognize a person's assigned sex (not gender identity). Sometimes called "designated sex at birth" (DSAB) or "sex coercively assigned at birth" (SCAB), or specifically used as "assigned male at birth" (AMAB) or "assigned female at birth" (AFAB): *Jenny was assigned male at birth, but identifies as a woman.*
Transgender	**1** *Adj.*: A gender description for someone who has transitioned (or is transitioning) from living as one gender to another. **2** *adj.*: An umbrella term for anyone whose sex assigned at birth and gender identity do not correspond in the expected way (e.g., someone who was assigned male at birth, but does not identify as a man).

History and Culture

For students to be able to picture 1518 Strasbourg and the characters' cultures, exposition is necessary. Teachers can divide students into groups and then conduct a jigsaw activity where students share their findings with a heterogeneous group. Students can take notes on a graphic organizer during the jigsaw, and then continue to take notes while reading to see how these elements manifest in the novel. The graphic organizer can have sections for recording (1) research topic, (2) research findings, (3) source, (4) pages in the novel, and (5) importance in the novel. Items 1–3 can be completed in this before reading activity, while items 4–5 can be filled out while students read and serve as topics for ongoing class discussions. Figure 8.1 offers suggestions for research topics and sources.

If time or other issues prevent teachers from asking students to research all topics in the figure 8.1 (A–E), I suggest focusing pre-reading research on Romani culture (topic C) as it plays the largest role in the narrative. Teachers can further scaffold this activity by asking students to look up the definitions and/or images for the following terms found in the novel: vitsa (kinship group), Gadje (non-Roma people), Romanipen (Roma spirit), drabarni (a woman who is a healer), dikhle (head covering), vardo (Romani-style horse-drawn wagon), and Sara la Kali (a saint). Students should find images of the last three terms so that those who are not Romani or are unfamiliar with the culture can correctly picture the characters and setting as they read, to prevent them from subconsciously imagining objects and figures more familiar to them. Once they have the definitions and images, teachers can ask students to sort the terms into categories. These can be provided, or students can come up with their own. Suggested categories are community beliefs, physical objects, and people in the community. The sorting activity helps students

Research Topic	Suggested Online Sources
Strasbourg in the 1500s (especially the dancing plague)	• History.com: What was the dancing plague of 1518? • BBC: The Town that Danced itself to Death • Britannica: Strasbourg
Romani history (persecution in Europe, especially in the 1500s)	• Roma Support Group • The National WWII Museum: Fascination and Hatred: The Roma in European Culture • Britannica: Roma • Rombase
Romani culture (such as traditional dress and foods, belief system including mourning practices)	• The National WWII Museum: Fascination and Hatred: The Roma in European Culture • Britannica: Roma • Rombase
Transgender history (such as transgender people throughout history, contemporary figures, civil rights in the US)	• The Proud Trust: Trans History • glaad: Timeline: A Look Back at the History of Transgender Visibility • National Park Service: Transgender History in the US and the Places that Matter
Maquiladoras	• Britannica: Maquiladora • PBS: Maquilapolis: Examining Incentives in a Market Economy

Figure 8.1   Research Topics and Suggested Sources.

conceptualize these terms and ideas. Students can also create a shared online folder to store their images and research findings so that students can refer back to these when they encounter these terms or topics in the novel.

"The Red Shoes"

Students will also need some familiarity with Hans Christian Andersen's fairy tale "The Red Shoes" to analyze how McLemore adapted this tale to a contemporary setting. There are free versions of the fairy tale online (e.g., Andersen, n.d.), as well as films (Powell & Pressburger, 1948) and dance adaptations (e.g., The Kennedy Center, 2020) students could view. The basic premise is that a poor girl is adopted by a rich woman and becomes spoiled. She begs for a pair of red shoes and insists on wearing them to church, which her mother tells her is improper. The shoes become possessed and make the girl dance. She cannot take the shoes off and eventually asks an executioner to cut off her feet, and from then on, she lives a pious life. It is considered a morality tale for vain and selfish children, but more contemporary readers note the extreme punishment for the crime. As McLemore (2020) wrote in their author's note, "red shoes signified the bright fire of being a girl, a woman, who is unafraid of her own body and what it wants" (p. 303). This gives much to discuss about how women are punished for being proud of their bodies, and for students to predict how the fairy tale might be used throughout the narrative. Similarly to the suggested handout in the previous section, as students read, they could annotate the text in places that this retelling manifests itself during reading (discussed more in the following section, and seen in figure 8.1).

WHILE READING *DARK AND DEEPEST RED*

In the before reading section, ideas for students to make ongoing comparisons and analyses about the references to Romani culture and "The Red Shoes" throughout the novel were offered. In this section, two ideas for how to analyze the text more holistically are suggested. McLemore is a talented remixer of fairy tales, and one of the ways they do this is through their vivid imagery. Students can conduct close readings of their use of imagery to consider how it affects their ability to retell the fairy tale and remix it with historical and contemporary events. Both the "imagery" and "retellings and remixes" teaching ideas can be used in tandem for students to gain a full picture of McLemore's craft and the effects the author's writing choices have on the novel's meaning(s), which will be explored further in the "after reading" section.

Imagery

When we hear the word *imagery* we typically think of visual imagery. However, imagery is used by authors to describe smell, touch, taste, and sounds as well as sight. McLemore uses rich imagery throughout the novel to convey atmosphere and mood to the reader, as well as remix the fairy tale and historical events with the experiences of marginalized people. Teachers can choose passages based on their instructional goals. For example, students could conduct close readings to examine the following topics: setting (pp. 79–80, 88–89, 139–141), mood (pp. 18–22, 54–57, 59–62, 79–80, 87, 200–201), characterization (pp. 47–52, 79–80, 200–201, 252–255), social class (pp. 42–44), or the experiences of facing sexism (pp. 90–92, 247), racism (pp. 18–22, 31–33, 90–92), and/or religious persecution (pp. 18–22, 31–33, 79–80, 90–92, 119–121). Teachers may also wish to ask students which types of analysis they are most interested in and have students conduct close readings in small groups. Students, or student groups, can then present findings to the class so that a rich classroom discussion about craft and theme can occur.

Conversely, there are also times when imagery is notably lacking, and the focus is on dialogue. These are moments of high tension, and students can discuss the effect of lack of imagery on these sections. For example, on pages 180–181, Emil asks his parents for details about what happened to his ancestors in Strasbourg. The dialogue is nearly constant, without a lot of imagery interspersed, as is typical elsewhere in the novels. Another example is on pages 186–190, when Lala is questioned by the bailiff who accuses her of causing the dancing plague through witchcraft. Teachers can ask students the following questions for both passages: *What is the effect on the reader of this dialogue compared to others? Why do you think McLemore makes this choice? What does this lack of imagery emphasize? What is the mood in the passage, and how is that created?*

Retellings and Remixes

In fairy tales, characters are typically described sparingly while more attention is spent on the plot and setting. In a young adult novel, characterization tends to carry more weight, and McLemore's characters have rich personal lives and cultural backgrounds that are essential to their retelling. These in-depth characters allow McLemore to remix the tale to incorporate issues of race, ethnicity, gender, and queer sexuality that are often absent from the original fairy tales, or at least remain unnoticed by contemporary audiences removed from the original social context. In the case of *Dark and Deepest Red,* "The Red Shoes" are not used to shame girls for their bodies, but to show how social forces try to control girls and women, especially women of color (see figure 8.2).

Pages	Reference to original fairy tale	Changes from the original	Social Issues
18-22	• Customer visits a shoemaker's shop. • Customer sees red shoes and wants them.	• Shoes were made for this customer (not someone else). • Customer is a man shopping for daughter, not a woman with her adopted daughter. • Shoemaker's wife cuts up the shoes so the customer can't take them without paying.	• Racism: customer is a white man, tries to assert power over Mexican shoemaker. • Value of labor: Rosella knows how much work went into making the shoes, which the customer wants to take for free.
38-41	• Red shoes correlated with changes in behavior.	• Instead of 1 girl wearing red shoes, women and girls all over Briar Meadow wear them. • Shoes are not purchased but appear magically for each wearer. • Shoes cause variety of indulgent behavior: kissing, eating sweets, being adventurous.	• Labor: Rosella must sew her own shoes, taking part in her family's trade. • Outsider status: Rosella making her own shoes marks her as an outsider (due to her race and social class) from her white, upper-class friends and neighbors.
59-62	• Red shoes force the wearer to dance	• Rather than dancing past a church, Rosella dances in the road and is nearly hit by a truck.	• Chapter is between two chapters about the dancing plague, suggesting a comparison to societal control of women's bodies and desires. Rosella is thinking of kissing Emil before the shoes take control.
113-115	• Red shoes cannot be removed	• Rosella looks to her family for help, rather than an executioner or a religious figure.	• Exploitation of labor: Rosella remembers her grandparents' past in maquiladoras. • Family honor: Rosella worries if the townspeople learn her shoes are controlling her, it will ruin her family's business. She has pride in their craft. • Parental relationships: Rosella is conflicted over lying to her father about the shoes
132-133	• Red shoes cannot be removed, force the wearer to dance	• Rosella experiences physical (not just emotional) pain when she tries to remove the shoes.	• Cultural identity: Trying to remove the shoes is symbolic for Rosella hiding her cultural identity to fit in with the majority-white Briar Meadow. The shoes are "mapped onto [her] own body" (p. 132).
248-251	• Red shoes and sexuality	• Emil joins Rosella in her dance, and they have sex without shame.	• Sexuality: Rosella is in control of her body and her desire. • Consent: Rosella and Emil verbally check in with each other throughout their encounter.

Figure 8.2 "The Red Shoes" References and Remixes in *Dark and Deepest Red.*

In figure 8.2, suggested passages from the novel that relate to the fairy tale retelling sections are provided. This is not an exhaustive list, as the shoes are mentioned in other passages, but these suggestions have strong ties to the original story and showcase places where McLemore subverts the classic tale's messages of morality. Students can conduct close readings to note how the passage relates to the source material, and what contemporary social issues McLemore is introducing. For some of the passages, the contemporary issues may be harder for students to identify, or will come from passages before or after the fairy tale sections listed below. Teachers could provide a blank table with only the column headings or provide the headings and page numbers so students can focus on analyzing rather than identifying. Further differentiation and modification are possible by including more or less information in the table.

AFTER READING *DEEPEST AND DARKEST RED*

Overall, McLemore's mastery of imagery, retelling, and remixing allows students to explore the lives of marginalized peoples (Romani, queer and transgender, and Mexican people) in history and the present day. The novel offers readers an opportunity to imagine what life can be like when those who are marginalized feel safe to be their full selves. To bring together the study of imagery and retellings and remixes, students can share their findings from the previous activities through a facilitated small group and/or whole class discussion. Then, the teacher can ask students to examine together moments in the novel where marginalization is explicitly addressed outside of those used in the previous activities. Suggestions are shown in table 8.1, and there are enough that teachers may divide students into groups and give each a different passage or discuss a few of them altogether. Teachers can pose questions such as:

- In what ways does McLemore use imagery in this passage, and to what effect?
- How does this passage portray the marginalized group(s)?
- How does this passage portray the oppressors?
- In what ways do marginalized people triumph in both the Strasbourg and Briar Meadow narratives?
- In what ways does this passage connect to plot lines and characters in the other narrative timeline?
- How, in our society, can we support people in marginalized groups (see figure 8.3)?

Rewriting the Tale

Beyond the above discussion, students can move forward in their understanding by rewriting "The Red Shoes" to address another character's perspective. Students can complete this in groups or individually and focus on a character who is part of one of the marginalized groups they previously investigated. They may also consult the research and resources investigated in the before-reading activities. As students will have already discussed the social issues McLemore brings up through Rosella's narrative, ask them to brainstorm the additional social issues that characters of other identities may face. They should choose a single character whose perspective they will use to reimagine and remix a part of "The Red Shoes" as written in *Deep and Darkest Red*. Possible characters include (from the contemporary chapters) Emil, Aubrey, or Graham, or (from the Strasbourg chapters) Alifair, Dorenia, or minor characters who joined them in their new community. Students can choose a chapter from figure 8.3 (or other Rosella chapters in the novel) that interests them, using this chapter as an anchor text for both plot and imagery. Teachers can pose the following questions to students for brainstorming: *What group(s) does this character belong to? What issues does this character*

Pages	Marginalized group(s)
25	Romani
71- 76	Romani, women
109- 110	Queer and trans people, Romani, women
150	Women, Romani
158-159	Transgender people, transgender men specifically
194-199	Queer couples
280-281	Women and girls, especially women and girls of color
282- 285	Romani, queer and transgender people

Figure 8.3   Passages Where Marginalization is Addressed in *Dark and Deepest Red*.

face in mainstream society due to their identit(ies)? What social issues are you interested in exploring through this character?

Teachers can also lead students through an exercise to practice imagery. Ask students to choose an object or image that has meaning for them. Prompt students to (1) concentrate on the object, and jot down what feeling you get while looking and thinking about it; (2) write down words or phrases that describe the feeling; and (3) use as many senses as possible in describing your chosen feeling. Once students have completed this exercise and received feedback (from their teacher and/or peers), they can write a fast draft using imagery to describe an emotion experienced by their chosen character. Questions to consider include the following: *How does this character react to the red shoes or the dancing plague? What is the characters' response to others? How do these reactions and responses relate to their marginalization? How does the character relate to your chosen social issue?*

Creating their new version of "The Red Shoes" can occur through a variety of methods. Students could write a short story to share with their classmates. They might compose a multimodal fairy tale using video, music, visuals, or other media. Those who like drawing may wish to create a graphic novel, so that readers can see the marginalized people portrayed exactly how the student envisions them. As with all the activities described in this chapter, there is ample room for flexibility to best meet the diverse needs of students and cater to differing instructional goals. If possible, sharing the fairy tales with elementary students would be a rewarding experience for everyone, as the younger students would get to learn about different kinds of people than are typically portrayed in fairy tales, and the older students can see the impact of diverse reads.

BEYOND *DEEP AND DARKEST RED*

Emil's Journey

While the during-reading activities focused on Rosella in Briar Meadow and Lala and Alifair in Strasbourg, Emil is crucial to the novel. His journey from denial of his Romani heritage due to the pain of being misunderstood and discriminated against, to pride and interest in his family history, is worth exploring. Students could write a continuation of Emil's narrative, imagining his continued journey learning about his culture. This would require students to refer back to their research in the "before reading" activity, and to possibly conduct more research on contemporary traditions within Romani communities in the United States (see figure 8.4). Besides searching for news stories on the topic, students can look to the suggested sources in figure 8.4. Questions to consider include the following: *What further information on his ancestors do you imagine Emil might find? How can Emil find materials to dye fabric with woad like his ancestors, or where can he learn about dying textiles today? How will Emil's friends react to his new interests? How will Emil's relationship with his parents be affected by*

Source	Source Type	Description
The Dikhlo Collective	Instagram, Website	Provide free Dikhlo's to Roma people, serve as a cultural community.
Voice of Roma	Website	Celebrates Roma history and culture, advocates for human rights
Roma/Romani- North America	Facebook Page	Offers support, community, and shared resources for Romani people living in North America
Local Color Dyes: Dyeing with Woad	Website	Instructions for dying with woad

Figure 8.4   Suggested Sources on Romani-American Culture.

his new interests in their history? What might Emil gain from seeking out a larger Romani community?

Queer Communities Past and Present

One of the important messages of this text is that queer and transgender people have existed throughout history and have found ways to form relationships and communities despite attempts to silence them (at best) or violently deny their rights to exist (at worse). Students can research queer communities in other historical time periods and/or other geographical locations. Or, to learn about present-day queer and transgender people, students could research queer communities and community spaces (such as LGBTQ centers in their town, queer-straight alliances at their school, etc.). Students can create a resource to educate others about their queer and/or transgender community. This might be a website, a pamphlet, a video, or a community presentation. Some questions to consider, for all options, are the following: *Who created this community? How was it created? Who was/is this community for? Who did/does this community exclude? What barriers did/does this community face? How did/does this community overcome these barriers? These questions will allow students to gain a nuanced picture of a queer community, and gain ideas for how it (or other communities in the future) can be more inclusive* (see figure 8.5). Suggestions for resources are listed in the figure below.

Source	Source Type	Description
CenterLink: The Community of LGBT Centers	LGBTQ+ Center Directory (website)	Search for LGBTQ+ centers by geographic location
LGBT History	Stories tagged as LGBT History on History.com	Repository of articles on LGBT culture and communities throughout history
OSU Queer Archives: LGBTQ+ Archival Repositories	Library Guide (website)	Includes links and brief descriptions to several LGBTQ+ Archives
The Overlooked Queer History of Medieval Christianity	Article (from Time)	A historian discusses same-gender relationships in Medieval Europe
What is Trans History?	Article (from Perspectives on History, published by the American Historical Association)	Discusses how the history of transgender people is studied

Figure 8.5   Queer Community Sources.

CONCLUSION

McLemore's *Dark and Deepest Red* is a rich text that will capture the interest of many students. While it is a great addition to any secondary classroom library, teaching it allows one to cover the standard content areas of examining an author's craft, analyzing imagery, and analyzing retellings of so-called classic works. Furthermore, the novel can assist teachers in the necessary work of creating an anti-racist classroom through centering People of Color, like the Romani, in textual analysis (Ebarvia, Germán, Parker, & Torres, 2020), as well as a queer friendly classroom through examining Alifair and his relationship with Lala. While the book could technically be taught without this critical examination, this would be a great disservice to students, as well as a disservice to the book itself. Reading about complex, intersectional characters is beneficial to all students.

REFERENCES

Andersen, H. C. (n.d.). *The red shoes*. [folktale], annotated by D. Bill, in Children and Youth in History, Item #203. https://chnm.gmu.edu/cyh/items/show/203.

Cavender, B. (2019). In defense of fairy tales in high school. *The Educator's Room*. https://theeducatorsroom.com/in-defense-of-fairy-tales-in-high-school-3/.

Chapman, C. (2018). Cinderella goes global: The value of teaching fairy tales in high school. *mETAphor, 4*, 29–33.

Crenshaw, K. (1990). Mapping the margins: Intersectionality, identity politics, and violence against women of color. *Stanford Law Review, 43*, 1241.

Ebarvia, T., Germán, L., Parker, K. N., & Torres, J. (2020). # Disrupttexts. *English Journal, 110*(1), 100–102.

Hurley, D. (2005). Seeing white: Children of color and the Disney fairy tale princess. *The Journal of Negro Education, 74*(3), 221–232.

LGBTQ+ Vocabulary Glossary of Terms. *The Safe Zone Project*. https://thesafezoneproject.com/resources/vocabulary/.

McLemore, A. M. (2020). *Dark and deepest red*. Feiwel & Friends.

McLemore, A. M. (2021). #OWNVOICES & CWS. Anna-Marie. http://author.annamariemclemore.com/p/five-things.html.

Pennell, S. M. (2017). Training secondary teachers to support LGBTQ+ students: Practical applications from theory and research. *The High School Journal, 101*(1), 62–72.

Powell, M., & Pressburger, E. (Directors). 1948. *The red shoes* [Film]. UK: D & P Studios.

Seifert, L. C. (2015). Introduction: queer (ing) fairy tales. *Marvels & Tales, 29*(1), 15–20.

Sims Bishop, R. (1990). Mirrors, windows, and sliding glass doors. *Perspectives, 6*(3), ix–xi.

New Adventures. (Oct. 29, 2020). *The red shoes world ballet day 2020 exclusive clip* [Video]. YouTube. https://www.youtube.com/watch?v=3HdKwP84wMA.

Chapter 9

Queering Literary Close Reading with *The Fascinators*

Scott Storm

In Andrew Eliopulos's young adult fantasy novel, *The Fascinators,* casting magic spells not only requires knowing the denotations and pronunciations of the incantation words but also commands a laser-focus on those words' connotations and associations. Eliopulos's narrator described that spellcasting necessitates "feats of figurative language, metaphorical thinking" (p. 12). For the characters in *The Fascinators*, decoding and comprehending the words is not enough to make magic—one must also explore the words' figurative associations and nuanced meanings. In this way, Eliopulos's vision of magic is aligned with a practice of literary scholars known as *close reading.* When literary scholars conduct a close reading, they are not merely concerned with comprehending texts, but rather, with analyzing literary form. Although some scholars in education refer to close reading as just a way of looking closely at the literal meaning and comprehension in a text (see Lehman & Roberts, 2014, as a resource for this way of supporting student readers), this chapter draws on the work of literary scholars (Eagleton, 2014; Wolfe & Wilder, 2016) to define close reading as not only parsing what the text says, but also analyzing how the text is written. Literary close reading includes an exploration of literary elements like metaphor, hyperbole, personification, allusion, as well as linguistic forms like a focus on syntax or grammar. Just like spellcasting in Eliopulos's novel, close reading too requires metaphorical thinking, and when done well, close reading can feel joyous, cogent, and elegant—like magic.

This chapter illustrates how Andrew Eliopulos's *The Fascinators* can be used in classrooms to empower adolescents to conduct literary close readings that feel important and perhaps even magical. Eliopulos's novel is rich with figurative associations which are central to both the plot and the characterization of the novel. Thus, a focus on close reading is a compelling way to teach *The Fascinators* in ELA classrooms. Further, close reading is central to many ELA standards, assessments, and disciplinary content (Tyson, 2015). Still, when taught as a monotonous set of literary devices to be memorized and applied to texts, students may experience close reading as a tedious slog through a text. Instead of that approach, this chapter hopes to illustrate how Eliopulos's novel affords a chance to sustain the seemingly magical affordances of literary close reading, and to disrupt traditional ways of doing close reading in ELA classrooms to make these practices more engaging and empowering.

Teaching *The Fascinators* also encourages us to disrupt or to queer some traditional notions of close reading. The use of the infinitive form "to queer" here is to demonstrate that the idea of queering, not only references ways of infusing content about sexualities and genders, but also when used as a verb "to queer" refers to the process of questioning binaries in thinking, challenging long-held assumptions or beliefs, and imagining new ways to see and experience the world. For example, some people might assume that literary close reading can only be taught with a classic work from the Western canon. Even some teachers might think that using a young adult text by a contemporary author is not a worthy enough text to closely read. While even some literary scholars and English teachers may hold tight to these assumptions, the work of queering close reading means disrupting these beliefs. Queering close reading means embracing the idea that readers can conduct a literary close reading of any text. Queering close reading means seeing that novels, film scripts, poetry, and songs written by anyone may be worthy of analysis. Even multimodal texts like webpages, comics, and memes are appropriate for literary analysis. Similarly, students might have a belief that close reading is boring, is just about regurgitating the teacher's interpretation, or is only for students in Advanced Placement courses. Queering close reading as a teacher means disrupting these beliefs. Teachers queering close reading show that close reading can be exciting and can allow for multiple interpretations. Further, teachers who queer close reading illustrate not only that this practice is an inclusive one which can be accessible to all students, but also that close reading may even be a critical practice for liberation.

SUMMARY OF *THE FASCINATORS*
BY ANDREW ELIOPULOS

The fantasy world of *The Fascinators* is much like our own real world with one important exception: magic, the stuff of sorcerers and wizards, is real. Set in rural Georgia, *The Fascinators* follows a group of high school friends who participate in an afterschool magic club. Unlike more exclusionary imaginings of magic though, there are no non-magical people in Eliopulos's world. Instead, magic is much like calculus—everyone can learn it but it is difficult and time-consuming to do so. *The Fascinators* follows a group of friends trying to find their way through the social worlds of high school as they also practice spells together. Sam, the novel's protagonist and narrator, is an out gay cisgender man who has a crush on his seemingly straight-identifying best friend, James. The other member of their group, Delia, plays a Hermoine-esque role as the nerdy brains of the operation, and this year, the magic club grows in its membership when a new guy, Dean, moves to the school. Focused on the relationships between the four main characters, the novel explores not only queer identities but also how these intersect with class, gender, religion, and place-based (e.g., rural, urban) identities. At its core, *The Fascinators* explores the complexities of friendships in late high school especially as larger systemic forces sometimes make friendships shift and prompt people to grow in different directions.

BEFORE READING *THE FASCINATORS*

A Cognitive Apprenticeship in Close Reading

A cognitive apprenticeship—like an extended think-aloud—is a way to first model complex thinking practices and then empower the classroom community to take up these practices and make them their own. To teach close reading, avoid focusing on the individual literary terms but rather focus on the practices of close reading itself: noticing patterns, identifying strangeness, parsing connotative meanings, and unpacking literary effect.

Modeling Close Reading

To begin, move the chairs into a large horseshoe or semicircle facing the board. Then, using a projector or document camera, put up part of the text that you want students to analyze. A sentence or two is enough at this point because this activity focuses on depth of analysis. Next, talk through the patterns you are noticing and the strangeness you are seeing in just one line of the text. Try to pick a line that will allow students to access the larger themes in the text as well. With *The Fascinators*, the relationship between Sam and his best friend James is central to the novel so perhaps choosing a line focused on this complex relationship could be beneficial. For example, consider the following line from the text, "There had been infinite question marks between them over the years that they'd been friends, because the line between boys being boys and boys being attracted to boys was never easy to walk" (p. 72).

Explain that this line has the novel's protagonist, Sam, talking about his relationship with his best friend, James. Remind everyone that you are going to think aloud like a literary scholar and that they should note the kinds of intellectual moves that you make. It may sound like this:

This idea of 'infinite question marks' feels strange. I don't think he means there are literal question marks between them. There probably aren't cardboard cut-outs of a question mark lined up between the two of them and there certainly couldn't be an unending or infinite number of them anyway. So, it seems to me that this is metaphorical language. That for some reason the relationship between them feels like "infinite question marks." The image of question marks stretching into infinity seems to highlight uncertainty and confusion. So, the literary effect here is that it shapes the characterization—their relationship now feels more nebulous. This line seems to construct the characters as ones who are growing or changing. I'm wondering if themes of complex friendship relationships will be a key construct in this whole novel or if it is just going to be in this one section?

Metacognitive Discussion

At this point, stop the analysis and ask that everyone turns to talk to the person next to them about the literary moves they saw you make. A *literary move* refers to any use of describing not only what something might mean but also how it is written; focusing on literary devices, patterns of symbols, strange juxtaposed syntax, or connotative meaning are all literary moves. After students have had four minutes or so to discuss in pairs, come together and brainstorm a list of literary and intellectual moves. *Intellectual moves* are the kinds of general academic thinking that are necessary for rigorous close reading—these moves can include evaluating evidence quality and quantity, weighing multiple arguments, and constructing theses. Teachers should at this point write everyone's ideas at the side of the board and in order to create a running list of how communities of literary scholars closely read a text. Some of these ideas might include: "you broke down every word," "you said something wasn't literal so it must be metaphorical," "you didn't just identify that it was a metaphor, but rather you said what that metaphor did."

Collaboratively Close Reading

In the next iterations, ask students continue the think-aloud together. A student might point out the alliteration, repetition, and or parallel sentence structure in the phrase "between boys being boys and boys being attracted to boys." As a class, visualize or draw the metaphorical line and put "boys being boys" and "boys being attracted to boys" on opposite sides of the line. Then unpack the meaning. Students might point out that the tautological statement "boys being boys" brings up associations of "messing around," "joking," and "innocence" but "boys being attracted to boys" feels "sexual," "serious," and "more adult." Explore how Eliopulos's use of the line metaphor coupled with the alliteration, repetition, and parallel structure, create tension and highlight counterpoints between opposites—joking versus serious, childish versus adult, platonic friendship versus sexual relationship, and straight versus gay. Students would likely notice that the characters are not on one side of these dichotomies but rather are navigating the nebulous space between them. At this point, wonder together if Eliopulos's novel was going to be about this kind of navigation of uncertainty in character relationships or if it was just this one line.

At the end of this discussion, teachers could direct students back to the list in order to add their own list of intellectual moves. Finally, do not be overly worried if students do not pick up on all the practices the first time you do a cognitive apprenticeship. Teachers can help make the experience engaging and exciting by doing this intellectual work together across multiple immersive iterations.

Queer Identities and Experiences

The language in *The Fascinators* makes distinctions between queer identities and queer experiences. Identities are labels people use to describe sexualities while experiences are the sexual acts in which people engage. Before reading, teachers may want to introduce these ideas by having students think through multiple terms that describe identities, expressions, and experiences. One pedagogical resource to begin these conversations is the Genderbread Person (Killermann, 2017), a teaching tool that illustrates these points.

Teachers can also pull select passages from *The Fascinator* to underscore ideas about identities and experiences. For example, consider the passage on page 106 where Sam discusses James's sexuality:

He was ready for her to say that James was straight, or at least not into guys. He was ready for her to say that even if James did like guys—even if he was gay or bi or pan—Sam would be better off with a guy who wasn't closeted. He was ready for her to say that even if James did like guys, and even if he finally came out, there was still no way he'd ever be into some femme, flamboyant guy like Sam.

A close reading reveals that identities and experiences, for these characters, do not have to match. The passage shows that a character like James can be into guys and still identify as straight. This passage also explores other identities: gay, bi, pan, closeted, out, femme, flamboyant. A queer close reading would parse each of these terms, exploring the connotations and literary effect of Eliopulos including each word. A queer close reading would also question the absence of other identities from not only this passage, but the novel as a whole—for example, there is little discussion of asexual and agender identities in the text.

Map Analysis Activity

Teachers considering how to introduce *The Fascinators* in ELA classrooms may want to prime students to the upcoming content in a few key ways. First, have students look carefully at maps of Georgia and its demographics. For example, one could use any major news website's coverage of either the 2020 Presidential race or the 2021 senate elections in Georgia to notice the fault lines of political ideology in Georgia such as *The New York Times* (2021) color-coded county results map. Political ideology is often alluded to in the text. For example, Eliopulos's narrator explains:

> The closer you got to Atlanta—and for sure, the closer you got to the North—the more you encountered people who saw magic for its progressive and artistic possibilities. Down here, in the Deep South, you were still more likely to get an I-saw-Goody-Proctor-with-the-devil. (p. 27)

A map of voting patterns by Republican and Democrat in Georgia helps students to be able to notice the literary patterns in this quotation. For example, a student who might not otherwise be familiar with Georgia's political makeup, looking at this sentence, may notice the pattern in capitalization of "North" and "Deep South" which has the literary effect of marking these terms so readers read them figuratively and not necessarily literally. After all, Atlanta is not the northernmost part of Georgia, but the voting patterns map helps to illuminate that the word "North" here with a capital "N" signals not a cardinal direction per se but a change in ideology—that the cities and other blue areas are more aligned with "progressive" views on magic while the "Deep South," including the more rural areas has an oppositional view. Students will likely also notice the strangeness of the multiply hyphenated phrase "I-saw-Goody-Proctor-with-the-devil." Students who are familiar with Arthur Miller's *The Crucible* might use this background knowledge to explain that the allusion to Miller's work underscores the associations of ruralness and a particular ideology toward magic and religion.

WHILE READING *THE FASCINATORS*

Queering Socratic Seminars for Close Reading

In a traditional literature-based Socratic Seminar, students and teachers sit in a large circle and discuss their understandings of a text. Sometimes, this can turn into just a lecture in a circle as the talk ping-pongs between the teacher and one student at a time. Queering the Socratic Seminar means rethinking power relations. A queer Socratic Seminar radically values all members of the seminar and sees them all as capable intellectuals contributing to knowledge production. To these ends, try having a different member of the class prepare to facilitate the seminar each day. Before students facilitate, the teacher can model some facilitation routines and co-construct some guidelines. Some routines might include having time for everyone to read a short—a page or two at most—passage, spending six minutes or so having everyone annotate and think about their close reading of that passage, and sharing in pairs to rehearse ideas before talking as a whole group. A helpful resource may be Storm and Rainey's (2018) article which provides a step by step protocol and classroom examples of these pedagogic methods.

To prepare student facilitators, teachers may wish to meet briefly with facilitators—this can be done as an aside while other students might be reading independently or discussing their interpretations in small groups. Teachers should help facilitators to choose a passage for the seminar and construct some questions to get the conversation rolling. In *The Fascinators* good passages to choose are ones that interest the facilitators and include literary language. For example, pages 63–64 can be a powerful passage to use because it explores how spells don't work when the castors have "slightly different mental images" (p. 63). Exploring the connections between literary imagery and spellcasting can be fruitful here as can thinking about how the text builds these ideas into themes of "imagination and memory" (p. 64) because Eliopulos repeatedly returns to these themes throughout the novel.

During the class seminar, as the class community starts their close reading, the teacher steps back. However, teachers may find that students are still largely speaking to them. Our bodies and gaze give away the ways that power operates and show the strength of the idea that the teacher is the interpretive authority. Teachers can gently remind everyone to "speak to all the literary scholars in the room" Also, note the word "student" contains connotations that run counter to the project of queering the Socratic Seminar, thus teachers can refer to other group members as "literary scholars" instead. For some teachers, queering the Socratic Seminar is scary—one has to give up some of their own power. However, making space in the seminar empowers the other literary scholars in the room. For example, recall the exchange on page

106 where Delia and Sam discuss the reasons that Sam should get over his
infatuation with James. This is a particularly good passage for a student-led
seminar. Not only is this a poignant scene, but it includes queer terminology such as "pan," "closeted," and "femme" and as such, it positions queer
youth seminar participants who may be familiar with these terms to take on
identities as queer literary experts and unpack the denotative and connotative
meanings of these terms so that everyone can understand both these terms
and their literary effects.

Close Reading Identities

Conducting a queer close reading with *The Fascinators* means looking at how
language constructs queer identities and ideologies in the text. For example,
some aspects of the novel might not immediately seem like they are indexing
queer identities. For example, when discussing the rules of magic, Sam says,
"I thought it was 'Don't dream it, be it,'" (p. 90) to which Denver replies,
"No, that's Rocky Horror Picture Show" (p. 90). A literary close reading
might point out *The Rocky Horror Picture Show* is a cultural allusion to a
movie musical from the 1970s. However, a queer close reading would go
further to explain that this movie is also often thought of as important to queer
culture. It includes characters—even seemingly straight characters—fluidly
exploring their sexualities. Having youth literary scholars point out that the
use of *The Rocky Horror Picture Show* shapes the characterization highlighting Sam and Denver's shared cultural touchstones, thus creating more intimacy between these characters.

Discussing sexual and gender identities can be tricky terrain even for experienced teachers. Because queer Socratic Seminar share power, have the community of scholars create norms about how they want to talk with one another
and how they will work to first avoid and when necessary, address problematic
language in their shared space. Norm creation like this is a process that can
feel like a rubber stamp if it is rushed or feels inauthentic, so, if you are able
you may want to have the community of scholars spend an entire class day on
thinking through their norms, coming up with examples of what it looks like
to uphold these norms, and even roleplaying what to do and how to respond
after the norms are broken. A norm that my class has often found helpful is
one often called *three before me*, wherein seminar participants make sure
that after they speak in the whole group that they wait until three others have
gotten to speak before they add to the conversation a second time. This norm
allows more space for multiple voices to be heard in the seminar. My classes
have also sometimes enjoyed a norm we refer to as "*Ouch!*" When someone
in the seminar says something that another participant views as problematic
for being sexist, homophobic, or racist, a participant can interject, "ouch" as a

way to ask everyone to carefully consider their language. Interjecting "ouch" also alerts the facilitator to step in and help the class unpack what was just said in the seminar. However, this norm can become hokey or even detrimental if the class does not also constantly work on building trust with one another. The class community needs to take the interjection of ouch as a serious and loving critique that strives to strengthen our relationships and our communication with each other. Teachers need to underscore these ideals and continue building trusting communities for this to be an effective norm.

Close Reading as Critical Literacies

Much of the novel focuses on Sam's own close reading of the world around him. For example, Sam conducts a queer justice-driven critique of a play that he and Denver attend, and using these passages can not only help build student's sensitivity to language but also support seeing how to conduct queer literary analysis. He remarks, "Okay, I do think it's borderline homophobic that the prince seems like he is going to save the princess from this evil witch who *absolutely* also has a crush on the princess, but I'm willing to be surprised in act two" (p. 165). In this section, Sam models how to link up close reading with a critical analysis of power. Sam points to issues of characterization and plot structure while simultaneously calling the playout for being borderline homophobic. Later, Sam reacts to act two of the play: "Balling his hands into fists as the subtext became more anti-queer instead of less, with the evil witch masquerading as a prince to try to fend off the competition, only for the princess to see right through the disguise. Hard pass." (p. 167). A literary close reading might use an archetype to describe the kinds of often-reoccurring literary roles that these characters are fulfilling. A queer close reading though does exactly what the narration does here as it calls out particular archetypes as being "anti-queer" when they reify heteronormative ideas about which archetypal characters are allowed to fall in love with each other and which are relegated to the role of comedic relief at the expense of straight people. Connecting close reading with a critical consciousness is a goal of queer close reading and *The Fascinators* models this kind of close reading throughout the text. Analyzing these passages may help students to be able to closely read how texts in their world subtly inscribe anti-queer ideologies.

Activities for Close Reading at the Word Level

While the Socratic Seminar affords space to discuss in-depth themes, these activities help to focus on particular language in the text and help make the act of close reading more engaging.

"The Most Important Word" Activity

Close reading does not always have to involve using technical literary terminology like synecdoche and chiasmus. Instead, close reading can also involve students parsing language to describe the literary effect of an author's particular word choice or diction. This approach to close reading can feel more accessible to all learners and can be done in engaging and kinesthetic ways. For example, in the "Most Important Word" activity, every student is given a personal-sized whiteboard with markers and an erasure. Although these are easy enough to purchase in bulk, you can also use markers with either a legal pad or printer paper. In this activity, the teacher reveals a passage for close reading. This works best with a group of passages that are linked in some ways since there will be multiple rounds with short passages. This activity is well suited to *The Fascinators*, because the language of complex relationships is often charged with connotation. For example, take these sentences:

> James suddenly leaned up on his elbow, his eyes open wide and mere inches from Sam's eyes. The space between them was so small, so charged with electricity, that Sam felt it ignite all the air in his lungs. His chest went rigid. His heartbeat stopped. (pp. 133–134)

For starters, the teacher puts just the first of these sentences on the board. Then, they ask students to write the most important word in terms of the literary effect of the sentence. Everyone writes what they believe is the most important word and starts to formulate a robust argument for why this single word matters deeply. Have a drumroll and countdown and have all the students turn their whiteboards around at the same time. Have everyone take note of the variance among answers. Then, the fun really begins.

Any student who wants to gets a 30-second time period to stand up at their chair and argue for why their most important word is essential to the literary effect of the sentence. Make sure you have a loud and annoying timer that goes off at the end of 30 seconds and keep the pace brisk with only a short but enlivened applause between students. If you think your students will need an example, you can model the first one. It is fun to invite robust debate at this stage. My students have made arguments about everything from complex nouns to seemingly simple prepositions. Sometimes words like "of" and "with" can hold depths of meaning that we wouldn't notice unless we made a case for it. After several students have argued for different words, have everyone "vote with their feet" by having everyone get up and stand next to the person whose argument they thought was strongest for the most important word of the sentence. Have everyone sit back in the circle but maintain the voting groups (most people will be in a new chair). Then pose to the group, "Okay, so why did you vote how you did? What made each person's argument compelling?" Students should start to notice that compelling arguments come from a close reading of the text. For example, in this passage, a student might argue that "suddenly" is the most important word because it has the effect of accentuating the way that James quickly moves his body as if he has made an important decision and it further adds to the complex characterization of James as someone who is both deliberate and direct but also seeking intimacy—a possibly strange yet sophisticated pairing.

"Parse the Synonym!" Activity

Once everyone has gotten a chance to argue for the most important word, have everyone erase their whiteboards. Then, the teacher underlines one word in the sentence. Now instruct everyone to write a synonym for that word and prepare an argument for how this synonym greatly changes the connotative meaning. The first few times, this task might feel confusing, so feel free to model an example. For instance, in the second sentence above the teacher might underline the word "ignite." Instead of "ignite" Eliopulos could have written "burn" "spark" or even "kindle." How would these synonyms change the literary meaning? Let's take "ignite" and "kindle." The word "ignite" connotes a swiftness or suddenness while the word "kindle" connotes something more slow and subtle. Thus, the diction of the word "ignite" has the effect of having a feeling of immediacy and urgency which characterizes Sam's passionate and sudden feelings at that moment. When time is up, have another drumroll and have everyone turn around their whiteboards to see everyone's synonyms. Some of them will be the same and that's totally fine. One variation is to have students point and yell "great minds!" (for "great minds think alike") when they see they have the same word as someone else—though for some groups this may feel too cheesy. In any case, have students volunteer to present their arguments about the literary effect of the original word versus their synonyms. Again, have the presenting student stand in front of their chair and give them students 30 seconds to make a compelling case about their word. At the end of a few rounds of argument, have everyone choose who they thought was most compelling and stand by that person. Staying in these groups, have everyone take a new seat, and discuss what made the arguments compelling for this group of budding literary scholars.

AFTER READING *THE FASCINATORS*

Writing Close Reading Papers

Having students build on their ideas from the Socratic Seminars to write their own close reading papers can be an exciting and intellectually stimulating experience. One traditional method for having students write these papers is to assign a writing prompt that students must write about. However, instead of prompts, which may feel limiting, teachers could envision platforms, which are spaces on which students can bring their own passions instead of being coerced into writing about a teacher's prompt (Muhammad, 2015). However, teachers envisioning writing experiences as platforms also need to support students to think through their ideas and passions. One strategy to do this is to have the class brainstorm themes from the Socratic Seminars that they found most interesting. Some potential themes that students might list for *The Fascinators* include imagination, memory, queer identities, teenage friendship, independence, aesthetic beauty, queer desire, physical and emotional abuse, regeneration/healing, sacrifice, and giving. Then, ask students to brainstorm patterns and themes in the novel that the class did not have time to discuss in the seminar. Writing everyone's ideas on a large whiteboard and taking a picture is a good way to support students to think about many possible topics.

Once students choose a topic of interest, they can search through Eliopulos's text to find all the passages that are related to their themes. Then, students can write close reading memos—short paragraphs where they analyze one word, phrase, or sentence at a time from the passages they identified. Once students have written several close reading memos, have them print these and lay them all out on the floor. Then have students look for patterns in their memos. For example, a student writing about "memory" might notice that across their memos, Eliopulos uses imagery of shadows and dreams when he discusses memories relating to queer love and that in the same passages he uses magic as a counterpoint against memory—writing that "magic is very real" (p. 301) but that memory is fleeting, intangible, and representational. Drawing on patterns in their memos, have students construct a literary thesis that describes not only what the text is about but also how the text is written. For instance, the student writing about memory might construct a multi-sentence thesis such as:

> Although readers may usually experience memories as relatively real and magic as fantasy, Eliopulos's novel queers these assumptions. Eliopulos aligns *queer memory* with imagery of dreams and shadows and associates *queer magic* with words that connote reality and consequence. By queering traditional notions of memory and magic, Eliopulos argues that while memory may be ephemeral, memories are undergirded by lasting emotions, concretely felt, which seem to operate by magic. In this way, Eliopulos understands *queer love* to be not about fleeting memories, but rather lasting emotions felt in the body which ultimately signal resilience, authenticity, and hope.

To help teachers support students in their writing literary close readings, figure 9.1 offers a partial list of themes/motifs/topics with example page numbers from *The Fascinators* that students can refer to to find fruitful quotations to use as evidence. However, teachers should be careful not to give this table to students who do not need this kind of support. Part of the intellectual joy

Themes/Motifs/Topics	Example Page Numbers	Key Words and Phrases to Consider
Friendship/Bromance	72-73, 130-135, 233, 299-301	boys, infinite question marks, buddy, grabbing Sam's hand, talked him down a maze, charged with electricity, unmasked desire, change, safe,
Gender Expression	22, 31-32, 106, 258-259	ponytail, purple, curls, roguish grin, dimples, femme, flamboyant, Swan Princess, feminine, masculine, pants, skirt/dress boy, girl,
Homophobia/Hate Crimes/Homophobic Microaggressions	28, 95-97, 127, 165-167, 212-215	defund, disband, violently, smashed, dirty look, actively support, deigning to allow, bias, loudly objected, content warning, homophobic, subtext, anti-queer, bullied, welcome, stolen, vandalized, constant fear,
Memory, Imagination, and Dreams	11, 64, 73, 128, 135, 299-302	past, mind, real, spell, simulacrum, revisit, the moment passed, remember, not real, happen
Queer Identities	27, 90, 106, 213-215	Rocky Horror, straight, gay, bi, pan, closeted, out. rainbow, trans, pronouns, queer
Spellcasting/Magic	12, 63, 117-118, 148-151, 187-188, 225, 298-299	spell, metaphor, touchy-feely, associations, mental images, canvas, painting, storm, primordial, tarot deck, spell of giving

Figure 9.1   A Support for Helping Students Write Literary Close Reading Papers on *The Fascinators*.

of conducting a close reading for many students is finding the quotations and drawing the links between them themselves. When students get stuck though, teachers can first remind students to look back at all their annotations and notes from the Socratic Seminars that their peers led. If students still need support, then this table can be used to help point students in a concrete direction. Giving a table like this to students prematurely could make students feel that these are the *only* sanctioned topics. Even if the teacher says students can choose any topic, students may think that topics on this list are more legitimate in the teacher's eyes and may shy away from choosing something not on the list. Use this table as a support for the few students who need it, instead of as a starting place for all.

Literary Scholars Conference

Once students have written their close reading papers based on their chosen themes, as described above, teachers may want to hold a literary scholars conference. Instead of the traditional method of having students write their close readings of the novel to hand in to the teacher, queer this idea. Create a more authentic audience by holding your own academic conference. Group students into small "roundtables" with four or five at a table just like one might see at an academic conference for real literary scholars. One can even group student close reading papers by topics. For example, perhaps several students are interested in tracing words that describe gender expression through the novel to argue how Eliopulos's novel might reify or contest problematic ideologies (refer to figure 9.1 for specific examples of topics and areas of the text to find relevant evidence). These papers could be grouped together under the heading of "Close reading gender expression and identities." Sometimes it won't be so obvious, though. For example, maybe one student is doing a close reading of the language of dreams in the novel. Another scholar might be looking at the language of homophobic microaggressions in the novel and how that shapes the character's psyche. A third scholar might be interested in unpacking the novel's central "bromance" by looking at the diction and connotations of the words that Sam and James use to describe one another and thinking about how these words shape their relationships. These papers might be productively put together with a roundtable title of "Psychoanalytic approaches to *The Fascinators*."

On the day of the conference, encourage everyone to dress in their most flamboyant academic attire—tweed jackets and bow-ties picked up from the thrift store perhaps—and arrange the room into roundtables. In roundtables, have each scholar formally present their paper to the other members at their table. Include time for questions and feedback between each presentation. If groups have laptops, they can also write comments on each other's papers so as to capture everyone's thinking at that moment.

Before the conference, assign someone from each roundtable to serve as the "discussant." When roundtables finish, the whole class comes together in a large semicircle and each discussant speaks to the whole class for 2–4 minutes. The discussant shares the authors and titles of the close reading papers that were at their roundtable as well as each person's central argument and then the discussant tries to pull out larger themes and ideas that the papers at that table collectively tackled. Teachers should take careful notes during the discussant's short speeches because then they can serve as the meta-discussant to synthesize all of the roundtables and talk about the class's collective contribution to scholarship based on all their close readings of *The Fascinators*.

BEYOND *THE FASCINATORS*

Speculative Queer Futures

Fantasy and sci-fi genres have often been used to envision future worlds that rethink gender or sexuality in significant ways. For example, Ursula K. LeGuin's classic *The Left Hand of Darkness* describes an alien world where the people experience both biological sex and gender expression very differently in that each month both their biological sex and gender can shift. Similarly, Bruce Coville's short story "Am I Blue" imagines a world where a genie turns all queer people different shades of blue for a day and considers the possible ramifications of this magical act on society. A close reading of Eliopulos's novel may help students to start to envision how they might want to manipulate genre or fantastical elements to create stories in their own fantasy worlds.

For this activity have students write a short story that takes place in a fantastic world that somehow reimagines gender and sexualities. In addition, have each student compose an artist statement where they discuss how they used close reading practices to construct the short story and develop the way their fantasy world interacts with genders and sexualities. For example, completing a similar project, one of my former students created a storied world where magic was controlled by the gods and all the gods were queer icons from Sappho to RuPaul. As a longer extension activity, have students draw maps of their fantasy worlds and present their worlds at a "Speculative Worlds' Fair" where each person sets up a booth in the school cafeteria that represents their fantasy world and students take turns standing at their booth or looking at their classmates exhibits.

Fascinators Drag Ball

As an extension to the literary scholars conference, challenge every student to create an outfit inspired by their paper's thesis statement. I have done this activity in my own classroom and one person, whose thesis was about exploring dichotomies as they relate to identities, came to class with his left side completely painted blue and his right side completely red. Not only did he use fabric paint to paint the tunic and trousers he adorned but he also used body paint and hair dye to complete the head-to-toe look. Another student wrote about the material objects in the text that were connected to supernatural means like magic spellcasting. They used sketch pad paper backed with cardboard to create drawings of some of the material objects and then they used coat hangers to drape these all over their body like a living Calder mobile. To showcase these looks, in the classroom, create a runway and have each person walk down the runway in their outfit and then have everyone explain how their outfit represents the thesis from their close reading.

CONCLUSION

The Fascinators lends itself to teaching students literary close reading because it combines LGBTQ characters and themes with literary language and devices. Unfortunately, under some traditional pedagogies, literary close reading can feel tedious and uninteresting to students. This chapter offers tools for queering literary close reading in the ELA classroom so that interpretation can feel more meaningful, relevant, intellectually stimulating, and even joyful. By centering student's interests, injecting elements of play into pedagogical activities, and purposefully building a community of literary scholars, teachers can queer literary close reading and simultaneously support all students to exceed standards around traditional ELA content.

Near the end of Eliopulos's novel, Sam must attempt to save James who has been the victim of an insidious spell rendering him comatose. In many ways, some traditional ELA methods, when taken together, may metaphorically function like a spell that renders our youth figuratively comatose. Long monologic lectures, singular interpretations presented as the only supposedly correct understanding of the text, and narrow writing prompt that limit youth's passions have collectively contributed to this metaphorical spell. In *The Fascinators*, Sam realizes that to save James, "the counter spell needed to be about giving" (p. 298). This chapter tries to demonstrate how queering literary close reading might be counter spell for the harm that some traditional methods have done. Queering literary close reading, then, is also about giving. It involves giving space for students to talk through their ideas, giving youth time to explore their own multiple interpretations of the text based on their intellectual passions, giving students support when they are stuck, and giving platforms on which students can present their interpretations to authentic audiences that include their whole class community of literary scholars. However, one teacher casting this spell of giving will not be enough. In *The Fascinators*, spells become more powerful when they are cast by many people simultaneously. It will take many teachers working together to cast this spell of giving. I urge you to begin reciting the words of this figurative incantation with me. Because, if we work together, I know that we are capable of real magic.

REFERENCES

Eagleton, T. (2014). *How to read literature*. Yale University Press.

Eliopulos, A. (2020). *The fascinators*. Harper Teen.

Killermann, S. (2017). *The genderbread person v4*. The genderbread person. https://www.genderbread.org.

Lehman, C., & Roberts, K. (2014). *Falling in love with close reading: Lessons for analyzing texts—and life*. Heinemann.

Muhammad, G. (2015). Searching for full vision: Writing representations of African American adolescent girls. *Research in the Teaching of English, 49*(3), 224–247.

Storm, S., & Rainey, E. C. (2018). Striving toward woke English teaching and learning. *English Journal, 107*(6), 95–101.

The New York Times (2021). Georgia senate runoff election results. *The New York Times*. https://www.nytimes.com/interactive/2021/01/05/us/elections/results-georg ia-runoffs.html.

Tyson, L. (2015). *Critical theory today: A user-friendly guide* (3rd ed.). Routledge.

Wolfe, J. & Wilder, L. (2016). *Digging into literature: Strategies for reading, analysis, and writing.* Bedford/St. Martin's.

Chapter 10

Exploring Blackness, Queerness, and Liberation through *The Stars and the Blackness between Them*

Danelle Adeniji, Brittany Frieson,
Tatyana Jimenez-Macias, Kristin Rasbury,
Kyle Wright, and Amanda E. Vickery

And of course I am afraid, because the transformation of silence into language and action is an act of self-revelation, and that always seems fraught with danger. (Lorde, 2007, p. 42)

Writing is a liberatory and political act of resistance (hooks, 1994), and providing students the freedom to share their narratives intentionally decenters eurocentric literary practices. The narratives of queer, Black middle-, and high school students framed in a Black feminist lens are largely omitted in white, heteronormative coming-out stock stories (Martiniez, 2014). In contrast, Black feminism acknowledges the experiences of Black women and gender creative folks and emphasizes the value of those experiences (Collins, 1999; Evans-Winters, 2019). In secondary school contexts, generally, the principles of Black feminism are not affirmed nor given space. In thinking about the multilayered forms of oppression that Black girls face in their daily lives, such as racism, sexism, and agism of not knowing their truth at a young age, it is imperative that we manifest spaces in our curriculum where Black queer, trans, and gender creative youth can embrace their identities without pause. Therefore we are inspired to ask ourselves, how can the radicalness and joy of being Black and queer be celebrated and affirmed in oppressive secondary educational spaces? In addition, how can the richness of Black geological spaces, spiritualness, and liberation be given an active voice to dismantle spaces that are meant to spirit-murder them (Love, 2019)?

The Stars and the Blackness between Them (Petrus, 2019) is a young adult fiction book narrated through a queer Black feminist, the ancestral magic first-person lens of two Black high school girls from differing geographical regions. The book is a key to liberating literary reading and writing practices (Lyiscott, 2019) as it evokes revolutionary actions through queer, Afrofuturistic character development, and descriptive personification of nature. This is not a typical stock story about coming out. Alternatively, teachers can utilize the book's poetic features to critically teach youth by prioritizing abolitionist teaching that fosters literacy practices such as liberatory narrative writing. Students and teachers need to create an emotional, mental, and spiritual homeplace where they can return to process their identities freely (Love, 2019). According to Love (2019), bell hooks (1994) describes homeplaces as

> a space where Black folx truly matter to each other, where souls are nurtured, comforted, and fed. Homeplace is a community, typically led by women, where White power and the damages done by it are helped by loving Blackness and restoring dignity. (p. 63)

Homeplaces are one of the central themes throughout the book which invite the reader to process and heal with the characters. This aids the narrative of how queer, trans, and inclusive literature pedagogies create opportunities for students to see themselves in the literature and provides a healing and thriving community infrastructure (Blackburn et al., 2015). The chapter also leads teachers and students through literary elements of examining historical perspectives to understand characterization, analyzing astrological symbolism, and using poetry to close read and critically analyze themes throughout the book. Students and teachers will also create plans of community activism to understand the author's points of view.

SUMMARY OF *THE STARS AND THE BLACKNESS BETWEEN THEM*

Audre is in her world with nature, sand, and the crashing beach waves as she explores the intersections of continuing Black liberation and coming to terms with her first heartbreak. Audre's mom sends her away from her home in the Port of Spain, Trinidad, after discovering her relationship with the pastor's granddaughter. Audre runs to her grandmother, Queenie, for refuge but her mom snatches her away and heads to an unknown home in Minneapolis. In Minneapolis, Audre finally stops fighting against the tide and opens up to living her spiritual destiny.

Mabel is entering her junior school year while daydreaming about an intense and unsure hug between her and Jada, a high school associate, in the rain. Focusing on these unsure feelings, Mabel sets her sights on being basketball ready while avoiding constant, troubling stomach pains. Without being prepared for a whirlwind of change, Audre enters Mabel's world like winter changes to spring. The text merges two geographically different worlds into a realm of self-exploration and Black liberation throughout the connectedness of these two characters.

BEFORE READING *THE STARS AND THE BLACKNESS BETWEEN THEM*

Note to Teachers

The characters are often engaged with music such as Mabel's mom playing neo-soul or nineties R&B around their house. As students and teachers read the book, they can create a short playlist to accompany the vibes of each section they read. The authors have provided a few example songs and their purpose with each section.

Historical Background

To know where we are going, we must understand where we have come from and how historical narratives impacted the characters. In this section, students will investigate and research Audre Lorde's motivations and fundamental notions regarding LGBTQ rights, Civil Rights, and Feminism. This process will allow them to obtain background knowledge on what the main character's name symbolizes and how it fuels their characterization. For example, the reference shown here would be supported by Audre Lorde's biography page on the Poetry Foundation (2021) website and excerpts from *The Master's Tools Will Never Dismantle the Master's House* by Audre Lorde (2018).

An overall question to consider for this section is, how does the symbolism of historical figures factor into the characterization of the main characters? Using a virtual gallery walkthrough activity, students will investigate Audre Lorde and other historical figures and events, such as the Stonewall riots, Black Lives Matter Movement, East L.A. walkouts in 1968, Marsha P. Johnson, to scaffold knowledge before reading the text. The virtual gallery walkthrough is customizable for each teacher's preference, and as shown in figure 10.1, Google slides can be used to build a virtual space. Each slide can contain a different figure or event with customizable questions. Also, teachers must include relevant research sources for their students to investigate with each title.

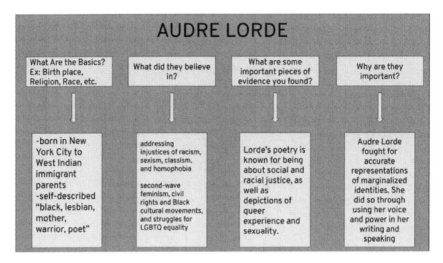

Figure 10.1   Virtual Gallery Walk Sample (created by authors).

Symbolism and Astrology

Throughout the book, spirituality and astrology are essential to connecting the character's journey to the events in their lives. For example, Audre's grandmother, Queenie, relies on nature and spiritual guides throughout her life. While Audre's mom is heavy into the church on their island and the peace she seeks from it. In this section, students will create astrology charts to understand Queenie, Audre's mom, and the spiritual journey of other characters.

Students can be asked how the symbolism of astrological signs factor into the characterization of the main characters? Students will encounter Petrus' intentionally placed poems titled with astrology signs while reading the text. Petrus utilizes these poems and their accompanying signs to symbolize underlying themes, tones, and events to foreshadow what is coming. Students could front-load the necessary knowledge to understand the symbolism behind these poems. Astrology sites, such as Space.com (see *Your Astrological Sign May Not Be What You Think It Is* by Braganca, n.d.) or Astrology.com (see *12 Zodiac Signs: All You Need to Know*), can be utilized to discover their signs and their correlation with the seasons.

Students can create and display their astrology chart using Google slides or jamboard. This activity is designed to help students understand astrology, the signs, and how the author uses symbolism to represent change. As shown in figure 10.2, the teacher may create another set of slides on Google to allow students to fill in the information on each given sign.

A Playlist for Before Reading

The following are three songs that flow with this section. The first song is *All the Stars* by Kendrick Lamar ft. SZA. This song is featured on the official soundtrack for the movie *Black Panther*, an Afrofuturistic themed film. The song's lyrics feature both space symbols and the struggle Black individuals experience in a world dominated by whiteness. It speaks on the emotions felt as trials and tribulations get thrown into the faces of so many Black individuals. The second song is *Milky Way* by GGK (Vo. Madison McFerrin) as the essence of this song from the anime *Carole & Tuesday* speaks to the themes of astronomy and love, which are prevalent within this novel. The third song is *Moonglow* by Billie Holiday because the novel discusses the strength of multiple Black individuals, but especially the strength between Audre and Mabel and the love they have for one another.

WHILE READING *THE STARS AND THE BLACKNESS BETWEEN THEM*

Queer Character Mapping

Throughout the book, Audre often draws on the ocean, moon, and earth forces to feel closer to the important women in her life and to understand herself as she navigates the space she is in: "The ocean witnessed us, and as I sat there with Neri, I felt shy. The water blue was loud and welcoming, like

Figure 10.2 Sample Astrology Display (created by authors).

a long-lost tantie" (p. 23). For this section, students could continue to follow astrological signs, geography, and nature to understand descriptive and figurative language and character development. Additionally, students can annotate and journal about the personification of nature and its connections to woman empowerment.

Students could consider the ways Audre and Mabel navigate their understanding of queerness. Students can write or draw out character maps for various characters to engage the students and visualize the diverse identities illustrated throughout *The Stars and the Blackness between Them* (see figure 10.3). Character mapping focuses on a singular character and analyzes the various details of what makes up a character. Textual evidence to support claims is encouraged. To focus on this novel, the students can form groups, assign a character, and explore how the novel's themes of queer identities, culture, and race make up these characters.

Assign the first group Audre as one of the characters the story is told through. Students can look at how Audre's character is made up of queerness, culture, and identity as a Black woman. Students should not focus solely on the surface-level characteristics of Audre, but look deeper as to who exactly she is and why these aspects are essential. Students could consider some questions while mapping out the characters: *What is Audre's identity in Trinidad? What is Audre's identity in Minneapolis? How are these two identities different, and how does it affect Audre? What about Audre's name itself? How does Audre's religious upbringing affect her queerness?* For example, Mabel goes with Audre to a thrift store to help Mabel look for winter clothes. While there, the shop clerk compliments Mabel's accent. This leads Mabel into a conversation about Trinidad, the carnival, music, and weather (Petrus, 2019, p. 107).

Another group will map out Mabel, and students should focus on how her identity revolves around being a young Black woman in the United States as shown in figure 10.3. Trinidad's and U.S. cultures are vastly different, so students should see the differences between Audre and Mabel. Additional questions students should consider while mapping out Mabel are: *What similarities do you see between Mabel and Black women in the United States currently? If there are any, why/how are they important to Mabel's character as a whole? What about Mabel's queerness and the intersectionality between her Blackness?*

Due to the novel chapters being split in narration, the students can discern between them as they read the book. Students should be taking notes on their readings and utilizing these notes in the character mapping activity as they read. Since there is a focus on only Audre and Mabel, textual evidence such as direct quotes helps solidify any observations the students make regarding the characters. Students will begin in their small groups working together to

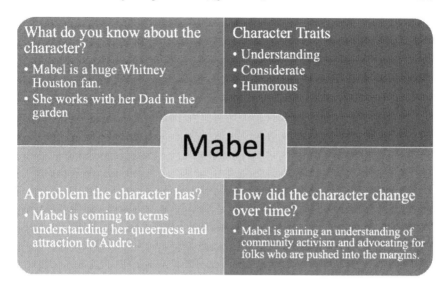

What do you know about the character?

- Mabel is a huge Whitney Houston fan.
- She works with her Dad in the garden

Character Traits

- Understanding
- Considerate
- Humorous

Mabel

A problem the character has?

- Mabel is coming to terms understanding her queerness and attraction to Audre.

How did the character change over time?

- Mabel is gaining an understanding of community activism and advocating for folks who are pushed into the margins.

Figure 10.3   Sample Character Map (created by authors).

create the map and will be offered the ability to do it on paper or digital mapping. Afterward, the class will come together and present their observations.

Intersectionality and Being Black

Some students may have been exposed to the term intersectionality (Crenshaw, 1989), but it is crucial to understand what it means and how it applies to *The Stars and the Blackness between Them*. Intersectionality was coined by Kimberle Crenshaw (1989) to purposely name the distinct racial and gender discrimination Black women face and live through. This novel centers on Audre's and Mabel's intersectional experiences because every setting forces them to rely on multiple identity markers to survive or thrive in numerous situations. Embracing intersectionality as a lens of interacting with the characters and the world means to include the oppression of folks who are othered by the dominant society. Mabel's mom, a Black woman, thrives despite this oppressive narrative by sharing rich knowledge with Mabel, embracing her roots, and relying on the spiritual ancestors to guide her. Therefore, she sees her mom embrace womanhood and Blackness. Mabel's family doctor is an Indigenous woman who started practicing with other Indigenous women doctors to serve underserved communities. Mabel feels safe with her doctor because she can relate and trust the doctor with her medical needs. *In what ways do these connections empower their womanhood and queerness?*

It is important to note that while the story is told through the eyes of various Black characters, being Black is not a monolith. Not any one person, tribe, country, or culture will be the same as another. Multiple visible and invisible identity markers of what it means to be Black for the characters are illustrated throughout the novel. It is important to note that while the story is told through the eyes of various Black characters, being Black is not a monolithic experience. Not any one person, tribe, country, or culture will be the same as another. Multiple visible and invisible identity markers of what it means to be Black for the characters transpire throughout the novel. During her first day at a new school, Audre asks a teacher why her country's history (Trinidad) isn't included with critical historical events they are taught in history class. The teacher responds, "[I] only cover the events that have global impact and not regional incidents" (Petrus, 2019, p. 103). Audre walked away, disregarded and irritated by the teachers' response. Character mapping is one way students can look at various Black identities between the characters of *The Stars and the Blackness between Them* (Petrus, 2019), as mentioned above with Audre and Mabel. However, students could also research other local, national, and international Black identities and communities.

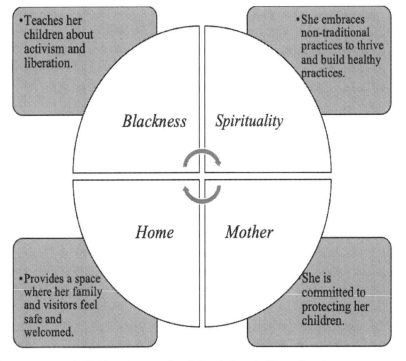

Figure 10.4   Mabel's Mom Intersectional Graph (created by authors).

Character mapping is one manner that students can look at different Black identities between the characters of *The Stars and the Blackness between Them*, as mentioned above with Audre and Mabel. However, students could also research other local, national, and international Black identities and communities.

Students can organize the information they find into various maps such as a Venn Diagram, compare and contrast, or even make a PowerPoint presentation with different imagery. While looking into the multiple Black identities, both inside and outside of the novel, it is important to note how culture and identity change from one place to another, shifting away preconceived biases of Black identities being the same. Students can create an image to represent supporting characters' visible and invisible intersections and their importance in these in the characters' lives (see figure 10.4 for an example).

Poetry Analyzation

The book flows chronologically with flashbacks at effective intervals that provide the reader with insight into the characters' pasts. The passage of time is marked by poems that coincide with the astrological seasons. These spiritually influenced poems offer an understanding of the attributes associated with their particular season. Students should find that symbolism and characteristics typically linked with the sign and season being spotlighted will be distinguishable in the poem. Students should also note how the poems and themes relate to the Black, Indigenous, brown queer, and trans community by drawing connections among the queer, trans, and gender creative community, astrology, and revolutionist concepts and movements. For example, the use of the word "pride" in "Leo Season" is not only an allusion to the LGBTQ community, but the revolutionary Pride movement sparked by the Stonewall riots (p. 38). Additionally, it refers to a common definition for a group of lions and further represents the sign of Leo season: the lion. Likewise, it depicts a correlation with the animal and the vibrant symbolic embodiment of the fierceness of a lion's pride. Dissecting language in the poetry will allow for students to connect the mentioning of spirituality and astrology with other similar wordings in the book.

A couple of overarching questions for this section include: *how does the novel's poetry reflect aspects of the Black, Indigenous, brown, queer, trans, and gender creative community? How does poetry impact the telling and experiencing of the story?* Students can be assigned a poem from the book and asked to close read it and identify an overall theme. Students decode language to detect poetic elements, allusions, metaphors, similes, alliteration, and any other literary device that may appear in the text (see figure 10.5). Through this assignment, students can invoke critical-thinking skills that

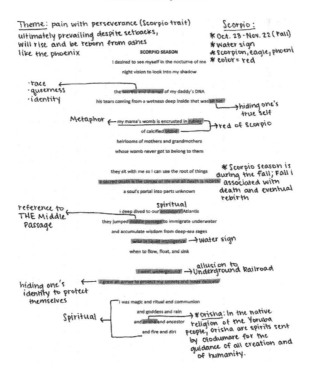

Figure 10.5 Close-Reading Example (created by authors).

push them to dig deeper into the language of the poetry and dissect literary elements that deal with the bigger concepts discussed in the lessons.

A Playlist While Reading

The following three songs flow with this section. *Song About You* by Chika. This song's singer, Chika, is a female, Black, queer artist singing about the success she has and the pride she takes in; what she's doing without worrying about the hate, criticism, and unimportant comments made about who she is. She's living her life and making moves to become even more successful while she knows there are people who don't want her to thrive and people who don't like how unapologetic she is in loving herself. The second song, *Thinkin Bout You* by Frank Ocean, is about unrequited love and how it influenced and continues to influence his life. This is similar to Audre and the love she felt for another girl in her home of Trinidad. Although it didn't work out, it influenced her life when she went to the United States. She never stopped thinking about this love, just as Ocean continues to remember his love. The third song is *Cranes in the Sky* by Solange. In this song, she sings about her attempts at numbing a difficult pain through various methods. This difficult pain goes unaddressed and there's no resolution seen nor acknowledged. When Mabel gets diagnosed with a life-threatening illness and causes her to fall into a deep depression where she isolates herself and attempts to ignore it.

AFTER READING *THE STARS AND THE BLACKNESS BETWEEN THEM*

Community Activism

The overall questions for this section include: *how can community activism support Black, Indigenous, brown, queer, trans, and gender creative individuals? In what ways can we reach out to our communities in order to provide justice for all folks?*

As students prepare to translate their ideas into action, they can connect their knowledge of the characters' experiences to their understanding of creating change. Using a graphic organizer, such as the one pictured in figure 10.6, students will connect scenes from the book with the theme of community activism. They must cite instances that portray the image of individuals

Figure 10.6   Community Activism (created by authors).

coming together to promote social justice and equality. Students should identify a quote, the speaker, and the page number from which the quote was drawn. Themes of togetherness, community, and transformation should be seen throughout students' responses. After filling in the graphic organizer, students can brainstorm how they plan to involve the community in matters of social justice and equality. Gathering insight from the book and their knowledge or experiences with community activism, they will use this activity as a steppingstone to enact change in their extension activity.

An After Reading Playlist

The following three songs could accompany the during-reading activities. *Heart-Shaped Box* by Amber Mark shares the story of Mark's reinvention of the song, originally sung by Nirvana. One could read this song as looking at the relationship between Audre and Mabel, from their first meeting to eventually romantic involvement. The second song, *Pink + White* by Frank Ocean is about the experiences and lessons Ocean learned with a friend who unfortunately passed away. Mortality is a theme of the song, something that can also be seen within the novel with Mabel's illness. Audre ends up in the same position, as Mabel teaches her so much about love and life, and passes along her knowledge as Mabel deals with her own mortality. The third song, *Skin* by Rag'n'Bone Man speaks about missing out on a love that might have blossomed.

A Note to Teachers

Before this post-reading activity, it is imperative that the class reconvene in their mental, emotional, physical, and spiritual homeplaces (Love, 2019) and return to it as needed. As mentioned earlier in the chapter, a homeplace is a physical, mental, and emotional space teachers and students can return to process and wonder safely and without judgment.

BEYOND READING *THE STARS AND THE BLACKNESS BETWEEN THEM*

Young Revolutionists

Flashbacks that occur in the story highlight distressing experiences, such as a Black father who is afraid to turn around and soothe his teething child when pulled over "in case the cops reacted with bullets" (p. 164). Students may relate to these emotions and feel these encounters accurately depict their feelings in difficult situations. Therefore, it is prevalent that these matters of police brutality and trauma are acknowledged, given their significance to today's society.

A question for teachers and students to consider after they read the book is how can we learn from Audre's and Mabel's community activism to promote equity in our schools and communities? Mabel is drawn to community activism by reading about an imprisoned Black man, Afua. This pushes Mabel to take action and call for the release of Afua from prison by bringing attention to his situation. With revolution on the mind, consider how students are significantly impacted by policies and decisions that have been implemented by administrators. To challenge students' critical thinking, have them contemplate in what ways their school may be revolutionized.

The prominence of liberatory actions in young adult settings featured in Petrus's novel paves the way for students, as the future of our world, to seek social justice in their schools and communities. A walkout is first mentioned in the book by Mabel when she describes to Audre, who is unaware of the term, what it means and represents. Mabel explains that it occurs "[w]hen folks walk the heck up out of class when some real stuff has gone down" like "police brutality and political ish" (p. 103). The reader is then keyed into a conversation that highlights the differences between the U.S. civil liberties versus that of Trinidad. Audre lets Mabel know "[t]hat would never happen in Trinidad" because "teachers would be in the hallway cuffing the kids down and de parents would be at the school, beating they children back into the building" (p. 103). To better understand revolutionary change, it is important that students are introduced to walkouts and protests that have occurred throughout history. Some examples would be the East L.A. walkouts in 1968, the queer Black women who founded Black Lives Matter and the Stonewall Riots. These demonstrations paint a vital picture for students to correlate with events in the book. A discussion can then take place covering the purpose of these protests in relation to the walkout in the novel.

Amid the continued awareness of injustices being brought to the forefront of our society today, our nation has created a blooming culture focused on the fight for equality. To establish a more just learning space, students can gather information via student handbooks, code of conduct, and other school or classroom policy materials. They can use these materials to analyze oppressive policies and articulate how they limit students' individualities or hurt their identities. Simply, students should be concerned with policies that could be interpreted as harmful to members of the queer, trans, and gender creative community, especially Black, Indigenous, brown, and other folks of Color. Using the information gathered, students will create and host a podcast or host a virtual gallery walk and critically call out the school's harmful educational policies. Utilizing this approach to adolescent literacy that results in social justice action, students can create inclusive spaces that are accepting of all and united against inequality.

Proposal for Change

An overarching question for students to consider is, *how can we work to amplify student voices and call out the racism, sexism, homophobia, xenophobia, and so forth embedded in school policies?* Going a step further and taking action, students can curate a proposal for change. It is vital that students feel they are being seen and heard and that authoritative figures value students' thoughts in their presentations. If students don't believe their concerns are being recognized and acknowledged, the extension activity will not amount to enacting change toward a diverse, inclusive learning environment. "What if we plan a walkout at school?" Audre asks her group of friends (p. 243). For Audre, the walkout represents call attention to carceral, prison, and school systems. Students have the power to speak up and incite action for change. Planned walkouts are effective such as the historical 1968 East L.A. walkouts where Chicano students protested racist curriculum and educational spaces. Protest, speaking up, and taking action for basic human rights can lead to abolishing an unjust system that is inherently racist (Delgado & Stefancic, 2001). Malcolm X said, "so early in life, I had learned that if you want something, you had better make some noise" (Malcolm X & Haley, 1964, p. 39). Students can continue to express their genius through writing letters to their administration, superintendent, local and national officials. Some topics that students may address in these letters could include anti-racist and inclusive pedagogy, freedom from carcel dress codes, language that acknowledges gender and sexual diversity, and the creation of justice driving educational spaces.

A Playlist Beyond Reading

To close out the extension activities, students there are several songs that students could listen to. *Fight the Power* by Public Enemy is a highly political conversation about revolutionizing and fighting against injustice. The group criticizes the military for fighting for a country "built on freedom" but allows marginalized people to be trampled, exploited, beaten, and killed. The second song is *Changes* by Tupac. Because. Tupac's songs are poetry being performed for the masses as he raps about the oppressive violence he faced alongside so many other Black people. He speaks about police violence, injustice, and how there are unjustified wars happening. He reminds listeners that these things need to change, but questions if they will. *Get Up, Stand Up* by Bob Marley encourages standing up and fighting for your rights instead of waiting for them to come. His message is not to give up the fight. More and more people are having their eyes opened to the racism that is so prevalent in this society and it's time to fight against it.

CONCLUSION

The Stars and the Blackness between Them is a coming-of-age story of two Black queer girls who are given the space to explore their intersectional identities and familial homeplaces, while becoming radicalized in their outlooks. This book actively disrupts monolithic Black trauma stories and representations. It is essential for Black and brown queer, trans, and gender creative students to have representation that goes beyond eurocentric stories. The framework of Black feminism, astrology, and radicalness of this book offers readers an access point to dream about a world where they can freely live and thrive.

Dr. Bettina Love (2019) said,

> I do not mean just to teach dark children their ABCs and 123s; I mean to teach them to demand what Anna Julia Cooper called "undisputed dignity." To call for the "recognition of one's inherent humanity" with the courage, persistence, vigilance, and the visionary imagination of an abolitionist. (p. 51)

This is an opportunity for folks who are often pushed to the margins and silenced to rise up and dismantle social "controversies" and move beyond heteronormative, cisgender, patriarchal literature.

REFERENCES

12 zodiac signs: All you need to know (n.d.). Astrology.com. https://www.astrology.com/zodiac-signs.

Blackburn, M. V., Clark, C. T., & Nemeth, E. A. (2015). Examining queer elements and ideologies in LGBT-themed literature: What queer literature can offer young adult readers. *Journal of Literacy Research*, *47*(1), 11–48.

Braganca, P. (n.d.). *Your astrological sign may not be what you think it is*. Space.Com. https://www.space.com/4477-astrological-sign.html.

Collins, P. H. (1999). *Black feminist thought: Knowledge, consciousness, and the politics of empowerment* (2nd Ed.). Routledge.

Crenshaw, K. (2015). Demarginalizing the intersection of race and sex: A black feminist critique of antidiscrimination doctrine, feminist theory and antiracist politics. *University of Chicago Legal Forum, 1989*, article 8.

Delgado, R., & Stefancic, J. (2001). *Critical race theory: An introduction*. New York University Press.

Evans-Winters, V. E. (2019). *Black feminism in qualitative inquiry: A mosaic for writing our daughter's body* (1st Ed.). Routledge.

hooks, b. (1994). *Teaching to trangress: Education as the practice of freedom*. Routledge.

Lorde, A. (2007). *Sister outsider: Essays and speeches*. Crossing Press.

Lorde, A. (2018). *The master's tools will never dismantle the master's house* (1st Ed.). Penguin.

Love, B. (2019). *We want to do more than survive: Abolitionist teaching and the pursuit of educational freedom*. Beacon Press.

Lyiscott, J. (2019). *Black appetite. White food: Issues of race, voice, and justice within and beyond the classroom* (1st Ed.). Routledge.

Malcolm, X., & Haley, A. (1964). *The autobiography of Malcolm X*. The Random House Publishing Group.

Martinez, A. Y. (2014). A plea for critical race theory counterstory: Stock story versus counterstory dialogues concerning Alejandra's "Fit" in the academy. *Composition Studies, 42*(2), 33–55.

Petrus, J. (2019). *The stars and the blackness between them*. Penguin Books.

Poetry Foundation. (2021). *Audre Lorde*. Poetry Foundation https://www.poetryfoundation.org/poets/audre-lorde.

Chapter 11

Felix Ever After

A Mystery in Progress

Lucy A. Garcia and Megan Lynn Isaac

The mystery tale has a long history. As literary critic Porter (1981) pointed out, many of the most commonly taught Western texts circulate around mysteries—Sophocles' Oedipus struggles to figure out who his parents might be; Shakespeare's Hamlet pursues the secret behind his father's death; and in early American literature, Edgar Allan Poe popularized thrilling mysteries with his short stories (pp. 11–12). Using a mystery novel in class provides instructors the opportunity to teach literary analysis at the level of plot, character, and sentence, and, perhaps even more importantly, to focus student attention on process rather than solution. The goal of a mystery novel is never a secret—discover who committed the crime or what happened to missing treasure or when a triggering event occurred. The heart of the mystery novel is in the "how" and "why" questions, and this is true of literary analysis as well. Inviting students to approach literary analysis as detectives developing potential hypotheses and interpretations leads them toward understanding the ways we create meaning as readers, sometimes competing meanings, and that the interpretations we arrive at are not so often right or wrong as much as they are reflections of ourselves and what we value. Kacen Callender's *Felix Ever After* (2020) is a book ripe for such explorations as well as for introducing literary strategies and tools that are used by authors both to build and unravel mysteries, including allusions, foil characters, and first-person narratives.

SUMMARY OF *FELIX EVER AFTER* BY KACEN CALLENDER

During a summer program at a prestigious arts high school in New York City, Felix Love, a Black, queer, trans high school student, is faced with the pressures of senior year and complicated relationships with his classmates. The summer has barely begun when a gallery of photos stolen from his Instagram before he transitioned is plastered on a wall for all the school to see. There are some obvious suspects; so Felix and his best friend Ezra vow to solve the mystery of who did it—no matter the emotional cost. While navigating his own feelings and shouldering the hurt of a mother who abandoned him, a father who doesn't understand him, and romances that elude him, Felix must figure out how much he is willing to sacrifice to get his answers, all while finishing the art portfolio he needs to win a college scholarship.

BEFORE READING *FELIX EVER AFTER*

A Note to Teachers

Felix Ever After covers serious topics like bullying and transphobia, which must be handled with care and intentionality during class discussions. Before reading the novel, teachers should consider facilitating a session wherein students negotiate their own standards or community agreements for turn-taking, classroom vocabulary (e.g., queer vs. homosexual), and using "I" statements instead of "you" or "they" statements to express their ideas. Reading the Southern Poverty Law Center's online guide *Let's Talk: Facilitating Critical Conversations with Students* (Teaching Tolerance, 2019) or Svrecek and Miller's (2021) article *Developing Critical Communities for Critical Conversations in K-12 Classrooms* can help educators develop confidence in leading these discussions. Three basic guidelines students might begin with as they work together to craft classroom expectations could include:

1. Listen to learn, not to debate.
2. Engage with ideas or assumptions, not people.
3. Be attentive to how others perceive what you are saying rather than focusing only on your intentions.

Some of the vocabulary terms students will need to engage in discussion of *Felix Ever After* are listed and defined in figure 11.1. This list is organized to facilitate the first discussion of gender identity and then sexual identity.

Building Vocabulary Activity

Assign students one term and refer them to the organization websites such as GLADD and for The National Center for Transgender Equity to research the term's meaning. (Each term will likely be researched by more than one

Term	Definition
gender identity	A person's internal sense of their gender. Sometimes this changes from what a person is assigned at birth (see transgender), and some people don't fit into the gender binary (see nonbinary).
transgender/trans	Someone whose gender identity differs from the gender they were assigned at birth.
nonbinary and/or genderqueer	A person whose gender identity does not fall within the accepted gender binary. They may identify as both male and female, neither, or a mixture of the two.
agender	A nonbinary person who is genderless, who has no gender.
bigender	A person who has both masculine and feminine gender identities.
transmasculine or transfeminine	A transmasculine person's gender expression is masculine. A transfeminine person's gender expression is feminine.
gender nonconforming	Someone who does not conform to society's definitions of male and female.
deadname/birth name	The name given to a transgender person when they were born, but which they no longer use.
demiboy or demigirl	A demiboy identifies primarily, but not exclusively, with a masculine identity. A demigirl identifies primarily, but not exclusively, with a feminine identity. Demiboys and demigirls may also identify as nonbinary.
sexual orientation	The term for an individual's enduring physical, romantic and/or emotional attraction to other people.
queer	An adjective used for people whose sexual orientation is not exclusively heterosexual. Some people may use queer to describe their gender identity and/or gender expression.
gay	The adjective used to describe people whose enduring physical, romantic, and/or emotional attractions are to people of the same gender.
lesbian	A woman whose enduring physical, romantic, and/or emotional attraction is to other women.
bisexual/bi	A person who has the capacity to form enduring physical, romantic, and/or emotional attractions to those of the same gender or to those of another gender.

Figure 11.1   Vocabulary List.

student.) Encourage students to look at the vast number of identities held by the LGBTQIA+ communities. Ask students to volunteer to present their definition to the class and add each term to a slide deck full of definitions to use as a shared reference tool during the study of *Felix Ever After*. Teachers should be sure to scan the slides for any violation of agreed-upon terms, inaccurate definitions, or malicious content. Teachers still developing a sense of community in their classrooms may choose to take a more active role in leading this research experience.

Additionally, providing students contact information for The National Center for Transgender Equity or GLAAD will enable curious students to pursue questions or support on their own if they choose. Teachers can also reference Callender's resources in the author's note at the end of the novel for a list of online sites about gender identity.

Genre and Mystery

Porter (1981) explained the draw of mysteries and detective fiction by pointing to the two emotions they feed: curiosity, as a reader seeks to discover "whodunit," and fear as the reader wonders whether the culprit will do it again (pp. 28–29). Prior to reading *Felix Ever After*, teachers can initiate a discussion about the genre of mystery. Some questions to pose might include: *What do you know about the genre? What are some mysteries you're familiar with? What words would you use to describe the genre?*

Once students have a working definition of the genre, teachers can next help students understand the structural features of this type of novel. Mystery works by varying a formula in ways that surprise, tease, or delight the reader. In employing this strategy, mysteries are no different than many other genres. For example, sonnets require the poet to say or do something fresh while confining themselves to fourteen lines each of which contains merely ten syllables. The typical features of a mystery include discovering a crime, searching for evidence, unearthing small clues, following leads, recognizing false leads, revising theories, making unexpected connections, experiencing a revelation, and resolving the case. Readers consciously or unconsciously pit themselves against a detective in the tale (and by extension against the author) to see if they can figure out the culprit or the solution before the protagonist. Listing and discussing these features prior to reading can prepare students to understand the ways Callender both uses the mystery formula in *Felix Ever After* and plays with it. Table 11.1 is a chart that some instructors might find helpful for guiding students through the elements of mystery employed in *Felix Ever After*.

Yet, not all mysteries concede to rational explanation. In an analysis of mystery in books for young readers, Gavin and Routledge (2001) distinguished between explicable (or rational) and inexplicable (or supernatural) mysteries (p. 2). Explicable mysteries are those that can be solved by logic, sleuthing, gathering clues, and analyzing evidence. Inexplicable mysteries are those that cannot be explained by a single answer or, perhaps, adequately explained at all. In short, they are the questions that often consume adolescent readers (and a fair number of adult readers): *Who am I? What does life mean? How do I make my life purposeful?* Some mystery writers focus on the concrete questions of the explicable mystery and others place more emphasis on the unknowable or contingent questions of the inexplicable mystery. Callender balances both kinds of mystery. In addition to discovering who is bullying him by stealing his Instagram images and sending him hateful texts, Felix is also exploring other mysteries including: *Why isn't his mother answering his emails, why won't his father address him as "Felix," and what does it mean to fall in love?* Discussing the fact mystery novels address two different sorts of questions—those that we can answer through exploration and those that we learn to accept even without achieving concrete, correct, or immutable answers—will prepare readers to recognize the complexity of Callender's novel.

Image Analysis

In some ways, all of the mysteries in *Felix Ever After* contribute to a larger exploration of identity. In addition to investigating Felix's personal relationships to figure out who he is and how other people reinforce or undermine his sense of self, worth, pride, and happiness, Callender invites readers to think about art, especially photographic and artistic portraits, as methods of understanding personal identity. Early in the novel, Felix is hurt when old images of him are displayed publicly without his permission. Felix says, "What does surprise me are the images. . . . Photos of who I used to be. . . . Pictures of me with these forced smiles. Expressions showing just how uncomfortable I always felt. The physical pain is strained across my face in those photos" (p. 31). Sometimes, photos or representations of ourselves that do not capture who we are can be off-putting and upsetting. Seeing images of ourselves that someone took without our permission or that are not edited to our liking can be difficult. At the same time, self-portraits can be useful in exploring the gap between how we perceive ourselves and how others perceive us.

Images and Reactions

We like to control how others see us, especially through images. This activity invites the class to consider the many ways we do not, or cannot, control representations of ourselves. It reminds us how central visual images and forms of presentation are to identity—whether we want to fit in or stand out, be transparent to the world or maintain a sense of mystery.

Teachers can begin by prompting a discussion of the distinctions among an unflattering, inaccurate, and malicious representation in photographs. Consider selfies, formal portraits, candid shots, and other kinds of portraits. As a way to model the activity, teachers can bring to class a photographic image that misrepresents them. It could be a candid photo or a posed photo like a yearbook photo. It could be a photo someone posted on social media without permission or a photo that was once beloved but now is embarrassing or simply seems awkward. Instructors can share their image with the class and reasons for disliking it.

Next, have students select an image of themselves that they dislike; prompt students to reflect on how their image was inaccurately constructed or presented in this photo. In this reflection, have students describe the image in detail and consider if there is a specific feature of the photo that misrepresents them. If students can recall, prompt them to think about how the image captures or fails to capture their mood from that day. For example, if a student regards themselves as a confident leader, but a friend takes a picture during a losing match where they look shrunken and defeated, what does that mean

Table 11.1   Partial List of Mystery Elements by Plotline

	Mystery of Secret Student Bully	*Mystery of Mother's Abandonment*	*Mystery of Father's Behavior*	*Mystery of Falling in Love*
Discovering the *mystery*	Felix discovers the stolen photos in the school lobby (p. 31).	Felix's mother has divorced his father and left the family (p. 20).	Felix's Father stumbles over how to address Felix and defers to calling him "Kid" (p. 22).	Felix wonders what love feels like after spying on some graffiti (p. 2).
Searching for evidence	Felix thinks it could be anyone (p. 35). Felix decides it must be Declan (pp. 39, 47). Felix is sure the trolling messages are from Declan (p. 123).	Felix writes to his mom about falling out of love and whether a mother can fall out of love with a child (p. 179).	Felix's dad asks to keep old pictures (p. 25). Dad is annoyed by Felix's absence (p. 60).	Felix discusses love with Ezra (p. 56). Felix admits he wants to fall in love while catfishing Declan (p. 88).
Unearthing small clues	Felix rethinks his brief dating history with Marisol (p. 75).	Felix considers why his mother never responded to the news of his transition and why she might prefer Florida and her new family over him (p. 24).	Felix and his dad spar about appropriate behavior with boys (p. 67). Dad asks Felix to be patient with him (p. 68).	Ezra asks to cuddle with Felix (p. 90). Ezra tells Felix he loves him (p. 107). Ezra tells Felix he is worthy of respect and love (p. 122). Austin assumes Felix and Ezra are a couple (p. 191).
Following leads	Felix asks Leah for information and help (p. 163).	[Felix's mother provides no information to help him understand her behavior.]	Felix expects his father to stop "trying" and start using the right pronouns (p. 127).	Felix asks Ezra whether he was ever in love with Declan (p. 92).
Recognizing false leads	Felix considers the absence of proof that Declan is behind the gallery and trolling (p. 129). Felix realizes Declan is nnocent (p. 141).	[Felix still has no leads—useful or false—to explain his mother's behavior.]	Listening to the rejection Declan has experienced from his father helps Ezra appreciate his own father (pp. 304–305).	Felix realizes Austin is the sort of person "the world adores" but that he cannot and does not want to be like him (pp. 154–155).

Revising theories	Felix decides James must be the bully (p. 159). Felix again feels it could be anyone, including Marisol (p. 160). Felix wonders if it is Hazel (p. 234).	Texts from the troll force Felix to confront his mother's abandonment of him (pp. 264–265).	Felix admits that even when his dad messes up, he still knows his dad loves him (p. 111). Dad tells Felix about the risks of falling in love and chasing someone who doesn't love you (p. 225).	Felix admits he is jealous of Austin and Ezra as a couple (p. 210).
Making unexpected connections	Felix realizes Marisol has always slandered him, even calling him a misogynist (pp. 207–209).	Felix thinks he has lost two friends and realizes how much his mother's abandonment has harmed him (pp. 283–284).	Felix's dad talks to him about love, loss, and feelings (pp. 286–287).	Felix admits to Declan (while in his guise of Lucky) how much he wants love (p. 217).
Experiencing a revelation	Felix realizes Leah is helping him solve the mystery because she wants to be his friend (p. 290). Felix realizes Austin shares some of the same interests as the person who has been sending him vicious texts (p. 318).	Felix realizes he has been angry at himself more than his mother (p. 327).	Felix and his dad talk about gender identity (pp. 327–330).	Declan tells Lucky that Ezra is in love with Felix (p. 244). Felix and Ezra dance together (p. 250). Felix and Ezra kiss (p. 255). A painful conversation with Declan reveals to Felix the depth of his love for Ezra (pp. 311–314).
Solving the case	Felix understands how ignorance and privilege fueled Austin's behavior and reports him to the school authorities (pp. 323–324).	Felix deletes the hundreds of unsent emails he has written to his mother (p. 327).	Felix's father begins to use Felix's name (pp. 330–332).	Felix tells Ezra he loves him at the Pride parade (pp. 336–337).

to them? Ask students to explore the impact that the creation of this image has for them. Focus on feelings and reactions rather than on the intentions or skills of the photographer. Remind students that Felix often evaluates images of himself in the novel in this way—he considers both images other people take and ones he creates himself. He also has to come to terms with the fact that the same image can mean different things to different people—old photos of him taken before he transitioned are used viciously by the bully, are reminders of pain and discomfort to Felix, and are nostalgic for his father. Felix gains confidence when he learns to focus less on how others portray him and more on how he portrays himself.

Communication

In the novel, Felix uses unsent emails to delve into personal mysteries. Writing helps him frame his concerns. In order to prepare for a brief discussion about the significance of questions versus answers, ask each student to write an email of at least 300 words (one double-spaced page) in response to the prompt below. Reassure students that while they will need to show their instructor they have completed the email, they will not have to let anyone (including the teacher) read it unless they want to. Ideally, teachers will do this exercise with their students and use their own letter and experience writing it to facilitate class participation:

> Think of someone you no longer see or have a close relationship with by their choice rather than yours or by circumstances beyond your control. This person could be a friend from elementary school, a sports team, or your neighborhood. This person could be a relative. This person could be someone from a job, a camp, a religious organization, or anywhere else you have spent a significant portion of your time. This person could be living or dead. Write a letter articulating what you wish they could explain to you and letting them know what you wish you could share with them.

Once the emails are complete, let students know they are welcome to read a few sentences from their emails aloud if they wish and discuss the following questions:

- What did you learn about yourself from writing this email?
- Was it more helpful to put into words the questions you have about the other person or the things you wish you could tell them?
- If you could send this email, would you? Why or why not?
- What value is there in crafting communications knowing they won't ever be sent?

In this novel, different communication strategies contribute to the various mysteries in different ways. For example, written communications are a particular frustration for Felix. He doesn't receive emails from his mother answering his many questions, yet he receives rafts of unwanted texts from an unknown bully that only serve to provoke questions of a different sort. Later in the novel, once Felix adopts the pseudonym of "luckyliquid95" and begins texting with "thekeanster123," the mysteries of communication get even more complicated. Felix knows there is a problematic gap between how he presents himself in words typed on a screen versus how he presents himself in face-to-face interactions. Letters, texts, conversations, and self-portraits are all strategies that Felix uses to reveal and hide his identity; at the same time, they are clues to other people's identity. Students might conclude this exercise by discussing what mediums they prefer to communicate through and analyzing the choices Felix makes in his communications with suspects, family, friends, and romantic interests.

Allusions as Mini-Mysteries

One way to look at an allusion in a work of literature is as a brief, coded message. Rather than use a lengthy description, the author includes a well-known artwork, object, person, place, or historic event and leaves the reader to figure out how to apply all the connotations that flow from the allusion to their understanding of the current scene. When a reader is already familiar with the allusion, this literary technique is easy to understand. When the reader is unfamiliar with the allusion, the sudden appearance of an object or idea with no direct connection to the action or dialogue can be mysterious.

To prepare students to interpret allusions, make sure they understand the distinction between the denotative meaning of a word and its connotative associations. For example, explain that both "childish" and "childlike" have the same denotative meaning: "having the features or behaviors appropriate to a child." Yet, most of us would much rather be described as "childlike" than "childish" due to the connotative meanings that collect around each of these words. Ask students to brainstorm what connotations they have for both terms. Students might say:

childlike: youthful, fun, imaginative, playful, creative
childish: immature, temperamental, uninformed, tiresome

To practice understanding the denotative and connotative levels of words and how they work together to create an allusion, ask students to find a partner and work through the following three steps:

1. Each team should come up with a person, place, object, and artwork. For example, one group might choose Beyoncé, the Grand Canyon, crayons, and the Mona Lisa. Another group might choose Shakespeare, Starbucks, Nike Yeezy shoes, and Lil Nas X's "Old Town Road."

2. Next, the pair should list the denotative definition and connotative associations that attach to their choices. For example:
   crayons (denotative): inexpensive-colored wax sticks for drawing
   crayons (connotative): kindergarten, enticing, easily broken, nostalgic smell

3. Ask each group to share with the whole class the allusion for which they developed the most interesting set of connotations. For some students, an allusion might be interesting when it is easy to agree on connotations, but others might prefer allusions that are complicated and open to a range of connotations. Encourage students to consider that one reason novels are open to interpretation is that we all bring our own experiences into our understanding of the material, and allusions are a great example of this phenomenon.

> Finally, explain that Callender's novel is rich in allusions, especially to works of art and music. Some of these allusions will be easily understood by readers, and many students will be able to unpack more layers of connotative meaning in them than their teachers. Other allusions may be less familiar. Using the graphic organizer (see table 11.2), assign each student to explore the connotative meaning of a small number of allusions from this list of twenty-five terms employed in *Felix Ever After*. As the class reading proceeds, students can serve as experts sharing their interpretations with the rest of the class as each allusion is discovered in the novel.

WHILE READING *FELIX EVER AFTER*

Connecting Allusions to Meaning

After students have begun the reading and developed connotative meanings for some of the allusions, use class discussion to demonstrate how allusions are important to understanding the plot, characters, and themes. For example, Miles Morales is a biracial teenager growing up in New York City. Like Felix, he is hesitant to embrace his identity as a superhero, but when he finally does accept himself, he becomes powerful. Or, readers might see Miles as a parallel to Ezra who shares his biracial identity. For both Felix and Ezra, Miles is an inspiration—a person of color newly empowered to fight injustice in society, whether that means taking on powerful villains or high school bullies.

Allusions can also aid in uncovering themes. For instance, the show *Downton Abbey* is used to demonstrate how Felix feels as if he does not fit into Ezra's upper-class world when he accompanies his friend to the elaborate Patel party in their elegant apartment (pp. 113–119). Remind students that allusions serve as mini-mysteries and that authors employ them to provide depth and complexity without having to use long explanations. When students are able to suggest a variety of interpretations for an allusion, they are demonstrating how much material the author is able to pack into a book through a single well-chosen word or phrase. Unexpected connections to the book and creative interpretations should be encouraged. After all, untangling the mystery of an allusion is an opportunity for readers to relate to the characters and make the text more personally meaningful.

Foil Characters and Identity

Central to the plot and its mysteries are the complex characters and relationships in this novel. Felix frequently compares himself to his best friend Ezra, who provides one kind of foil; his nemesis, Declan, provides a different kind. Foils are often used in literature to reveal information about a character, as well as motivations. Some famous character foils potentially familiar to students include Sherlock and Dr. Watson from Conan Doyle's *Sherlock Holmes* stories, Harry Potter, Neville Longbottom, and Draco Malfoy from J.K. Rowling's *Harry Potter* books, and Celie and Sofia from *The Color Purple* by Alice Walker. Each of these examples is an intentional juxtaposition of differing personalities that shows a contrast and strengthens the individual aspects of characters, making them clearer to the reader. In Callender's novel, Felix's primary motivation to get into Brown on an art scholarship clashes with Declan's plan to do the same. The artistic skills and personal traits of the two boys also deepen their function as rivals and foils. Another foil is set up by the distinctions between Felix's socioeconomic background and that of his best friend Ezra. Foil comparisons also unfold among each of the three characters' familial and romantic relationships. The dynamics of these comparisons functioning beneath the surface of the plot chip away at the mystery of Felix's identity and reveal his complexities.

Foil Analysis

Felix, Ezra, and Declan have different motivations, desires, and circumstances. Working in small groups, maintain a graphic organizer of notes and ideas analyzing moments in the novel that illuminate foil characters and reveal Felix as a more layered protagonist (see figure 11.2). Include page numbers and be sure to explain your insights in the last column.

Table 11.2   Graphic Organizer for Allusions (Denotative Meaning Already Provided)

Page	Term	Denotative Definition
p. 5	Klimt	Gustav Klimt (1862–1918) was an Austrian artist famous for his representations of the female body and the use of gold leaf to augment his paintings.
p. 5	Andy Warhol	American artist (1928–1987) was famous for incorporating advertising and celebrities into his works.
p. 8	Cara Delevingne eyebrows	English model, actress, musician, and writer who celebrates her own gender fluidity and critiques narrow gender restrictions.
p. 12	RISD	The acronym for the Rhode Island School of Design in Providence, Rhode Island, a college noted for outstanding arts education.
p. 16	Langston Hughes	Black poet and activist (1901–1967) who lived in Harlem and helped anchor the Harlem Renaissance. Biographers differ in describing him as gay, straight, or asexual, but all agree he celebrated the lives and passions of Black people.
p. 16	Claude McKay	Jamaican-American poet and writer (1889–1948) and another anchor of the Harlem Renaissance in NYC. McKay pursued personal relationships with men and women, and while he never identified as bisexual, the narrators of his poems are often ungendered and open to interpretation.
p. 16	Harlem Renaissance	An artistic and cultural movement celebrating the work of Black artists and intellectuals centered in NYC during the 1920s and 1930s.
p. 16	Fleetwood Mac	A British-American band formed in 1967 with hits that regularly experience a resurgence, most recently as part of TikTok videos.
p. 17	*The Shining*	A 1980 horror movie directed by Stanley Kubrick based on the novel by Stephen King. Isolation and frustration cause Jack, the main character, to go insane.
p. 24	Cris Beam	An author and educator best known for *I Am J* (2011), one of the first widely recognized YA novels to feature a transgender character.
p. 66	*Akira*	A six-volume Japanese manga series written and illustrated by Katsuhiro Otomo and published between 1982 and 1990. Otomo's work is credited with popularizing both the artistic style of manga in the United States and elevating themes of dystopian isolation and social corruption.
p. 73	Hayley Kiyoko	A lesbian pop artist popularly alluded to in queer culture. Her music video "Girls Like Girls" is a cult classic of queer music videos, with more than 130M views on YouTube.
p. 114	*Downton Abbey*	A historical television drama that focuses thematically on class and the inability to move up a preexisting social hierarchy.

(Continued)

Table 11.2 Graphic Organizer for Allusions (Denotative Meaning Already Provided) (*Continued*)

Page	Term	Denotative Definition
p. 136	Boruto, FMA: Brotherhood, Death Note	Japanese manga series, which have all been adapted into movies and video games. All of these have queer-coded characters (the subtextual coding of a character as queer), even when they are not in queer relationships or given explicitly queer storylines.
p. 180	Laverne Cox	A transgender activist and actor known for a 2020 documentary on trans representation called *Disclosure* as well as her work in the popular Netflix show *Orange Is the New Black*.
p. 180	Janet Mock	A writer, producer, and television host. Importantly, Mock was an executive producer on *POSE*, a show about the 1980s NYC ballroom culture and chosen families, centering Black, queer, and trans stories.
p. 223	Steve and Bucky	Steve Rogers and Bucky Barnes, or Captain America and The Winter Soldier, respectively. Superheroes in the Marvel Cinematic Universe that many fans "ship" together, or want to be together, because of their close friendship.
p. 223	Billie Holiday	A jazz and swing music singer and pioneer (1915–1959) who was persecuted in the 1940s by the U.S. government. Her song, "Strange Fruit," protested the lynchings of Black Americans that were common at the time.
p. 223	Sigur Ros	An Icelandic post-rock band with ambient, minimal, floaty sounds.
p. 246	Stonewall Inn	A bar in Greenwich Village, NYC: the location for a key turning point in the gay rights movement, when bar patrons and community members fought back against a police raid in 1969.
p. 246	Marsha P. Johnson	A prominent figure in the Stonewall Uprising (1945–1992). She was a self-identified drag queen, an activist, and a survivor.
p. 246	Sylvia Rivera	Another prominent figure at Stonewall, Rivera (1951–2002) was a gay rights activist and community worker in NYC.
p. 247	Mariah Carey	An international pop star who was huge in the late 90s, now known as a "gay icon," or a figure who is highly regarded in the LGBTQIA+ communities for her support.
p. 272	Miles Morales	Created in 2011 by Brian Michael Bendis and Sara Pichelli, Miles is the biracial son of a Black father and Puerto Rican mother who assumes the role of Spider-Man following the death of Peter Parker.
p. 318	Ariana Grande	A pop music star whose lyrics celebrate gender fluidity and who also refuses to label herself.

Identity and First-Person Narration

In *Felix Ever After*, readers are invited to share Felix's perceptions of NYC, his judgments of his peers, and even his self-doubts as he narrates his experiences in and out of school. For example, Felix recounts his ride on the L train and walk through the farmer's market (pp. 4–6), describes Declan's demeanor and physical appearance (pp. 8–10), details his home in Harlem (pp. 16–18), critiques his unfinished art portfolio (p. 28), and catalogs the activity in his acrylics class (pp. 38–40). On one hand, readers feel as if they are getting a robust vision of his world because they see through Felix's eyes and "hear" everything he is thinking. On the other hand, first-person narration also lends itself to hiding gaps in the story. Whatever oversights or errors Felix makes are shared by the reader as well. Consequently, the astute reader of first-person narration must become a detective, deciding how and why their narrator might be omitting important information, making unwarranted assumptions, or falling into errors of judgment.

In many ways, Felix Love is an excellent example of a well-intentioned but unreliable narrator. His initial hunch about the identity of the culprit behind the illicit photo gallery leads readers to believe that Declan is a villain for much of the book. If the reader has any suspicions that the gallery may not have been put up by Declan, they are due to their own intuition. Another area of unreliability, or incomplete information, concerns Felix's father. Readers might not understand his motivations or behaviors. For example, why won't Mr. Love call Felix by his name or why doesn't he want to destroy old photos? Readers are unlikely to sympathize with Mr. Love or explore his motivations because Felix doesn't ask the audience to consider his father's point of view or challenges. Instead, readers are likely to adopt Felix's frustration.

Like all narrators in fiction, Felix is not a real person. As Cadden (2000) insists, the narrator is always unreliable in this genre because the first-person point of view is really that of an adult writing about being an adolescent from the vantage point of being an adult. For some critics and readers, skilled imitation of the teenage voice is not enough. Since the young adult author Corinne Duyvis coined the hashtag #ownvoices in 2015, challenging publishers to support not just books with a diverse range of protagonists but books with a diverse range of authors, questions about the reliability of narration in young adult literature have become even more focused (Vanderhage, 2019). In an interview published in *Broad Recognition*, Callender noted,

> If a queer character of color was in a book, we were only the side character, or if we were featured in a novel, that queer character was white. . . . We need to see our stories reflected to feel validated and seen, and to begin healing from

Foil Moment	Felix	Ezra	Declan	Analysis of foil feature	Relation to Mystery
The group art project	Felix doesn't care that he and Ezra are going to be late for the group art project (p. 4)	Ezra knows Declan will be mad, but spends extra time with Felix anyway (p. 8)	Declan likes to be on time and organized (p. 9)	The differing priorities of Declan and Felix pit them against each other and create mistrust.	At the beginning of the novel, Felix does not care about Declan's feelings, which makes it easy for him to emphasize their distinctions and make negative assumptions about him—even blaming him for the bullying.
Felix texts Declan while talking to Ezra	Felix is texting Declan while with Ezra, not really paying attention to Ezra (p. 193)	While Ezra is being vulnerable with Felix, Felix is not being very responsive and doesn't immediately tell Ezra who he is texting with (p. 195)	Declan expresses vulnerability to Lucky/Felix by saying "I'm scared I'm not living my life to my full potential." (p. 194)	Since Declan and Ezra used to date, Felix struggles to hide his conflicted feelings for each of them.	Felix shifts from catfishing Declan to genuine curiosity about him.
Parental relationship realizations	Felix is bitter about Ezra taking so much for granted at his family's party (p. 119)	Ezra's penthouse party reveals he lives in "a whole other world" than Felix (p. 123) but the financial privilege is not matched by emotional support from his family	Declan tells Felix his biggest secret: that his father disowned him, which puts Felix's struggles into perspective (p. 241)	Felix's relationship with his parents is crucial to the story. However, he realizes throughout the novel that his friends have family issues too. This is a point of growth for Felix.	Felix makes assumptions about how easy Declan and Ezra's lives are and fails to see that they are dealing with mysteries of their own. Why did Declan's dad disown him if he's supposed to love him? Why do Ezra's parents treat him like an accessory?

Figure 11.2   Graphic Organizer for Foil Characters with Sample Entries.

collective traumas of racism and anti-queerness and how these two traumas can be linked. (Jackson, 2021, para 2)

Reliability in a first-person narrator sometimes comes from the author's lived experiences, especially in underrepresented cultures, communities, and identities.

In the end, readers evaluating the use of first-person narration in the novel might consider at least three different levels of reliability. First, when is the character of Felix reliable and when are readers tempted by the use of first-person narration to accept his errors or oversights? Second, when is the representation of Felix's perspective as a young adult reliable and when does it seem to reflect adult perceptions or expectations? Third, and finally, what insights does Callender bring or leave out in the representation of Felix as a Black, queer, trans person?

Figure 11.3 provides opportunities for evaluating Felix's narrative reliability. Analyze each quotation (examples are provided) and explain why you find Felix reliable or unreliable. Finally, choose a passage yourself from the novel that illustrates interesting issues in terms of reliability and add it to the chart. When everyone has completed the chart, share your work with the class.

AFTER READING *FELIX EVER AFTER*

Foil Characters and First-Person Narration

One way to better understand the freedoms and limits of first-person narration is to practice it—especially by narrating the same situation from the point of view of different people. Instruct students to find a section of Felix's thoughts or dialogue from the book (3–6 lines) and copy them out on a sheet of paper along with the page number where they are found. For example, students might choose Felix's description of Declan's artwork (pp. 50–51), the discussion of Harry Potter vs. astrology (pp. 61–62), or the physical altercation between Felix and Declan (p. 96). On the back of the paper ask students to rewrite the same section from the point of view and in the voice of Ezra or Declan using what they have learned about foil characters and narration. Students can also be encouraged to employ an allusion that might be appropriate to the voice of the speaker in their rewritten version. Here's an example:

Original Text: "I type on my phone, asking Ezra if I should meet him at his apartment, but he tells me no—he wants me to meet him at Stonewall. I hold in a groan. Stonewall Inn? Really? It's ten days into Pride month, so it's going to be packed. A few years ago, I was totally obsessed with the place." (p. 246)

Rewritten Text: "Pride Month is the best part of the year. It's like a giant party! We are meeting up at Stonewall Inn, one of the most iconic places in queer history. We'll dance like wild things. I love the crowds of people here; I feel right at home." (From Ezra's perspective)

Invite students to present their revised quotation to the class and have classmates guess the speaker. Then, discuss how this activity shows the power of perspective. Instructors can prompt deeper discussion by asking: *How did the meaning of your quotation change when the same idea was presented from Declan or Ezra's point of view? How might Callender's novel change if the book were told from the perspective of someone other than Felix?*

Discussing the Features of Mystery

In many traditional mysteries, the detective's job is to discover who killed the victim. In *Felix Ever After*, Callender has turned this convention upside down. Felix's former identity is long dead when the novel begins, and instead of trying to figure out why or who ended it, he's determined to figure out who is trying to resurrect it. Facilitate a discussion with the entire class

Quotation	Reliable or unreliable?	Explanation
"[Declan] talks crap about us every chance he gets." (p. 8)	Unreliable	In the scene, Declan is mad at Felix because he's late, and Felix is being preemptively defensive because he knows he is about to be criticized. Felix is unreliable because he is attacking Declan's character rather than accurately reporting the cause of conflict. Also, there is no evidence in the book that "everyone" hates Felix and Ezra.
"I always try to forget that Ezra and Declan used to go out." (p. 47)	Reliable	Here, Felix is just conveying to the reader the history between Ezra and Declan. They did date, and it is a point of contention throughout the book. Felix is not being biased, just giving the reader some necessary backstory information.
"Why am I always the person who just sits on the side and watches?" (p. 74)	Unreliable	Felix is throwing a pity party here. He wants people to feel bad for him when, really, he is the only one responsible for not going after what he wants (a love interest).
"Why did you leave? Dad doesn't really like to talk about it." (p. 179)	Reliable	Felix is genuinely curious about why his mom left. This is a huge mystery in the book, and a lot of his sadness about not being loved comes from his mother's inexplicable absence. We never hear Felix's dad talk about his mom.

Figure 11.3   Graphic Organizer for Charting Reliability.

that compares the typical features and tropes of a mystery with the choices Callender makes in this novel. Ask students how Callender's use, adaptation, or rejection of expected mystery features and strategies impacts the development of plot, character, and theme. Below is a list of questions to jumpstart this discussion:

- What qualifies the protagonist to act as a detective?
- What role does the detective's sidekick serve? Does this novel have a Watson as well as a Sherlock Holmes? More than one Watson?
- What kinds of "crimes" do readers expect in mysteries? What kinds of crimes are explored here?
- Crime scenes often set the tone for a mystery. How is the scene of the crime important in this novel?
- What weapons are typical in a mystery? What weapons are used by the culprit here?
- Some detectives excel at solving mysteries by following physical clues. Other detectives rely mostly on psychological analysis and clues. What type of detective is Felix?

- For many readers of mysteries, half the pleasure comes from solving the crime before the writer fully reveals the solution. Did you figure out who was bullying Felix before he did? If so, what details in the book enabled you to accurately predict which character was to blame?
- The mystery genre is prone to sequels. If Callender wrote a follow-up volume about Felix, what new mystery would you like to see him investigate?

BEYOND *FELIX EVER AFTER*

Self-Portraits

Felix's portraits and his final gallery presentation give closure to his journey with identity and wrap up many of the mysteries that circulate throughout the book. Felix says,

> But then I started these paintings . . . . And it was more helpful than I expected. More . . . empowering, to put up these paintings I created, of who I know I am, instead of what someone else sees me as. I am Felix. No one else gets to define who I am. Only me. (p. 350)

Self-portraits can legitimize and celebrate the individual. There is so much mystery within us, about who we are aside from the expectations others have of us, and visual art is one way to bring this internal mystery to the surface and flesh it out. In this activity, students create a self-portrait. Teachers can ask the following of students:

> Revisit your first portrait, the one that felt inaccurate or unappealing. You will now have a chance to create a self-portrait that better captures your own sense of personal identity. Begin by reflecting on any aspect of your life or personality that is important to you and that you want others to see. Then, present yourself in a way that feels truthful and empowering. Your self-portrait can be
>
> - a printed photograph of yourself, created with intention;
> - a painting or drawing of yourself; and
> - a collage composed of words and/or images.

For example, if you regard yourself as a confident leader, create a collage filled with magazine clippings of powerful people, evoke images of leadership, and use colors that bring to life your ideas. When you have finished creating your self-portrait, attach a written reflection articulating how this work of art celebrates you. The written reflection can act as the gallery tag, which is a recurring image in the novel. Hang the portraits (even if only temporarily for a single class session) in your classroom. Take a few minutes of class time to tour the class gallery and appreciate each person's work.

This self-portrait can be created from virtually any medium. Students who do not feel strong in their drawing or painting skills should be assured that they can use collages or digital art to create their own unique self-portrait. For example, in the book, Declan is strongest in photography, and Felix is strongest with paint—they create college portfolios out of the medium they are strongest at. If students need inspiration, they can imitate the style of artists that were alluded to in the book: Kahlo, Klimt, Warhol, and even the cover artist Wiley. This is a thematic exercise, not graded on artistic skill but thoughtful consideration about celebrating the true self.

Transferable Skills

Throughout the novel, Felix worries about his future. He is concerned about his art portfolio, the scholarship application he needs to complete, and his college applications. Although his anxiety is not helpful, his ability to think ahead and make plans is worth emulating. For this activity, students should consider their summer or post-high school plans and draft an application, essay, or personal statement for college, a job, an internship, or an apprenticeship program. Teachers can help students by providing them with sample essay questions from the college Common Application or job applications from local employers like a junior counselor position at a YMCA day camp.

CONCLUSION

Callender's *Felix Ever After* both employs and exploits the features of the mystery novel in order to craft a contemporary YA tale rich with traditional themes and contemporary topics. Felix's work in the novel involves discovering the identity of both the student who has been bullying him and his own. Felix considers many possible culprits—peers who disdain him and peers who have proffered friendship, likely candidates and unlikely ones. Similarly, Felix considers his own identity from many angles—he attends a gender-identity discussion group, reflects on his brief relationship with Marisol, and experiments with dating Declan. Eventually, Felix finds answers to both his questions, and in the tradition of many novels, the answers to the mysteries are to be found in words, especially in names. Decoding the pseudonym of the bully and claiming the demiboy identity for himself brings both plot lines to a conclusion. Even readers who don't love a good mystery may find much to appreciate in *Felix Ever After*, however. Callender renders a host of experiences typical for older high school students with nuance and accuracy: the anxiety of preparing not for college but simply for applying to college, the complexity of large friend groups that shift and reconfigure with every break-up and new flirtation, the baffling absence of support (fiscal and emotional) many teens experience from their families, and the confidence that arises from putting love into practice—whether that is a love of art, love of a friend, or love of self. In the end, Callender's novel reminds readers that while some mysteries can be solved, the answers we discover only serve as stepping stones to help us navigate the new mysteries life inevitably hands us.

REFERENCES

Cadden, M. (2000). The irony of narration in the young adult novel. *Children's Literature Association Quarterly, 25*(4), 146–154.

Callender, K. (2020). *Felix ever after.* Balzer+Bray.

Gavin, A. E. and C. Routledge (2001). Mystery in children's literature from the rational to the supernatural: An introduction. In A. Gavin and C. Routledge (Eds). *Mystery in Children's Literature: From the Rational to the Supernatural* (pp. 1–13). Palgrave.

Jackson, L. (2021). Deserving the world: An interview with Kacen Callender. *Broad Recognition.* https://www.broadsatyale.com/kacen-callender/.

Koss, M. D. and W. H. Teale. (2009). What's happening in YA literature? Trends in books for adolescents. *Journal of Adolescent & Adult Literacy, 52*(7), 563–572.

Pavonetti, L. M. (1996). Joan Lowery Nixon: The grande dame of young adult mystery author(s). *Journal of Adolescent & Adult Literacy, 39*(6), 454–461.

Porter, D. (1981). *The pursuit of crime: Art and ideology in detective fiction.* Yale University Press.

Svrcek, N. S. and H. C. Miller (2021). Developing critical communities for critical conversations in K-12 classrooms. *The Language Arts Journal of Michigan*, Winter, 10–19.

Teaching Tolerance. (2019). *Let's talk: A guide to facilitating critical conversations with students.* The Southern Poverty Law Center. https://www.tolerance.org/sites/default/files/2019-12/TT-Lets-Talk-December-2019.pdf.

Vanderhage, G. (2019). What is #ownvoices? https://www.brodartbooks.com/newsletter/posts-in-2019/what-is-ownvoices.

Chapter 12

Exploring Characterization Narratives with *Chulito: A Novel*

Gabriel T. Acevedo Velázquez

"Pato!" "Maricón!" These are some of the derogatory words used for LGBTQ people in Puerto Rico. As a teacher on the island, I heard these words constantly said by students. I utilized these instances for the engagement around conversations of power, bullying, and homophobia. It was always my intention not only to reprimand students but also to give them the opportunity and space to grow, learn, and allow them to move on from using language that brings down others. We also engaged in conversations around the danger that rhetoric has on people. Talking about the rhetorical assimilation that occurs to kids and teenagers, and how those tend to follow into adulthood. This led to the implementation of LGBTQ texts in the classrooms as a tool, to not only enhance the conversations of equity and diversity but the ELA standards as well.

Therefore, my purpose of creating nontraditional units and bringing in LGBTQ texts into the classroom stems from the idea of affording students the opportunities to critically think about queerness, homophobia, and sexual orientation as well as expanding on their ELA content knowledge. This chapter utilizes *Chulito: A Novel* (Rice-González, 2011) as an entry point into characterization, storytelling, and narrative. *Chulito: A Novel* presents both heterosexual and queer characters; addresses topics of racism, skin color, masculinity; and deals with the issues of love, friendship, and trust. In those regards, *Chulito* has many commonly taught themes, which allows, not only LGBTQ or Latinx students to relate to the novel, but students and teachers, in general, as well.

SUMMARY OF *CHULITO: A NOVEL*

Charles Rice-González's *Chulito: A Novel* (2011) is a young adult novel about Chulito, which means "cutie," where we get a front-row seat to his struggle with identity in regards to his sexuality, ethnicity, race, and belonging. In this coming-of-age story, Chulito, a tough, macho, hip-hop-loving Puerto Rican living in the South Bronx, is best friends with Carlos, that is, until everyone starts calling Carlos "pato," which is the derogatory term for gay in Puerto Rican slang. After Carlos returns home from his first year in college, Carlos and Chulito share a kiss which forever changes Chulito's understanding of what he has been told throughout his life. After the kiss, Chulito's life turns upside down as he begins to question and understand his sexuality, what it means to navigate his Puerto Rican identity, masculinity, and his attraction toward Carlos.

BEFORE READING *CHULITO: A NOVEL*

Let's Talk About Identity!

Identity markers are an essential part of *Chulito: A Novel*. Not only does identity as a gay man come into play, but an array of intersectional identities like race, class, skin color, language, visual presentation, and others are explored in the novel. Conversations about gender, sexuality, race, class, and others are often regarded as "difficult" or "uncomfortable." Engaging in these conversations with students is necessary as it allows for culturally responsive pedagogical practices from both the teacher and the student. By having these conversations, we create "spaces of practice" (Talbert & Mor-Avi, 2019) that encourage students to be comfortable and open up about who they are and how they see the world around them. By fostering these spaces of practice, teachers can gain strategic facilities to foster expected and unexpected conversations around identity and incorporate those conversations in a meaningful way in the classroom.

Together with students, engage in conversations about Afro-Puerto Rican identities which directly connect with Chulito as he identifies as an Afro-Puerto Rican/Boricua. Teachers can begin by researching and talking about Afro-Latinidad in the classroom. Teachers can turn to Remezcla, a website with tons of resources that focus on identities around Afro-Latinidad.

Also, conversations around LGBTQ Puerto Rican and Nuyorican activists are encouraged. Important figures that should be discussed include Sylvia Rivera, who was a Puerto Rican transgender and gay liberation activist, and along with Marsha P. Johnson, cofounded the Street Transvestite Action Revolutionaries (STAR); Ritchie Torres who is a Nuyorican politician who was the first Afro-Latino elected to Congress and one of the nine cochairs of the Congressional LGBTQ Equality Caucus; and, Lawrence La Fountain-Strokes, who is a gay Puerto Rican author, scholar, and activist who writes about queer experiences in Puerto Rico and their relationships to machismo. Researching and having conversations about these important figures will help ground and understand the intersection of LGBTQ and Afro-Puerto Rican identities found in Chulito.

Who am I: Identity Self-Portrait?

Who am I? is a constant question that we ask ourselves, even after our adolescent years. However, it is a critical question for adolescents as they are searching for their identities, what defines them, and where they fit in. *Chulito: A Novel* speaks to the many facets of understanding one's identity. As the teacher, encourage your students to examine, understand, and engage with their own identities before reading the novel. Specifically, students could contemplate to which extent identity markers like gender, race, culture, language(s), sexual orientation, interests, social groups, physical traits, and others define how they frame their story. Engaging in the creation of identity self-portraits provides students an opportunity for self-understanding by encouraging them to reflect on different aspects of their identities. By looking inward and identifying aspects of who they are, students think deeply about their beliefs, self-presentation, and value. Also, by displaying their identities, students give insights into others' multilayered identities.

As the teacher, introduce the concept of identity self-portraits. Give students a model of an identity self-portrait, perhaps model this portrait with a teacher known to the class by writing and utilizing your self-portrait as an example to the students because it allows them to see you in a light other than just a teacher (see figure 12.1). It could allow students to feel more comfortable around you and their classmates. Make markers, crayons, colored pencils, paper, and any other materials available for students to work on their self-portraits. Have students draw any figure they want (stick figure, masks, face, entire body) representing who they are. Ask students to use smaller drawings, words, or phrases that reveal their identity's more profound levels. Remind students that their portraits will be shared with the class to feel safe, including identity markers they feel comfortable sharing.

Once self-portraits are finished, students can share them in small groups or with the entire class in a gallery walk. Utilize this gallery walk in conjunction with a 3-2-1 activity. A 3-2-1 is a quick reflective activity that helps students organize their thoughts and promote reflection. This activity will provide students an easy way to understand and gauge any questions about their classmates. The activity can be structured the following way: three things you

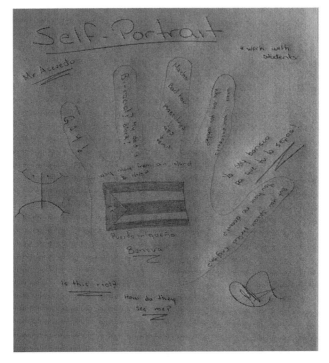

Figure 12.1   Mr. Acevedo's Self-Portrait Done in Class.

learned about a classmate, two things you found interesting, and one question students have for a classmate.

Identity is not always constant or static; our identity markers and how we see each other are constantly changing or evolving. Therefore, create a self-portrait museum. Hang students' self-portraits up in the classroom so while you are all reading *Chulito: A Novel*, students have the opportunity to visit their self-portraits and add or modify identity markers.

Rapid-Fire Writing: Assumptions & Stereotypes

Rapid-fire writing is a simple and highly structured way that guides students to think and write about any topic. This writing strategy is designed for students to organize and clarify their thoughts as they navigate thinking and writing. It guides students to think quickly on their feet and reflect on their initial thoughts about the prompts at hand. It also builds on the practice and skill of revision throughout the writing process. Employing a rapid-fire writing strategy helps students to brainstorm, narrow, and synthesize their thoughts on the topic at hand. The rapid-fire session should not be longer than 10 minutes for writing and an additional 5–10 minutes for the author's chair discussion.

For a rapid-fire writing session, you may want to choose prompts/texts that correlate with your primary text(s), lesson(s), or provoke deep thought and conversation in students' responses. For example, you can use TED talks relating to the power of stories, identity, relationships, and growth. Have students get materials for writing. These could be a combination of pen/paper, markers, crayons, or others that enhance the classroom setting. Students have been asked to scatter around the classroom for this rapid-fire writing session and find their cozy corners to write. Remind students that the rapid-fire session will follow a structure to guide their writing. This helps students think about specifics in their writing.

As a class, watch the TED Talk. After the video plays, be sure to answer/discuss any doubts or comments about it (this should be a quick discussion as students will write and discuss later on). As the teacher, you should guide students through the rapid-fire session using time markers. Students quietly think about what they will be writing about; no specific writing will be done (1 minute). Students begin writing. The teacher should emphasize that they should write non-stop (3–4 minutes). Students point out by circling three or four main ideas (words or phrases) from their writing. At this point, no other writing should occur. You can read and think about what you would write next but do not start writing (1 minute). Students expand on one or more of the ideas circled in their first part of writing (2–3 minutes).

Next, students go over their writing and select one idea that jumps out at them as the most important or relevant (1 minute). Students should do one final writing session expanding on that idea they previously selected (1 minute). After the rapid-fire writing session ends, the teacher guides the students in a conversation around what they wrote in their session. As the teacher, you should be ready for a deep and thought-provoking conversation about stereotypes, assumptions, and individual stories. Depending on the class size and your intended time limit, the author's chair discussion could also be done in small groups (5–10 minutes).

Inquiry into a Story

Chulito goes through a journey of identity and self-discovery with his sexual orientation. He struggles with self-acceptance while simultaneously thinking about how and if the world around him will accept him as a gay man. It is crucial to frame the idea of personal narratives into the reading and students as readers. Teachers can engage students in a process called "Inquiry into a Story" which has three main goals: students come to understand their place in the world better and better understand other people when they challenge a monolithic story; students get to share their own stories with others in ways that shape their power and the way they see the world; lastly, stories hold power, and as readers and writers, students can utilize stories to give agency to those who have been denied it. Teachers can connect the process to literacies students use daily by asking students to think about how people share their stories. Students can consider YouTube, Facebook, Twitter, text messages, books, journals, interviews, and other forms of media as story-sharing processes.

WHILE READING *CHULITO: A NOVEL*

Although the story revolves around Chulito and his struggles with identity, we also have Carlos as a counterpoint to Chulito. Apart from these two central characters, we are presented with additional and developed characters throughout that intersect and become essential to Chulito's development. The approaches offered in this section are intended to engage students more with identity and characterization issues as presented in the text.

Identity Markers in Characterization

While reading Chulito students will be asked to be aware and keep track of characters' identity markers and how they evolve throughout the novel. The focus on character identities will allow students to be aware of how characters' identities are evolving throughout the novel. There are identity markers that are concurrently identified through the text in relation to the characters. Students are given the identity markers that are mostly seen throughout the text. They will have to keep track of who exhibits those identity traits and where in the text you can see them. Prevalent identity markers that are relevant and will be discussed in class are:

- Masculinity—this identity marker is essential to Chulito. Not only is this marker throughout the text but the main character of Chulito struggles with his identity as a gay man and how this might affect his notions of masculine identities.
- Cultural identity—the characters in the novel struggle with the notions of cultural identity and fitting in while being Puerto Ricans living in New York. They find themselves constantly trying to navigate what is Puerto Rican enough versus "American" enough.
- Physicality/Physical acceptance—the text opens up with Chulito staring at himself in the mirror. This sets up the way he thinks about himself and how body image becomes essential to how people perceive his masculinity and heterosexuality throughout.

- Love relationships—one of the main reasons Chulito is navigating his identities is his realization that he is falling in love with his friend Carlos. Both Chulito and Carlos navigate notions of love through the lens of their identities as gay and Latinx men.
- Friendship—one of Chulito's fears throughout the novel is the possibility of losing both Carlos and Kamikaze as friends. All three men navigate ideas of friendship and how that is seen through the eyes of others and themselves once queer identities come into the forefront.

Table 12.1 provides some textual evidence from the novel that can be used throughout this lesson. The textual entry points offered in this table were created through a collaboration of both the teacher and students in my own classroom. Each class and discussion vary, so these can be contextualized and received differently by other readers.

Examining Relationships with Regard to Characterization

Examining character relationships in texts can be a powerful strategy for students to respond to what they are reading, gain writing fluency, and critically think about what they are reading, writing, and how they see the world. It encourages students to engage by expressing their thoughts and insights on the text and helps build on their ability to observe, take notes, reflect on those notes, and ask questions about the novel's characters and situations. Understanding character relations provide students the space and opportunity to express and locate their specific points of view about the themes evoked in the novel. It also encourages students to reflect on their beliefs about LGBTQ issues safely and honestly. This provides teachers a chance to observe what and how students are reading and opens the door for more complex and guided discussions around the novel. It is essential that teachers establish the appropriate rules in order to create a safe space for students to be honest about their thoughts and feelings. All ideas that come to mind about the novel while students read should be jotted down in the students' journals.

Figure 12.2 offers some discussion questions relating to characterization and identity that can be posed. These discussion questions and their respective chapters support close readings for the character of Chulito and his relationships throughout the novel.

Character Mapping

Another activity that teachers can implement is Character Mapping. This strategy lends itself very well to the approach of the characters and themes within *Chulito: A Novel*. A character map is a graphic organizer which

Table 12.1 Sample Textual Evidence, Possible Topics, and Activities

Textual Evidence	Chosen by the . . .	Possible Topics	Activity
"Chulito stood naked in front of the full-length mirror on the back of his door. That spring, with just some push-ups and sit-ups, smooth, hard muscles came out of nowhere, and he looked like a Latino, hip hop version of Michelangelo's David. He shifted his weight onto his right hip, tilted his head, tucked his chin into his neck, and contorted his pretty-boy face into a mean gangsta snarl." (p. 2)	Chosen by the teacher for being the first descriptors of Chulito as the protagonist of the novel. It is an entry point for conversations of physicality, cultural identity, and rhetorical identifiers.	Identity Masculinity Cultural Identity Physicality/Physical acceptance Rhetoric	Self or character portraits Character map Introspective journaling
"We should kick his faggot ass to show him a lesson," said Looney Tunes, referring to Carlos, Chulito's best friend. "Yo, Carlos is my boy and he from the 'hood, so cut that shit." —Chulito. "Protecting your boyfriend?"—Looney Tunes (p. 3)	Chosen by the teacher because it shows Chulito's protectiveness of Carlos that is tested throughout the novel. It is an entry point for conversations around bullying and derogatory rhetoric.	Homophobia Bullying Masculinity Aggressiveness	Personal narratives Introspective journaling
"Chulito liked it best when it was just the two of them, like that first day in his room, or when they'd sit and watch *Scarface* in his crib and order his favorite rib tips and beef fried rice from the Chinese spot." (p. 30)	Chosen by the student(s) because of the sweet nature that it shows of Chulito and his relationship with Carlos. It engaged in a compare/contrast discussion of his aggressive masculinity vs. his loving nature.	Love Relationships Friendship	Introspective journaling Character Map Personal narratives

Carlos: "What are you saying? What are you doing?" Chulito: "Carlos, I been feeling you for a while. I just didn't know what to do. What we'd do? I don't know what to do next, but I figure I say what I got to say. Let you know how I feel, and then we can see wassup." (p. 121)	Chosen by the student(s) because it is the first time, we see Chulito cross the friendship line with Carlos. Conversations on letting his guard down around Carlos came up and how being with him creates safe spaces to be who you are and express your feelings.	Acceptance Confronting reality Identity	Character map Personal Narratives
Chulito: "I love you, Carlos. And I don't want to let go of you. You got me." (p. 315)	Chosen by the teacher because it is the final moment, we see Chulito and Carlos in the novel, and it represents Chulito's journey as a character.	Acceptance Love Identity	Self or character portraits Character map Personal narratives Introspective journaling
"His arms reached out as if he could embrace Carlos. And Chulito danced. He danced for Carlos. He danced for Puti. He danced for Lee. He danced for Julio and Brick. He danced for Kamikaze. He danced for all his friends on the pier. He danced for Davey and the fellas. He danced for his mother and Mari." (p. 317)	Chosen by the student(s) because they point out the sense of happiness, calm, and resolve to accept his identity and freedom.	Freedom Acceptance Self-love	Personal narratives Introspective journaling Podcast

helps students learn about a character and how that character impacts and is impacted by other characters, settings, and plot. Although character maps can be used after reading a text, they can be beneficial to use during the reading of texts as students are constantly adding or making changes to their character maps rather than having them think in retrospection after finishing a text. Teachers can and should keep the idea of identity markers present throughout the time the students engage with *Chulito: A Novel*. Teachers can do this by providing students with an identity mapping chart. Teachers can also assign students characters (or let them choose) and have them identify where in the text we get insights into the characters' identities. Encourage them, as well, to return to their self-identity portraits throughout the reading of *Chulito* so they can add or make changes to how they see themselves.

Tracing Marked Identities

Throughout reading *Chulito: A Novel*, pair up students so they can pinpoint and trace characters' identities with a word bank provided by the teacher. This is a straightforward way to help students navigate and understand the characters' identity and their growth throughout the text. Also, it encourages students to think about how they might bring up these identity markers and talk about them in a podcast they will be working with after reading the novel. Teachers can do this in one of two ways. First, teachers can have students do their own word wall based on the identity markers they pick up throughout the novel. Teachers can pair up students which will help them give feedback to each other in regards to the characters. Second, and the way I have approached it in my classes is, by providing a word bank of specific identities that relate to different characters in the novel. Throughout the reading, students could keep a detailed journal which notes where in the novel they see those identity markers and to which character they belong.

There are three characters in particular that the novel centers on: Chulito, Carlos, and Kamikaze. Figure 12.3 is the word bank that I used in class that relates to those three characters.

AFTER READING *CHULITO: A NOVEL*

Podcasting!

Podcasts have become an effective tool in teaching. Jarvis & Dickie (2010) argued that podcasts boost student's confidence and foster effective learning. This approach to Chulito has been to look at identity markers by others, break away from them, and create our own. After reading and reflecting

Chapters	Some Discussion Questions
Chapters 1-6	Right from the beginning, the author gives us a direct description of Chulito, "Chulito stood naked in front of the full-length mirror…he looked like a Latino, hip hop version of Michelangelo's David." (p. 2) What do the following passages reveal about Chulito? Why is it essential for us to know that specific descriptor from the beginning? What does this say about Chulito?
Chapters 7-13	Chulito and Carlos have a strong friendship. This is tested when Carlos is called "pato," and Chulito begins questioning his friendship with him because of his identity insecurities. What do you think Chulito should do? What do you think Carlos should do? How might this impact their friendship going forward? Was there ever a time that you second-guessed a friendship because of what others thought?
Chapters 12-19	When Carlos returns from college, he and Chulito share a kiss; how do you think both Carlos and Chulito felt when this happened? What do you predict will happen going forward?
Chapters 18-23	How do you see Chulito now compared to where he was when you began reading the novel? What other struggles, if any, do you think Chulito will face? What has been a moment in which you have had to face your own identity? What are some elements of Chulito's journey that you can relate to and/or see on your own?
Chapter 24	In the novel's final scene, we know that Chulito is on the rooftop dancing and feeling liberated after coming out and being in a loving relationship. When have you had a moment and feeling of liberation that made you feel complete?

Figure 12.2   Discussion Questions—Chulito and His Relationships.

upon *Chulito: A Novel*, it is time for students to engage in conversations about the characters in the novel. By offering fun and creative ways of engaging with the characters from the novel, students think deeper about the specifics of what is being asked of them. They tend to put themselves at the forefront of conversations rather than submitting an assignment for a grade.

Instructions for the Podcast Assignment

Students create a 20- to 30-minute podcast about how they see identity play out throughout the novel with the characters of Chulito, Carlos, and Kamikaze. Teachers can pair students up and give them the option to choose a character, or directly assign them one of those characters, for the podcast. Although this is a creative way to do character analysis, it is also a formal assignment for the course and you should ask students to follow a format. Podcasts should flow like a conversation between two friends. As such, the goal is for students to take listeners on a short audio narrative about the novel and their assigned or chosen character. Provide students time to plan and do an outline on a specific point, or points, they wish to talk about, and think about how they want to divide time between them.

To begin their podcast, ask students to introduce themselves and give listeners a sense of who they are. This should take anywhere from 3 to 5

Chulito	Carlos	Kamikaze
Puerto Rican	Gay	Heterosexual
Gay (closeted)	Nuyorican	Machista
Latinx	White/Latinx	Latinx
Afro-boricua	Bi-racial	Nuyorican
Macho	Sentimental	Aggressiveness
Aggressiveness		

Figure 12.3   Character Word Bank.

minutes. Toward the end of this introduction, ask students to let listeners know about *Chulito: A Novel*— an overview about the novel so the listener is with them when they refer back to it throughout the podcast. Students should also let listeners know about the characters of Chulito, Carlos, and Kamikaze.

Throughout the podcast, students should be referring back to the novel and its characters. This assignment's ideas relate to the characters' stories and their identity. Therefore, each participant should paraphrase at least two situations in the book that relate to their character and the issues they are addressing. These connections should be done in a way that fits naturally within students' discussions. As a pair, there should be a minimum of three (3) quotes from the book. Students should refer to the specifics of the novel and let the listener know these by mentioning the chapter and page of the book.

This podcast is meant to amplify students' voices. Teachers should assure students understand that they want students to express their stories, thoughts, and opinions about the novel and the characters in the most honest way. Provide them the space to be honest as long as they are respectful to their teammate, classmates, and teacher. At the end of the podcast, ask students to give their honest recommendations of the novel. *Do they recommend it to listeners? Why or Why not?* Remember to let students know to conclude and say goodbye to their listeners instead of just cutting off the podcast. Let them know they are social media influencers and have thousands of listeners who are interested in their thoughts about the novel and characters.

Note to Teachers on Podcasting

First, it is critical to give feedback to students continuously. There may come a time that works for the podcast are out of the school, so teachers should include checkpoints to see how students are doing with recorded sessions they may already have. Also, encourage students to share and hear each other's podcasts through the process of recording. This allows feedback from potential listeners on how it is coming together, how it presents the novel, and if the podcasters' intentions are coming through. In the end, each student will have an even stronger project because of it. When all podcasts are submitted, the teacher can have a class where everyone listens to all of the podcasts or specific sections students found exciting to have a group discussion about what their peers shared in them.

Second, the podcast is an activity that can be done beyond the text. This shift to the podcast would focus on students' identities and conversations around their identity markers after reading the novel. Teachers could follow the same steps as with the regular after-reading podcast but this time direct the students to discuss their identity markers and how those markers shape who they are as students and people. Teachers can also have students talk about the novel by relating their identities to the characters in the novel. Teachers can expand the podcast activity to have students do further research on other important figures within the LGBTQ, Latinx, and Puerto Rican communities in order to connect the ideas to *Chulito*.

Movie Casting!

After finishing Chulito and the podcast assignment, another after-reading activity that allows students to explore LGBTQ and Latinx identities is casting a film version of the novel. For this short assignment, ask students to cast the main characters of the novel with Latinx and openly gay actors. They can create a casting sheet for the actors they see fit for the roles. Have students research the actors' profiles in relation to their background, filmography, and any tidbits they see as important for them to be cast as a specific character. When students complete this assignment, pair students into small groups in order for them to have discussions around their casting decisions. This assignment offers students an opportunity to go back to previous conversations regarding Remezcla, LGBTQ Puerto Rican activists, and expand on those important figures.

BEYOND *CHULITO: A NOVEL*

Not a single activity can do justice when engaging with topics and texts about queer, gender, sexual or cultural identity. Instead of attempting to give a one-size-fits-all approach to teaching *Chulito: A Novel* or any other LGBTQ texts for that matter, this chapter was designed to help teachers and students understand that we get to live outside of monolithic representation. Below are a few suggested extension activities that you can also use when teaching *Chulito*.

Ignorance Isn't Bliss—Why We need LGBTQ Education

Watch *Ignorance Isn't Bliss—Why We need LGBTQ Education* by Grace James (2013). Teachers can include a transcript of the video and a read-aloud strategy can be implemented when engaging with this text. In this video, James explained her experience with reading LGBTQ texts in her classrooms. She expanded on the importance of reading books with characters that feel, talk, look, and identify like her. She also mentioned how the incorporation of such texts created a more safe and open environment in her school, something that is also talked about in *Chulito*. Guiding questions discussed in my classroom with this video have been: *Why is it important for us, as students, to read and learn about LGBTQ stories? How do I relate to Grace's experience of LGBTQ issues in schools? Have I ever made school spaces safe or unsafe for LGBTQ students? and Have I ever disregarded stories because I explicitly do not see myself reflected in them?* Teachers can have students answer these questions in pairs before opening up the discussion to the entire class. After discussing the video, begin a benefits chart or table on the board. Lead the class in adding characteristics on why it is beneficial to discuss LGBTQ texts in schools.

Supplemental Texts—LGBTQ Short Stories and Poems

Teachers can also explore supplemental texts that enhance the conversation around LGBTQ and Latinx identities for students. There are LGBTQ short stories and poems that would enhance the conversations around queer and Latinx identity. Some suggested texts include the following:

- *Americano: Growing Up Gay and Latino in the USA* by Emanuel Xavier (2010) explores the duality of being gay and Latino through an examination of gender, sexuality, politics, and religion. Xavier examined the complexities of identity through a nuanced, relatable, and positivistic outlook that reflects real life.

• *Mundo Cruel* by Luis Negrón (2010) is a collection of stories that explores gayness, sexuality, and identity in Puerto Rico from a satirical, hilarious, and heartbreaking perspective.

These texts explore the relationship between individual queer, cultural, Latinx identities and how we define ourselves and allow others to define us. These texts enhance the discussion in *Chulito,* and strategies like the ones presented in this chapter can be modified to have discussions about these poems and short stories.

CONCLUSION

As an openly gay man, it was inconceivable that I, one day, would be able to teach and have a discussion regarding LGBTQ issues with students. Students, nowadays, are exposed to a variety of identities and perspectives that, I feel, are vital for them to comprehend and discuss. As teachers, we sometimes use texts to focus on or teach one specific aspect of English Language Arts or social issues. Reading *Chulito: A Novel* offers us an opportunity to step back and look at various identities that constitute one character in order for students to see how there are many ever-changing factors when it comes to discovering our identities. Studying this novel illustrates that we do not have to live within the parameters of what others set upon us, but instead, we have the opportunity to discover our path within the world. And just like Chulito does at the end, "Danced because it was alright and he felt it" (p. 37).

REFERENCES

James, G. [TEDx Talks]. (2016). *Ignorance Isn't Bliss* [Video]. YouTube. https://www.youtube.com/watch?v=dWieTvjkj0k&t=9s.

Jarvis, C. & Dickie, J. (2010). Podcasts in support of experiential field learning. *Journal of Geography in Higher Education, 34*(2), 173–186.

Negrón, L. (2010). *Mundo cruel.* Seven Stories Press.

Rice-Gonzalez, C. (2011). *Chulito: A novel.* Magnus Books.

Talbert, R. & Mor-Avi, A. (2019). A space for learning: An analysis of research on active learning spaces. *Heliyon Cell Press, 5*(12), 1–19.

Xavier, E. (2012). *Americano: Growing up gay and Latino in the USA.* Rebel Satori Press.

Chapter 13

Multimodal Exploration of Identity in *The Music of What Happens*

Anthony Celaya and Joseph D. Sweet

When students are asked to read texts about issues connected to their lived realities and are able to explore their engagement and processing through written texts that are accessible to a larger audience (someone other than their teacher), students have the opportunity to further develop their empathetic understanding and response to people of different cultures and identities. In order to do this, this chapter details how educators can use *The Music of What Happens* (Konigsberg, 2019) to engage students in multimodal composition while also exploring issues and themes relevant to students' lived realities.

We have taught *The Music of What Happens* to address a range of important issues including sexual assault and consent, toxic masculinities, and diverse representations in literature. Additionally, this novel lends itself to the teaching of multimodal writing and writing for specific audiences. The main characters in the novel, Max and Jordan, sometimes struggle to communicate with each other. However, the biggest breakthroughs in their relationship occur through the production, sharing, and consumption of multimodal texts, which are present throughout the novel.

NOTE TO TEACHERS

We want readers to be aware that a character in the novel is a victim of rape, and he struggles to accept that the act perpetrated on him is rape. The story contains flashbacks to his assault that may be difficult for some readers.

SUMMARY OF *THE MUSIC OF WHAT HAPPENS* BY BILL KONIGSBERG

After a night Max would rather forget, he runs into Jordan, a boy from his high school, at a local farmers market. Jordan would rather be anywhere else than working the window of his deceased father's food truck while his erratic mother tries to restart the family business to avoid losing their house. Max takes it upon himself to play the role of a hero, agreeing to work on the food truck with Jordan and save him and his mom from eviction. However, they both soon realize they know nothing about running a food truck, or each other. Through trial and error—and a bunch of YouTube videos—they learn how to cook and manage a food truck, and each learns that the other is gay.

Pressure cooked within the tight confines of a barely functional food truck in the scorching Arizona summer, Max and Jordan start to see past their initial assumptions and begin to understand each other from a new perspective. It takes some time, but Max and Jordan begin to date as they continue to raise money to save Jordan from eviction. As their relationship grows, Max and Jordan are forced to wrestle with their insecurities and traumas as they begin to let the other into their lives.

The novel is narrated through Max's and Jordan's alternating first-person perspectives, which allows the audience to inhabit the internal struggles of each character. The reader learns how the characters' different identities and life experiences have shaped and continue to influence their lives. These complex characters, processing through their trauma and learning how to love another person, help readers to understand their own complex identities and to empathize with others.

BEFORE READING *THE MUSIC OF WHAT HAPPENS*

Framing Identity Conversations

When having critical conversations with students about identity, it is important to provide a common framework to help students understand and be understood. For some, reading a story featuring two gay protagonists might conjure expectations of a narrative that focuses on the characters' sexual identity, instead of a story where their "identity is simply a given, as it is in stories about heterosexual characters" (Cart, 2011, p. 160). However, as Blackburn and Smith (2010) explained, "Sexual identities cannot be effectively separated from the race, class, gender, and other identities embodied by people since no one is solely sexual. Sexuality cannot be understood well in isolation from other identity markers" (p. 633). For example, when students begin to examine the character, Max, not only is he comfortably open with his heterosexual friends (p. 18), readers can identify several of his intersecting identities: male, half-white, half-Latino [the character's preferred term (p. 125)], teenager, athlete, artist, and gamer.

These identities create a multidimensional and complex character that may represent the variety of intersecting identities students bring to the classroom. Therefore, an intersectional analysis of these characters' experiences "might focus on how the sociocultural communities to which these youth belong construct sexuality and what these constructs reveal about the ways in which heterosexuality and heterosexism already function within these cultural communities (Durand, 2015, p. 75). Looking at Max again, Jordan, who at first only knows Max as a "dude bro" (p. 13), is shocked and moved to the brink of tears when Max shares his charcoal sketch that was inspired by a poem Jordan shared with him (p. 128). As Jordan learns more about Max and his identities, his preconceived idea that Max is a superhero, always confident, and ready to save others, begins to change as he recognizes the vulnerability Max displays in his artwork.

Before inviting the students to analyze the identities of characters, begin this process by critically reflecting on their own complex, overlapping identities. It's important to note that although we may talk about isolated identities, the intersection of these identities remains far more important than a sum of its parts. Though Max and Jordan may claim these disparate identities, they are also much more than all of those things.

Preparing to Compose Multimodal Texts

In *The Music of What Happens*, the characters communicate through a variety of multimodal texts, such as poetry and charcoal drawings (see pp. 113, 128). Prior to creating multimodal texts, students should examine the different texts and modalities they consume and produce for authentic audiences outside of school. With increased access to the internet, digital platforms, and sophisticated computers and cameras on their smartphones, students now produce more digital and multimodal texts than ever before. As a result, it is entirely possible that students may be more prepared to discuss and produce multimodal texts than teachers feel prepared to teach. We encourage teachers to facilitate discussions and opportunities that help students transfer their academic literacy skills to their everyday literacy experiences.

Students can explore talks on the TED website (e.g., Eldra Jackson's [2018] "How I unlearned dangerous lessons about masculinity") and identify features that make TED Talks a unique and engaging media. Students might point to the expertise of the speakers, the relevant topics, the conversational speaking style, the use of graphics, or the audience participation. Next, students can discuss the different processes and considerations that are required to produce an effective talk. Effective speakers are well organized, make research accessible, and meticulously plan and rehearse with the audience in mind. After this process of engaging in collaborative discussions about the genre, students may be ready to create their own TED-style talk.

To extend this analysis outside the classroom, students should turn an analytical eye toward their everyday texts. Some questions students can explore when examining their everyday texts include: *What are the distinguishing features of a media or text? How does an audience on social media influence texts such as tweets, memes, viral campaigns, and infographics? What skills, processes, and/or technologies are required to produce these different forms of texts? If a student wants to be successful in creating media or texts (e.g., YouTuber or blogger), what would their potential audience expect from them?*

Through these before-reading activities, students begin to critically examine the multimodal texts they consume and produce both in and out of school. Building upon this multimodal awareness, students will analyze the genres and modalities in the novel, and then write in those genres and modalities to demonstrate their understanding of the text and characters. Additionally, some of the genres are deeply personal, therefore analyzing the different genres in the novel supports the students' understanding of characterization and identity. By using *The Music of What Happens* to explore multimodal composition, we intend to create opportunities for students to engage in authentic writing experiences.

WHILE READING *THE MUSIC OF WHAT HAPPENS*

While recognizing that lived experience cannot be reduced to a monolith, the experiences of Max and Jordan likewise comprise a complicated and woven patchwork. Just like the students who read this book, the characters' lived experiences are multifaceted. This section presents multimodal engagements with the text that educators can use while their students read the novel. Upon completion of the book, the students will have produced a variety of texts that together comprise a multimodal representation of the characters' identities and experiences.

Digital Composition of Annotated Menu

Aligning with the spirit of a food truck, teachers could ask students to compose an alternate food truck menu. We suggest that students create menus that reflect the characterization present in the book. That is, students choose a character and design a menu indicative of the character's food choices.

Food emerges as a prominent motif throughout the novel, and each of the main characters expresses their personalities through their dietary choices. For instance, Jordan's mother, Lydia, appears to eat mostly drinkable yogurt and candy (p. 54), and Jordan has never eaten bone-in chicken until Max orders it for him at a restaurant (p. 162). Additionally, Max's mom is "the favorite mom; she grills the best hot dogs and makes the best tamales" (p. 86). Max and his amigos share convenience store ice cream (p. 86), and Max and Jordan change the food truck menu from preparing "Italian things with chicken" (p. 5) to blended lemonade and cloud eggs. Given that food runs through the novel and hints toward characterization, students can express their understanding of the characters through the menu design.

Teachers can provide examples of food truck menus to show students their contents, and to expose them to how food truck owners use elements of digital composition. In chapter 32, Max and Jordan change the truck's inherited name from "Coq au Vinny" to "Poultry in Motion" and consequently redesign the composition of the truck's exterior. Along with designing the menu, students can name the food truck and design its physical appearance. We encourage teachers to engage in these types of digital compositions with their students to engender creative multimodal composition as a way of highlighting various identity markers. We further suggest that this assignment includes a written analysis that explains what moments from the text compelled students to make the menu choices they did.

Poetic Expression—Genre Blending

The novel highlights the profound significance that friend groups have on the lives of teenagers. While the protagonists of *The Music of What Happens* are cisgender gay young men, all of their friends are cisgender and heterosexual. The dynamics of Max's friend group comprise diverse representations of masculinities. For instance, Max's "amigos," Betts and Zay-Rod, appear at first as caricatures of high school jocks, who make crude (occasionally homophobic) jokes, sometimes objectify girls, and tend to uphold patriarchal notions of masculinity and femininity (see pp. 17, 20, 89, 91, 299, 300). However, as the novel continues, readers learn of their insecurities, vulnerabilities, and sensitivities (pp. 299, 301, 303–4). It is noteworthy that this group of superficially stereotypical high school jocks include an openly gay member. Incidentally, readers learn about all of the male characters, including Jordan, through multiple and layered storying where the reader begins to recognize multiple and complex subjectivities and masculinities within one person's lived experience. Taken together, the four teenage boys offer a diverse representation of masculinity.

While the characters offer multifaceted examples of masculinities, at times they risk being viewed monolithically. At the beginning of the novel,

Jordan's "wives," Pam and Kayla, project gay best friend (GBF) stereotypes onto him (p. 244); for instance, they consistently express their desire to give him a makeover (p. 27), and Jordan reports to Max that they expect him to adhere to GBF stereotypes such as being "[c]ampy and snarky and all on the surface (p. 244). Also, Zay-Rod and Max constantly tease Betts about his intelligence (pp. 87, 338), and it's not until the very end of the novel that Betts expresses that he doesn't like it, because he fears he will grow into a man like his father (pp. 301–303). Similarly, the novel characterizes Jordan's mother as an incompetent basket case, but as the novel progresses, we learn that she suffers from a gambling addiction. In these few examples, the reader learns that the characters break apart the monolithic views through open communication. Thus, we suggest that teachers ask students to track how they perceive the characters and how these perceptions shift as they progress through the novel and learn multiple stories about the characters.

With this in mind, we suggest that students compose a letter poem after reading chapters 7–14. During those chapters, readers learn that both Max and Jordan are missing their fathers; Jordan's died, and Max's lives outside of the state. Readers also learn that their mothers have different parenting styles, and readers get a strong sense of the dynamics of the particular friend groups. In order to engage with the boys' relationships with their parents and/ or friends, we suggest that students take either Max's or Jordan's perspective and write a letter to another character in the novel. For instance, Jordan composes a mental letter to his deceased father during which the reader learns that his father was a handyman and cowboy boot-wearing provider (p. 14). He also composes a poem that he states he thinks his father may have liked on p. 252, which begins, "Because to me you're the sun / I cannot shine without you." On the other hand, Max consistently displays hesitancy when speaking with his father while his father often performs homophobic behaviors associated with toxic masculinity (pp. 187, 328), when a more open and honest conversation may have proved more helpful. For this assignment, students could take Max's perspective and write a letter to his father that critiques his father's toxic masculinity and homophobic behaviors.

Students could also compose a letter between either of the protagonists and their friend groups. Jordan's wives consistently ignore him, make his desires secondary to theirs, and remain oblivious to the kind of support he needs. For example, Jordan expresses his insecurities regarding his attractiveness, and Pam and Kayla insist on giving him a makeover, even after he states clearly that he doesn't want one (p. 25). Rather than listen and offer empathy, they make fun of the way he looks. On the other hand, Max's amigos offer heartfelt support after learning of his sexual assault, but they consistently make homophobic remarks throughout the novel (see, for example, pp. 17, 18, 20). For instance, Max narrates: "'Do you know how I know you're gay? . . . It's because you had gay sex with a gay guy last night.' I crack up and say, 'Do you know how I know you're straight? Your T-shirt'" (p. 17). The kind of underlying homophobia they display is profoundly insidious partially because Max appears to accept it uncritically. It is not until chapter 41 that Max expresses his feelings about yet another homophobic remark (p. 300). As Max says, this is the first and only time he asks his friends to stop, but he also states that their remarks don't bother him. Further, he states that what bothers him is joking around in general, not the homophobic nature of the jokes. His letter to them, then, might negotiate their love and support for each other while simultaneously casting a critical eye on the sometimes subtle (but always harmful) homophobia Max's amigos perform. The letters would provide opportunities for students to demonstrate deep understandings of the complexity of the characters and also allow them to be highly critical of the issue at the focus of each letter (see figure 13.1).

These kinds of letters have proved a powerful modality in the spoken word, which is a genre of poetry that Jordan performs in the novel (p. 258). Teachers can blend genres into a hybrid letter poem. In order to enrich the reading and writing, teachers might consider including mentor texts such as, "Letter to the Girl I used to Be" by Ethan Smith, "Letter to the Playground

Speaker	Audience	Prompt
Max	Father	Toxic Masculinities
Jordan	Mother	Needs from his Parent
Max	Amigos	Homophobia
Jordan	Wives	Reciprocal Friendship

Figure 13.1   Prompts for Letter Poem Pairings.

Bully, from Andrea," and "A Letter to White Queers, A Letter to Myself," both of the latter by Andrea Gibson. These spoken-word letter poems provide models for genre blending while also enriching the reading of the text which includes slam and confessional poetry (see, for instance, pp. 103, 113, 252).

Confessional Poetry

Throughout the novel, Jordan composes confessional poetry (pp. 103, 113, 252). Despite the fact that Jordan narrates half the chapters as a first-person limited narrator, readers learn most about Jordan's inner thoughts through his poetry. For example, on page 103, Max discovers a poem in Jordan's poetry notebook that begins, "Fuck my life / S.O.S. / I am stuck / On a food truck / With a guy / Guy smiley." Jordan's confession teaches the reader and Max about Jordan's feelings regarding working on the food truck with Max. That said, we suggest teachers highlight that confessional poetry carries an important potential for students to understand the complexity of human emotion, for as the name implies, confessional poetry "renders personal experience as candidly as possible" (Kennedy & Gioia, p. 883). Thus, we recommend that teachers and their students analyze an example of confessional poetry to help contextualize Jordan's and Max's relationship.

In order to do this, teachers can use Robert Lowell's poem "Man and Wife" to examine some of confessional poetry's characteristics. "Man and Wife" contains twenty-eight lines in two stanzas. The first (22-line) stanza focuses on the speaker's and his wife's courtship, but the tone and setting shift when stanza two considers the speaker's perspective after twelve years of marriage. Over the course of the poem, the speaker confesses intimate details of his and his wife's relationship, including its challenges and difficulties. In this way, the analysis reveals that the genre can be deeply personal and can center on somewhat taboo subjects where the speaker articulates their most intimate feelings. Foregrounding the genre will provide students insight into Jordan's character development. For instance, pairing "Man and Wife" with Jordan's poem on page 103, the first six lines of which are detailed above. Max reads this poem without Jordan's permission, which proves important for how students and readers recognize the potential intimacy that confessional poetry carries. Further, during this lesson, teachers might consider highlighting Jordan's choice to share his poetry notebook with Max. After Max reads Jordan's poem on pages 113–114, he narrated, "He showed me his poem. No one has ever entrusted me with something so delicate before" (p. 116). Given the nature of confessional poetry, this action expresses the potential that confessional poetry can have on the development of their relationship and the deep intimacy the two boys share.

Lyric Poetry

The novel gets its title from Seamus Heaney's two-quatrain lyric poem, "Song," which Jordan reads to Max on page 257. The last stanza of the poem, "There are the mud flowers dialect / And the immortelles of perfect pitch / And that moment when the bird sings very close / To the music of what happens," draws from an Irish legend where hero Finn MacCool states that the music of what happens is the finest music in the world. According to Vendler (2015), Heaney described himself "as a poet of the everyday" (p. 238), and Vendler argued the last stanza of "Song" exemplified the ways in which Heaney engaged with the quotidian, the ways he transformed the ordinary, often overlooked aspects of nature, into the extraordinary. Moreover, and particular to the last line of the poem, Booth (1997) wrote that Heaney "never loses his sense that 'the best music in the world is the music of what happens'" (p. 375). In this context, Booth highlighted the ways in which Heaney's poetry focuses on the hard work of everyday existence where the words of the poem reflect the daily happenings of life. Furthermore, Booth contextualized the best music in the world with the notion that "the music of 'what happens' becomes the music of 'what is'" (p. 376). That is to say, the writing and reading of poetry, for Heaney, is more about the process of discovery than it is about the act of composing or the composition itself; it is a matter of revealing the subject.

With this in mind, teachers could lead students through an analysis of "Song" while also considering how it reflects and inspires events of the novel. Jordan's accompanying poem, which he titles "The Music of What Happens" (p. 258), considers the wonder of everyday occurrences; it focuses on the magic and the beauty that can be found in what we sometimes take for granted. By analyzing the poem through this lens, teachers prompt students to also consider the beauty and magic of their everyday lives, thus creating an opportunity for introspection. Some guidelines to consider amid the lesson include thinking about how Max describes Jordan at the beginning of the book (pp. 3–4). Max pays particular interest in Jordan's facial features and his school-assigned podcast. Despite readers learning this exposition, Max still feels compelled to introduce himself. Even though Max had so many complimentary things to say about Jordan, he also took Jordan for granted. For example, after spending a year in class together, Max only introduced himself after bumping into him at a farmer's market. This clearly indicates that they did not have a previous relationship. Max would have overlooked Jordan but for a chance meeting that sets the events of the novel in motion. This is how the music of what happens becomes the music of what is; it is about the process of discovery rather than the process of composition. Similarly, Jordan's poem "The Music of What Happens" also offers a close examination of the often overlooked. Unlike Jordan's other poetry, "The Music of What Happens" is not confessional. Rather, this poem focuses sharply on the everyday occurrences of his suburban neighborhood. In this way, Jordan finds beauty, tragedy, and hope in the everyday, and provides the reader a profound sense of possibilities for discovery. We encourage teachers to help their students engage with "Song" with "The Music of What Happens" to also consider the possibilities of the everyday in their own lives.

AFTER READING *THE MUSIC OF WHAT HAPPENS*

After exploring characterization through the composition of different genres and modes that Max and Jordan use, students can apply those skills to compose a multimodal project in which they further explore the identities and relationships among the characters of the novel. This project asks students to compose a variety of multimodal texts to demonstrate their critical understanding of the characters by inhabiting the characters' perspectives in their writing. Additionally, the project requires students to infer with textual evidence how the character may express themselves or interact with other characters.

There are several ways to structure and organize this multimodal composition project, depending on your students and curricula needs. First, students might choose one character to focus on for their whole project, inviting them to conduct a thorough analysis of a character. Another option is to ask students to explore the relationship between two characters. This option offers an opportunity for students to explore the complications and tensions between characters, which may not have received much attention in the novel. Teachers may want to exclude the relationship of Max and Jordan from this option as it is well documented in the novel. The third option for this project combines the benefits of the previous two options. Students can be paired up to produce a collaborative multimodal project in which each student inhabits the perspective of a character and compose their pieces interacting with the other character. This option encourages students to collaboratively engage with the text and throughout the writing process. However, this option requires dedicated time from both partners to effectively collaborate, which most likely requires in-person class time.

Teachers can provide students a list of possible genres and modes to begin their projects (see figure 13.2 for a list of possible genres). Ask students to select genres and modes that will effectively present the character's perspective and position to their audience. Some students may want to use some of the genres they practiced while reading the novel, such as writing a confessional poem or composing a letter to another character. Students may want to

Annotated Menu	Annotated Music Playlist	Sketch
Letter-poem	Text message chain	Instagram post
Confessional poetry	Journal entry	TikTok video
Lyrical poetry	Dialogue	YouTube video
Podcast/Oral report	Recipe	Art installation

Figure 13.2   List of Potential Multimodal Genres.

apply the digital composition skills they practiced while designing food truck menus to create other digital texts such as an annotated playlist for their character or a series of Instagram photos and captions. However, students have to propose additional genres and texts for their multimodal project. When students propose a genre or text, it is important to discuss with the students the piece's potential contribution to the project, the genre's rules, and conventions, and if the student will need support or guidance from the teacher.

The multimodal composition project gives students the opportunity to demonstrate their understanding of the text and characters in a creative, authentic way. However, teachers may also require that students demonstrate their ability to cite textual evidence to support their claims or decisions. Rather than asking students to include textual references or parenthetical citations in their multimodal texts, which would often be in opposition to the genre's conventions, teachers can ask students to write brief reflections about their pieces. In these reflections, students can discuss the decisions they made with the text, and cite textual evidence to support their characterization in the project. This way, teachers can assess the students' ability to support their ideas and decisions with textual evidence within an academic genre, while maintaining the conventions of the multimodal genres.

At the end of the project, make time for students to celebrate and enjoy their peers' work. Depending on how the project is structured, there are a variety of possibilities for how students might share their writing. If the projects were completed digitally, students could create their own blog to show off their work, or the class can make one together for their projects. Websites like Weebly.com are free and easy to use to create personal blogs. More simply, if your school uses an LMS with a discussion board feature, students can upload their projects to the discussion board. Another option could be a project-reading day. Plan a day where students can bring their projects to the class and spend time reading their classmates' projects. The teacher might play soft music, provide snacks or refreshments, and "thank you" cards for students to fill out and leave behind for the authors. Additionally, if a project was composed with a partner, with each inhabiting a different character, then the teacher might ask each pairing to read and share a few pieces from their project that explore the relationship between the two characters. This could be done as a gallery walk where each pair displays their selected pieces for other people to stop by and read. It can also be done performatively with each pair reading their work for the class.

When it comes to assessing the multimodal project, we encourage teachers to prepare different grading rubrics for different aspects of the project. An analytic rubric would work naturally for the written reflections if teachers are assessing the students' ability to cite relevant textual evidence. However, the analytic rubric would not work well with multimodal texts. Prescriptive rubrics limit the creative possibilities these authentic writing experiences offer. We suggest using a holistic rubric to evaluate the overall feel and effect that project has on its audience. While this approach may be new for both teachers and students, when given the opportunity to make their own creative choices and express themselves without worrying about whether or not they have checked all the boxes, students more often than not rise to the occasion and produce projects they find personally meaningful and memorable.

BEYOND *THE MUSIC OF WHAT HAPPENS*

Hooligan Do-goodery

In the novel, Jordan and Max engage in "hooligan do-goodery," which, "combine[s] the chaotic energy of hooligan culture with do-goodery–acts of kindness" (p. 164). Examples of this from the book include an installation art project about animal rights at the public zoo (p. 172) and spending an afternoon feeding people experiencing homelessness from their food truck (p. 206). Borrowing from Jordan and Max, invite students reading this book to design a hooligan do-goodery project. To do this, students first identify a problem that they might want to address. The teacher can help by identifying community issues by using local newspapers, or by facilitating a collaborative brainstorm session with students about what they see as issues in their communities, creating a long generative list of issues and ideas. However students arrive at a focus for their hooligan do-goodery project, it is essential that they are given the opportunity to have ownership of their issues and ideas. Whether this project is facilitated individually or as a group or a whole-class project, students must believe their work is meaningful for themselves and their communities. While service projects or civic action projects are intricate and deserve discussion beyond a few paragraphs, what follows are two extension activities that connect the hooligan do-goodery to multimodal composition.

Once students identify an issue and the potential action they can take, they can write a proposal to share their hooligan do-goodery project. Proposals often include research that identifies problems as well as research that supports the proposed solution. They also include budgets, calendars, goals, and projected outcomes. Asking students to write a proposal for their hooligan do-goodery project gives teachers an opportunity to provide guidance and support for student projects; it also gives teachers a writing assessment for the project that isn't tied to whether or not the action was "successful."

Another multimodal activity that can be included in the project is a multimodal presentation to celebrate students' engagement as hooligan do-gooders. These can include pictures and videos of the project, a presentation of the research or results, it can be an opportunity to share stories, whatever the students feel the best to showcase and celebrate their experiences. Just like with the proposal, encourage composition assignments that can be assessed without providing a score to the action. Some projects will produce positive results, some will be good first attempts, some may run into bureaucratic roadblocks and issues, but all these projects deserve to be celebrated. The students deserve to be celebrated for their efforts because that is always the hardest first step.

This I Believe Podcast

In addition to the genres and modes explored while reading the novel, another possible text for a multimodal project that can further students' digital composition skills while exploring their identities is to write and produce a "This I Believe" podcast (2021), like the one Jordan completed in his English class (p. 4). For the podcasts, teachers can turn to the several examples from This I Believe (see figure 13.3) and invite students to listen to others prior to brainstorming and selecting a belief topic.

Some teachers might be hesitant to ask students to produce podcasts or other forms of digital texts because they don't feel prepared to teach them. When introducing this project, show students an audio-editing program such as Audacity (audacityteam.org) which is free, open-source editing software that has many tutorials on YouTube. However, Audacity is computer-based, which means students would need access to a computer to download and use the software. If your students don't have access to a computer, then

Podcast Title and Author	Distinguishing Features	Essay Number
Returning to What's Natural by Amelia Baxter-Stoltzfus	• High school student's essay • Frames belief around temporary hair coloring	13023
A Goal of Service to Humankind by Anthony Fauci	• Prominent public figure • Uses an outline structure to organize the essay/podcast	15
There is No Such Thing as Too much Barbecue by Jason Sheehan	• Author draws from personal expertise rather than trying to make a grand belief statement. • Uses a repetitive structure to organize	5322

Figure 13.3　Podcast Examples with Unique Speakers and Features.

encourage students to use their other resources when making their podcasts. Students can watch YouTube videos to learn about programs on their smartphones such as the Voice Memos application or the Garageband application on Apple iOS. Or explore easily accessible web-based applications such as AudioMass (audiomass.co), which is also free and open-sourced but doesn't require a software installation. Students' resourcefulness and familiarity with digital tools should allow them to quickly adapt and produce podcasts.

To celebrate their podcasts, have students present their audio compositions over the course of several days. Some students may cringe and cover their ears at the sound of their recorded voice, while others might wait to show their peers their editing skills. In the end, students with whom this activity has been done commented that they enjoyed listening to the podcasts and learning more about their peers.

CONCLUSION

From texting friends to writing poetry, to watching YouTube videos, Max and Jordan participate in many of the literacy experiences that students engage in today. *The Music of What Happens* presents opportunities for teachers to connect the real-world writing of students to the literacy skills being taught in school through multimodal composition. By understanding the speaker and audience of a text, students are better prepared to compose for an intended purpose and audience to engage in effective written communication in and out of school. Additionally, the two main characters of the novel, through their complex identities and relationships, challenge students to explore how different speakers and audiences, shape different texts. These composition skills go beyond the reading of a novel or demonstrating one's understanding of characterization. These analytical and rhetorical skills are essential to becoming more critical consumers and producers of texts in our increasingly online and digital world.

REFERENCES

Blackburn, M. V., & Smith, J. M. (2010). Moving beyond the inclusion of LGBT-themed literature in English Language Arts classrooms: Interrogating heteronormativity and exploring intersectionality. *Journal of Adolescent and Adult Literacy, 53*(8), 625–634.

Booth, J. (1997). The turf cutter and the nine-to-five man: Heaney, Larkin, and "The spiritual intellect's great work". *Twentieth Century Literature, 43*(4), 369–393.

Cart, M. (2011). *Young adult literature: From romance to realism.* American Library Association.

Durand, E. S. (2016). At the intersections of identity: Race and sexuality in LGBTQ young adult literature. In D. Linville & D. L. Carlson (Eds.), *Beyond borders: Queer eros and ethos (ethics) in LGBTQ young adult literature* (pp. 73–84). Peter Lang.

Jackson, E. (2018). *How I unlearned dangerous lessons about masculinity.* TED.

Kennedy, X. J., & Gioia, D. (2016). *Literature: An introduction to fiction, poetry, drama, and writing* (13th Ed.). Pearson.

Konigsberg, B. (2019). *The music of what happens.* Scholastic Inc.

This I Believe Inc. (2021). *This I believe essay writing suggestions.* https://thisi-believe.org/guidelines/.

Vendler, H. (2015). Seamus Justin Heaney: 13 April 1939–30 august 2013. *Proceedings of the American Philosophical Society, 159*(2), 233–240.

Chapter 14

Multimodal Analysis of Characters and Settings in *Little & Lion* by Brandy Colbert

E. Sybil Durand

Reading *Little & Lion* by Brandy Colbert (2017) offers opportunities for students to reflect on the intersections of sexuality, race, socioeconomic class, religion, and mental health. The story explores how step-siblings from an affluent biracial Jewish family navigate one sibling's emerging bisexuality and the other's Bipolar-2 diagnosis. This chapter highlights multiple ways that students can engage in the sociocultural contexts of the story by focusing on the literary elements of characterization and setting, which guides students to consider the characters' identities as multidimensional and contextual.

Although *Little & Lion* is not a visual narrative, this chapter also provides a blueprint for analyzing texts in multimodal ways, by having students compose the reflections and essays using both images and words. Examining a story in multimodal ways challenges students to pay close attention to details, including characters, objects, and spaces (Levy, 2001). Levy (2001) argued that, although reading can seem like a linear activity, that is rarely the case for the narrative structure. Multimodal composition, whether annotations, reflections, or essays, allows students to map a text to reveal its narrative structure: "one steps back, sketches out the boundaries, marks the contours, and decides on the essential elements—where to place them, and how to connect them" (p. 195). Included in this chapter are student-centered activities that invite students to record their responses to the story and conduct research, including writing/drawing weekly reflections during reading, as well as exploring the book's settings and characterization through a research jigsaw, a character portrait, and a critical map of the story's settings. The culminating activity is a graphic essay, which builds on these skills by having students analyze characters in context through multimodal composition.

Little & Lion is set in contemporary Los Angeles, and the author refers to landmarks and well-known street names like Sunset Boulevard as the characters navigate through the city. These places, along with private spaces such as bedrooms, cars, and even a treehouse, lend themselves well to an analysis of settings. In addition, the diverse cast of characters grapples with social issues that are often stigmatized, making this story ideal for exploring how contexts shape identities.

SUMMARY OF *LITTLE & LION* BY BRANDY COLBERT

Narrated in a first-person present perspective, the story opens with sixteen-year-old Suzette at the Los Angeles airport, back home for the summer after spending a year away at a boarding school on the east coast. She is waiting with some apprehension for her older brother Lionel to pick her up. Lionel was diagnosed with Bipolar-2 disorder a year ago and was the reason their parents sent her away. A week into summer vacation, Lionel confesses that he has stopped taking his medications because none of the combinations his doctor has prescribed are working, and he swears Suzette to secrecy. The story primarily takes place in Los Angeles during the summer of Suzette's homecoming, with flashbacks of Suzette's childhood memories and her time at boarding school in chapters titled "then."

In addition to keeping her brother's secret and worrying about his mental health, Suzette is also questioning her sexuality. At boarding school, she developed feelings for and was in a secret relationship with her roommate Iris. Back home, Suzette questions whether she is bisexual because she is attracted to her childhood friend Emil as well as a new girl she met at a party, Rafaela. Suzette knows that no one in LA would take issue with her liking girls—her best friend is a lesbian and she knows her parents would express unconditional support. She feels unsure, however, about claiming a bisexual identity because of "all the jokes and assumptions [she had] heard about bisexual people: that they're just being greedy or doing it for attention or trying it on for size 'before they cross over to full-on gay'" (p. 88). Suzette has to navigate these feelings as she adjusts to being home and not quite fitting back into family life or her old circle of friends after being gone for so long.

Suzette's intersecting identities bring additional layers of complexity to the narrative. Her family is blended in several ways—she and her mother Nadine are Black and Lionel and his father Saul are white. Nadine and Saul have been living together for a decade and, although they were never married, Suzette and Lionel consider themselves siblings and call each other by their respective nicknames, Little and Lion. Lionel and Saul are Jewish, and Suzette and Nadine converted when Suzette was eleven, although Suzette avoids telling people this because "people have too many questions when you're black and Jewish [. . .] like you must offer up an extra-special reason for converting to Judaism if you have a certain type of brown skin" (p. 33). Suzette's family is affluent: Nadine is a screenwriter, Saul is a carpenter, and they all live in an upper-middle-class neighborhood, in an old Victorian house, where Suzette's bedroom is located in a turret.

A Note to Teachers: Addressing Sexuality and Mental Health with Students

This story contains mature themes and might not be suitable for all classrooms. The characters often use curse words and frequently consume alcohol even though they are underage. In addition, the story describes two of the main character's sexual encounters. These representations lend the story a sense of realism about youth who are largely unsupervised and mobile due to their access to cars and disposable income. Although activities described in this chapter can be applied to many texts, this particular story offers opportunities for students to engage in conversations about diverse sexualities. As Renzi, Letcher, and Miraglia (2017) explained, representations of LGBTQ youth are "conspicuously absent from our nation's secondary classrooms" and, "bisexual and transgender adolescents are the least likely to see themselves in books" (p. 104). Of particular import, the narrative features characters who identify as lesbian, bisexual, and questioning, which fills an important gap in literary representation for LGBTQ youth.

In addition to sexuality, this story also explores mental illness, and both require using destigmatizing language in the classroom. Derogatory language often comes from a lack of factual information about mental health and results in perpetuating social stigma and further isolating those who struggle with mental health (Richmond, 2017). Richmond (2017) advocated for using literature with youth to combat stereotypes and develop empathy and argues that "Educators and others who work with adolescents should talk about the vocabulary used in YA novels and discuss how negative terms can influence beliefs and behaviors and perpetuate stigma" (para. 9). English Language Arts teachers could also collaborate with health and counseling staff at their schools to provide students with relevant resources and services.

BEFORE READING *LITTLE & LION*

To introduce the unit, teachers can review the objectives, introduce the main characters, and provide an overview of the plot. Afterward, the students can participate in a research jigsaw that will provide them with facts about topics they will encounter in the story, and in a multimodal journal activity that will prepare them for engaging the focal literary elements of the story.

Research Jigsaw: Understanding Characters in Context

Little & Lion presents a diverse cast of characters, and students might benefit from exploring in more depth the representations of mental health, disability, and sociocultural elements in the story. For example, Suzette's childhood friend and current crush, Emil, is a Black Korean boy who has Meniere's disease, an inner-ear condition that can cause vertigo and hearing loss, and that requires him to wear hearing aids. Students can research the disease to gain perspective on Emil's experiences of hypervisibility on multiple fronts.

The book also features Los Angeles as the predominant setting where the story takes place. Although other settings within and beyond Los Angeles are important (for instance, Avondale, Massachusetts—a fictional place—is mentioned in flashbacks), students can conduct research about the demographics of Los Angeles or specific neighborhoods, like Echo Park, Silverlake, or the Palisades. In chapter 16, Suzette goes on a walk to Echo Park Lake with Lionel. The landmark has historical significance in Los Angeles—it has been featured in movies as far back as the silent black and white film era, and the surrounding neighborhood has been the site of gentrification, shifting from a "predominantly blue-collar Latino community, also favored by artists and progressives, to one that's now sought out by wealthier and whiter individuals" (Oreskes & Smith, 2021, para. 12).

Teams can conduct research on their selected topics, using the suggested sources provided in figure 14.1. Each team creates lists of facts about the topic, including topic description or definition of terms, relevant statistics,

Research Topics	Resources
LGBTQ identities	Genderbread Person v4 infographic (Killermann, 2017) Gay, Lesbian, and Straight Education Network (GLSEN)
Bipolar 2 disorder	Bipolar Disorder in Children and Teens (NIMH, 2020)
Meniere's disease	Meniere's Disease (Mayo Clinic, n.d.)
Jewish traditions/ African American Jews in the United States	Celebrating African American Jews (NYPL, 2016)
Population demographics of Los Angeles/ LA neighborhoods (Silver Lake, Echo Park)	QuickFacts: Los Angeles City California (US Census, 2019) LA's Homelessness Crisis (Oreskes & Smith, 2021)

Figure 14.1 Topics and Resources for Research Jigsaw.

and an anecdote of a person or a picture of a place related to the topic. Teams then share the insights gained from their research by forming new groups with one member from each team. The teacher closes the activity with a whole-class discussion through which students collectively reflect on both the topics that were shared and the ways in which doing research helped them understand their topic.

Readers' Art Journal

In order to put literary devices to work and analyze the story, students should pay close attention to their responses to and interpretations of the narrative. Reflection is an important component of a reader's response. To support students in delving deep into reflection, teachers could ask students to keep a reading/art journal. A reading journal typically includes written entries, and an art journal includes images. A reading/art journal combines both modes of communication—print and visual—which will support students for a suggested multimodal final project. Readers need not be artists—the visual components can be collages from magazine cutouts, found objects glued to the page, photocopied pages of the book for whiteout/blackout poems, or doodling with pencils, pens, or markers.

Teachers could also introduce the connection between art and reading by examining book covers. For example, *Little & Lion* has two covers—one created for the hardback and the other for the paperback. Artist Stephanie Snow shares on her website the mock-up for the cover art, which features a treehouse on a palm tree. The interior pages include images—pill bottles, pills, flowers, palm trees, a book, and a *New Yorker* magazine—that look like scratched-off black paint over neon pink and green underpaint. The final version of the hardcover used many of these items, which are important elements of the story. The title is in large block letters with uneven borders in bright pink and green, overlaying scratched line drawings of a palm tree, a *New Yorker* magazine, a flower, a pill bottle, and a book in the background. The tagline at the top reads, "Was trusting each other their biggest mistake?" and the author's name is at the bottom, illustrating the effect of combining words and images to convey important ideas.

Artist Marcie Lawrence created another cover for the paperback. Suzette and her brother Lionel are standing back to back, wearing colorful casual clothes with their hands in their pockets and frowns on their faces, conveying the tension between the two. The medium looks like paint on paper, with visible brush strokes. The artist features many more book covers on her website, many of which are YA and middle-grade novels, including two others by Brandy Colbert. In addition to the book covers, fans often create art about book characters, and there are some notable examples online, which students can look up (see Tschetter, 2014).

Students spend one class period personalizing a composition notebook into their reading/art journals by decorating the covers and the first interior page. Teachers can provide materials like old magazines, scissors, glue, markers, or other art supplies. Students can decide whether or not their journals have a theme—the goal is to make reading a personal endeavor. Teachers in classrooms that are equipped with digital tools can offer students the option of keeping a digital art journal or book blog where students can include digital collages, soundbites, and original art or doodles to accompany their reflections.

WHILE READING *LITTLE & LION*

While they read *Little & Lion*, students will use their readers' art journals to track characterization and settings in the story by writing and drawing/ doodling reflections. As teachers set the pace for reading, they can encourage reflections by including time to read in class and having students respond in their journals to simple prompts such as: *What did you notice so far in your reading? What characters stand out to you and why? What questions do you have about the story so far?* In addition to writing and drawing regular reflections, students can engage in a variety of collaborative discussions—in pairs, teams of four, and whole-class discussions—to explore their individual and collective impressions of the unfolding narrative.

The activities described in the sections that follow provide additional opportunities for students to engage in characterization and setting by considering the characters' identities in context. The first activity examines social identities by exploring how individuals are multidimensional, with identities that are shaped by social contexts. With this understanding, students then create character portraits that highlight their selected character's multidimensionality. In the second activity, students consider the role that social contexts and settings play in shaping the characters by creating critical maps of inequity in the story related to race, sexuality, and mental health.

Characterization: Social Identity Wheels and Character Portraits

As students read the first half of the book (chapters 1 through 13) and record what they notice about the characters and the settings, the teacher can introduce social identities. Social categories include physical, mental, and social identities, such as race, gender identity and expression, sexuality, disability, language, and religion, among many others. The University of Michigan developed a "Social Identity Wheel" (n.d.) activity, which is modified here to focus on characters instead of students (see figure 14.2). While teachers can use the original activity and have students also reflect on their own social identities, focusing on literary characters will mitigate tensions and discomfort that might arise if students feel required to divulge sensitive information such as sexuality or citizenship status. The teacher can project or draw the identity wheel on the board and either review definitions of each identity category provided in the original activity or develop definitions with students. Using the board, the teacher and students then create an identity wheel for one of the characters together, answering questions such as *What are the selected character's social identities? Is this category ascribed to or chosen by the character? How do we know? (Provide textual evidence).* Afterward, students work in teams of three or four to create identity wheels for other characters and share their findings with the whole class. The teacher can close the activity with a discussion about what new insights students gained about the characters by thinking about their social identities.

By the end of chapter 13, students will have enough information to create initial character portraits that build on the social identity wheels. Students can select one of the characters from the story and make a list of the character's

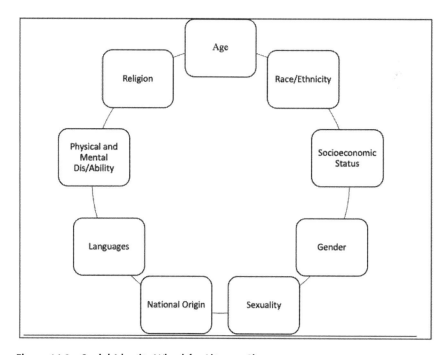

Figure 14.2   Social Identity Wheel for Literary Characters.

personality traits, actions, and motivations based on interactions with others. Because Suzette is the narrator, readers have access to her inner thoughts and her spoken words. Readers might notice a conflict between her worries and acting like she is fine all the time. For example, Suzette keeps Lionel's secret that he stopped taking his medication, which means lying to their parents while worrying that he might relapse. And, while she avoids talking about Lionel with most people, she admits to herself that,

> Lionel being off his meds is the biggest thing I've ever had to hide and it's heavy, a weight that's been stacked on my chest since the moment he confesses. I need to tell someone else. I need someone to talk to when I start to worry too much. (p. 203)

In addition, because Suzette is the narrator, all the other characters are filtered through her perspective, which means that students have to pay special attention to what characters say and do to draw their own conclusions. For example, readers are introduced to Rafaela from Suzette's perspective, who is largely focused on her attraction to the new girl. However, in dialogue, Rafaela reveals significant information about her background growing up in a small town in Texas, being pansexual, growing up in a single-parent household, getting pregnant at a young age and kicked out of her home, as well as feeling like she only attracts bad people in her life (pp. 187-193), standing in sharp contrast to Suzette's privileged upbringing.

Students create a one-page portrait using both words and images of their selected character. Visual components can be drawings of characters, profile portrait outlines, or collages of objects and spaces that reflect the character. For example, Lionel is an avid reader and Suzette describes his room as full of books (p. 26). He handed her *One Flew Over the Cuckoo's Nest* (p. 5) as a joke when she left for boarding school, and when she came back that summer, he was reading *Infinite Jest* (p. 27). When Lionel has his first breakdown, he wrecks his room, and books are everywhere (p. 178). Students could juxtapose the two rooms—tidy and wrecked—to illustrate Lionel's mental states, along with direct quotes of words and phrases that he and other characters use to describe him to substantiate their analysis. Some prompts to get students to think about characters in multidimensional ways include:

- What are your selected character's interests? What objects or places symbolize this?
- What words or phrases does your selected character use to describe him or herself? Include page numbers from the book.
- What words or phrases do others use to describe your selected character? Include page numbers from the book.

- Are there any conflicts between how characters view themselves and how others view them?

Students can share their character portraits in a gallery walk followed by a silent discussion—students use sticky notes to leave comments or ask questions, agreeing or challenging the analysis. Once they have completed the gallery walk, the teacher can lead a whole-class discussion on characterizations as well as prompt reflections on the multimodal process of analyzing characters. Some discussion prompts could include:

- Which character portraits stood out to you and why?
- Was any portrait of the character you analyzed very different from yours? What did you notice? In what ways do you agree with this characterization? In what ways do you disagree with this characterization?
- How do the visual components help you to understand the character? Any limitations?

Setting: Critical Geographies of Race, Sexuality, Socioeconomic Class, and Mental Health

Critical geographers examine inequity and oppression related to race, class, and gender, by mapping them over places such as cities or spaces such as homes (Brickell, 2012). Critical literary geographers do the same by examining the various settings—places and spaces—in a story (Piatti & Hurni, 2011; Levy, 2001). Mapping invites students to pay close attention to the text, synthesize key points, and represent their understanding in their own way (Levy, 2001). Students can conduct a critical geography of *Little & Lion* by exploring the main settings of the story and how the characters are shaped by and grow through these settings. Settings in the book include places like Los Angeles, where Suzette grew up, Massachusetts, where she attends boarding school, and Texas, where Rafaela is from. These settings enable and constrain Suzette in different ways. For example, to Suzette, L.A. is

a place where strangers openly discuss relationships that aren't just boy-girl, where a certain group of students don't whisper about the guys who were caught kissing in the woods behind Dinsmore Hall. And where two girls sleeping curled up in one bed wouldn't be gossip to make the rounds. (p. 57)

However, her dorm room at Dinsmore is also the space in which Suzette explored her attraction to Iris without questioning what it meant for her sexuality. The author describes Los Angeles in detail, with references to landmarks like Echo Park and well-known streets like Sunset Boulevard; in contrast, the setting of Suzette's boarding school is vague, Avondale is a fictional place, and only the dorm room Suzette shares with Iris is described in detail.

Spaces in the story include Suzette's storybook Victorian house, including her bedroom in the turret (pp. 9, 13), and the treehouse in the backyard (pp. 36, 60, 121, 160, 206), as well as the dorm room she shares with Iris at Dinsmore (pp. 149–157). Other spaces in which meaningful interactions between the characters occur include hiking trails and parks Suzette visits with Lionel (pp. 90–101), the pool where she and Emil have a racist encounter with a friend of a friend (pp. 107–117), and transitional spaces like cars, where important conversations happen (pp. 40–44, 211–214, 312–313).

Students can select settings that stand out to them and map them onto a double spread (two facing pages) in their art journals or use larger paper that they will later fold and glue into their journals. There are myriad ways to represent inequitable spaces and places through mapping, and one way is to sketch a map, or series of maps, that make up the settings of the story. Mapping inequity in Los Angeles, for instance, might mean drawing an outline of the city or the state of California and creating visual pop-outs of key locations accompanied by a legend and a narrative description or a direct quote from the story.

Similar to the character portrait activity, students can share their maps of *Little & Lion* in a gallery walk and reflect on the roles of settings for character or plot development in a whole-class discussion.

AFTER READING *LITTLE & LION*

After reading the book, and in preparation for the final project, students can synthesize and deepen the concepts they have been exploring in their journals during a whole-class discussion, using the Thoughts Questions Epiphanies (TQE) method (Thompson, n.d.) (see figure 14.3). During the first of two

Start Here:	Then Move Your Discussion Over Here:
What did you like or dislike about the story?	Why would the author ___ ?
What surprised you?	Why does the author keep mentioning the element of ___ ?
What settings and characters interested you? Why?	Who/what is ___ meant to represent, considering what happens/is said?
What social issues interested you? Why?	What is your favorite quote/life lesson from the book?
What questions do you still have about the story?	Draft statements, insights, and questions regarding social issues, characterization, and setting.

Figure 14.3 TQE Discussion (adapted from Thompson, n.d.).

Sociocultural Issue	Multimodal Prompts	Settings
Racism	What are moments in the story that highlight racial tensions or inequity? Draw the places where these events occur and include a direct quote from the book to illustrate.	• The pool party (pp. 107-117) • Shopping with Catie (pp. 67-76)
Homophobia	What are moments that highlight tensions or inequities about sexuality? Draw the places where these events occur and include a direct quote from the book to illustrate.	• Suzette's interactions with friends and family about being bisexual (pp. 92-96, 164-165, 322-324) • Rafaela's interactions with her family and previous heterosexual relationships (pp. 188-193)
Mental health stigma	What are moments that highlight tensions about mental health? Draw the places where these events occur and include a direct quote from the book to illustrate.	• Lionel's interactions with Suzette (pp. 96-101, chapter 16) • DeeDee's party (pp. 54-55) • Alicia's party (chapter 17)
Safe spaces	What are places and spaces where the characters feel safe or don't feel safe? Draw the places where these events occur and include a direct quote from the book to illustrate.	• The treehouse (pp. 36, 60, 121, 160, 206) • The dorm room (pp. 149-157)
Reflection Prompt: How do the characters grow or change in relation to these settings?		

Figure 14.4   Mapping Settings and Sociocultural Issues.

class sessions, students take 15 minutes to work in teams of 3 or 4 and discuss their thoughts, lingering questions, and epiphanies about the book to generate questions for the whole-class discussion. The teacher provides stem questions focused on characterization, setting, and social issues discussed during the unit to get students started (see figure 14.4), and students use their journals as sources to answer questions. By the end of 15 minutes, each team selects the top two questions and writes them on the board. The teacher uses the rest of the class time to edit all the questions on the board with students. These finalized student-generated questions are then used during the final whole-class discussion about the book. This approach complements the art journal activities by asking students to pay attention to their own thinking about the story and to contribute to the collective knowledge of the class.

Culminating Multimodal Project: Graphic Essay

After the class discussion, students are ready to tackle their final project: a graphic essay in which students conduct a multidimensional analysis of a character in context, examining both characterization and setting. Graphic essays are similar to infographics in that they both combine images and words; however, graphic essays are "more text-based and usually have a narrative arc or specific reading order" (DesignLab, 2021, para.1). They can have a variety of formats, including "comics, graphic novels, magazines, collages, artist books, textbooks, or even websites" (DesignLab, 2021, para. 1). A magazine feature, collage, artist book, or digital essay easily extends the work that students have been doing in their journals, and teachers can decide whether students will all use the same format or have options to choose from. Teachers can show students examples of final graphic essays from DesignLab or other sources, which might be helpful for those who are new to multimodal composition (Dallacqua, 2018).

A final project prompt such as this one could be suggested: *What are your selected character's social identities? (e.g., age, race/ethnicity, gender, sexuality, socioeconomic class, religion) How do various settings enable or constrain your selected character's growth?* However, students could also create their own prompts based on the TQE questions and discussion.

To complete their graphic essays, students can begin by revisiting their journal reflections, character portraits, and maps to decide which characters and settings they want to continue to explore. To connect the fictional narrative to contemporary issues and to substantiate students' arguments, the teacher might require students to locate and include an external source. Using their journals, students create an outline with bullet points of a thesis, arguments, and examples from the story. Once they have completed rough drafts of their essays, students then write a list of images of people, objects, and spaces that will illustrate their arguments. In their journals, students sketch their essay layout to visualize how words and images will be juxtaposed or overlaid. Then, they can create the final composition of their graphic essays using a poster board or a digital platform.

Similar to activities presented within this chapter, students can share their graphic essays in a gallery walk. If the final projects are completed on posters, teachers can have students circulate and leave comments and questions on posters with sticky notes. If the final projects are in digital formats on a shared platform, students can post comments that way. If a shared online platform is not available, teachers can include a presentation component to the final project where each student creates a 5-minute presentation of their graphic essays, highlighting key arguments and images. Teachers close the unit with a whole-class discussion reflecting on the process of composing a digital essay and its opportunities and challenges for literary analysis.

BEYOND *LITTLE & LION*

The activities in the sections that follow encourage students to move from text to world by considering how the social issues depicted in the novel impact the world around them. Students can deepen the skills and concepts they explored in the unit by connecting the places, social identities, and disabilities from the story to current events in news media or to concerns from the students' own neighborhood and school. In addition, students can develop projects to take action and make positive changes on issues that are meaningful to them.

Mapping Socioeconomic and Racial Inequities in Neighborhoods

Students extend their understanding of settings by building on the facts they learned about Los Angeles during the research jigsaw and critical mapping activities. First, students might examine current events related to socioeconomic inequities in the neighborhoods that Suzette navigates in Los Angeles. For example, in 2019, Echo Park saw exponential growth of homeless encampments, reflective of California's larger issues with housing insecurity, and coming to a point of crisis during the COVID-19 pandemic. Community members clashed as some protested camp removals and others signed petitions in favor of them. In March 2021, police removed the encampments and the park was closed indefinitely for renovations (CBS Los Angeles [CBSLA], 2021). Although *Little & Lion* was published in 2017, students can read the news articles cited in this chapter (see CSBLA, 2021; Oreskes & Smith, 2021) and reflect on Suzette's family's socioeconomic status—as affluent residents of the nearby neighborhood, on which side of the contentious issue would they fall?

Students could also create critical maps of inequities in their own communities. For the latter, students could conduct research about the socioeconomic and racial demographics of their neighborhoods and locate new articles that shed light on recent events about inequities their community members face. Then, students draw maps of their neighborhood and include pop-outs of specific spots in the neighborhood with direct quotes from their research to illustrate inequities.

Extending Understandings of Sexuality

In terms of sexuality, Suzette and most of her friends have supportive family and social networks. Such representations are important for readers to envision LGBTQ individuals in ways that do not reinforce their identities as a source of conflict. However, Rafaela, who is pansexual, has comparatively fewer sources of support. She grew up in a small Texas town and a religious household, and when she got pregnant and wanted to get an abortion, her mother "refused to even discuss any option other than having it" (p. 189). Rafaela ended up moving to Los Angeles to live with her aunt because her mom told her she "was a sinner, and that willful sinners aren't welcome under her roof" (p. 190). Rafaela also continued to meet people who are not accepting of her sexuality, such as the guy from the Palisades she dated and who showed signs of being abusive when he learned that she had previously been in homosexual relationships (p. 266). Students can look at the Gay, Lesbian, and Straight Education Network (GLSEN) report on the bullying LGBTQ youth of color face in schools (GLSEN, n.d.b.). In combination with the novel, students might create an anti-bullying awareness poster campaign to support LGBTQ students at their school. Other action-oriented projects could include conducting a climate survey to identify the challenges and needs of LGBTQ youth at their school, using GLSN's "Local School Climate Survey" tool (n.d.a). Students could then present their findings and recommendations for needed action to school faculty or distribute pamphlets with lists of locally available resources for LGBTQ youth, such as the local GLSN chapter or LGBTQ youth community centers.

Exploring Mental Health through Literature and Activism

Likewise, students can further explore and discuss approaches to destigmatize the mental health issues youth face. To understand how mental health affects youth like themselves, students could create a book group to read additional young adult fiction by authors who experience similar issues. There are a number of excellent titles for students to choose from (see Richmond, 2017). For example, in *Darius the Great is Not Okay* by Adib Khorram, Darius grapples with depression as he navigates different expressions of masculinity in a bicultural and biracial family. *Turtles All the Way Down* by John Green explores Aza's struggles with obsessive-compulsive disorder (OCD) and how it shapes her sense of self, as well as how it impacts her mother and best friend. In *Challenger Deep* by Neal Shusterman, Caden suffers from schizophrenia and his delusions are depicted through surrealism. In addition to reading fiction about mental health, students can take action on destigmatizing the perceptions of mental health at their school by creating an infographic of youth mental health statistics from data collected by the Centers for Disease Control and Prevention (CDC) or a critical map of resources available to youth at their school or in their city.

CONCLUSION

This chapter explored a variety of activities for students to engage in the sociocultural elements in *Little & Lion* through literary elements. Such an approach ensures that students understand and practice using literary tools to explore the representations of human experiences the author aims to convey as well as the narrative structure of the story. The multimodal journal also encourages students to begin with their own impressions of and responses to the story, which they then layer with research and literary analysis. The visual component of the readers' art journal and in most of the activities invites students to communicate their ideas in a highly personalized and creative way. Doing so illustrates how reading can be both a personal and academic endeavor, and an individual and collective process. In addition, analyzing the characters and settings in *Little & Lion* has the potential for LGBTQ youth to see themselves represented in literature and in the ELA curriculum, to reduce stigma related to nonnormative sexualities and mental health, and to increase students' empathy across multiple social categories.

REFERENCES

Brickell, K. (2012). "Mapping" and "doing" critical geographies of home. *Progress in Human Geography, 36*(2), 225–244.

CBS Los Angeles. (2021, March 26). Protesters clash with police over shutdown of Echo Park Lake homeless camps, 182 arrested. https://losangeles.cbslocal.com /2021/03/26/la-shutting-down-echo-park-lake-indefinitely-homeless-camps-being -cleared-out/.

Centers for Disease Control and Prevention (n.d.). Data and statistics on children's mental health. *CDC.* https://www.cdc.gov/childrensmentalhealth/data.html.

Dallacqua, A.K. (2018). "When I write, I picture it in my head": Graphic narratives as inspiration for multimodal compositions. *Language Arts, 95*(5), 273–286.

DesignLab (n.d.). Graphic essays and comics. University of Wisconsin-Madison. https://designlab.wisc.edu/resources/projects/graphic-essays-and-comics/.

Gay, Lesbian, and Straight Education Network. (n.d.a). Local school climate survey. *GLSEN.* https://localsurvey.glsen.org/.

Gay, Lesbian, and Straight Education Network. (n.d.b). Supporting LGBTQ youth of color. *GLSEN.* https://www.glsen.org/lgbtq-youth-color.

Killermann, S. (2017). Genderbread person v4: A teaching tool for breaking the big concept of gender down into bite-sized, digestible pieces. *The Genderbread Person.* https://www.genderbread.org/resource/genderbread-person-v4-0.

Levy, S.A. (2001). Traversing *terra incognita*: Mapping literary texts. *Teaching English in the Two-Year College, 29*(2), 193–203.

Mayo Clinic (n.d.) Meniere's disease. *Mayo Clinic.* https://www.mayoclinic.org/dis
 eases-conditions/menieres-disease/symptoms-causes/syc-20374910.

National Institute for Mental Health. (2020). Bipolar disorder in children and teens.
 NIMH. https://www.nimh.nih.gov/health/publications/bipolar-disorder-in-children
 -and-teens/.

New York Public Library. (2016). Celebrating African American Jews. *NYPL.* https:/
 /www.nypl.org/blog/2016/02/11/celebrating-african-american-jews.

Oreskes, B., & Smith, D. (2021, March 13). How a commune-like encampment
 in Echo Park became a flashpoint in L.A.'s homelessness crisis. *Los Angeles
 Times.* https://www.latimes.com/homeless-housing/story/2021-03-13/echo-park
 -encampment-exposes-bigger-la-homeless-issues.

Piatti, B., & Hurni, L. (2011). Cartographies of fictional worlds. *The Cartographic
 Journal, 48*(4), 218–223.

Renzi, L. J., Letcher, M., & Miraglia, K. (2017). Crossing boundaries: Exploring the
 fluidity of sexuality and gender in young adult literature. In J. A. Hayn, J.S. Kaplan,
 & K.R. Clemmons (Eds.), *Teaching young adult literature today: Insights, considerations, and perspectives for the classroom teacher* (pp. 101–121). Rowman &
 Littlefield.

Richmond, K. (2017). Language and symptoms of mental illness in young adult
 literature. *Dr. Bickmore's YA Wednesday.* http://www.yawednesday.com/blog/lan
 guage-and-symptoms-of-mental-illness-in-young-adult-literature.

Thompson, M. E. (n.d.). We're killing the love of reading, but here's an easy fix.
 Unlimited Teacher. https://www.unlimitedteacher.com/blog/were-killing-the-love-
 of-reading-but-heres-an-easy-fix.

Tschetter, A. (2014). Fanart inspired by YA books. *Young Adult Library Services
 Association.* http://www.yalsa.ala.org/thehub/2014/05/23/fanart-inspired-by-ya-
 books/.

United States Census Bureau (2019). QuickFacts: Los Angeles city, California. *US
 Census.* https://www.census.gov/quickfacts/losangelescitycalifornia.

University of Michigan (n.d.) Social Identity Wheel. *Inclusive Teaching at U-M.* https
 ://sites.lsa.umich.edu/inclusive-teaching/sample-activities/social-identity-wheel/.

Subject Index

About the Editors

Paula Greathouse is an associate professor of Secondary English Education at Tennessee Tech University. To date, she has coedited ten books including *Adolescent Literature as a Complement to the Content Areas* series (2017), *Breaking the Taboo with Young Adult Literature* (2020), *Young Adult and Canonical Literature: Pairing and Teaching* (2021), *Shakespeare and Young Adult Literature: Pairing and Teaching* (2021), and the first edition of *Queer Adolescent Literature as a Complement to the English Language Arts Curriculum* (2018). Her research on adolescent literacy and young adult literature has been published in books such as *Teaching, Affirming, and Recognizing Trans and Gender Creative Youth: A Queer Literacy Framework* (Miller, 2018) and journals such as *Educational Action Research, English Journal, The Clearing House*, and *Study and Scrutiny: Research on Young Adult Literature*. She has also guest coedited a special issue of *English Journal—Affirming LGBTQ+ Identities* (September 2020). She was a secondary ELA and Reading educator for sixteen years. She has received several teaching awards including the National Council of Teachers of English (NCTE) Teacher of Excellence and was the recipient of the University of South Florida Pride Award. She is an active member of the National Council of Teachers of English, International Literacy Association (ILA), and the Assembly of Literature for Adolescents of NCTE (ALAN).

Henry "Cody" Miller is an assistant professor of English education at SUNY Brockport. Prior to that role, he taught high school English in Florida for seven years. He was awarded the Teaching Tolerance Award for Excellence in Teaching in 2016. He served as the chair of the LGBTQ Advisory Board for the National Council of Teachers of English from 2018 to 2021 and currently serves on the Equity, Diversity, and Inclusion Committee for Assembly on Literature for Adolescents of NCTE. His scholarship has appeared in publications like *The English Journal, ALAN Review, Journal of Language and Literacy Education, Study and Scrutiny: Research on Young Adult Literature, The Clearing House,* and *Girlhood Studies,* among others. In 2019 his scholarship was awarded the Paul and Kate Farmer *English Journal* Writing Award. Additionally, he has guest edited special issues of *English Journal* and *Research on Diversity in Youth Literature.* Beginning in 2022, he will be the editor of the *English Leadership Quarterly.*

About the Contributors

Danelle Adeniji is a doctoral student at the University of North Texas studying Black queer preservice teachers and how intersectional identities impact and influence pedagogical practices. Danelle is a former elementary teacher.

Nicole Ann Amato is a PhD candidate in the Literacy, Language, and Culture program at The University of Iowa, where she teaches courses in children's and adolescent literature to preservice teachers. Nicole previously worked as a high school literature teacher for ten years. Her research interests include young adult literature analysis, literature discussion, feminist criticism, and critical youth studies. Her recent publications have appeared in *The Journal of Language & Literacy Education* and *Voices from the Middle*.

Ryan Burns is a doctoral candidate in the Literacy, Culture, and Language Education program at Indiana University, Bloomington. His current research involves autoethnography and exploring his stories and experiences in the classroom as both an educator and a queer, white man. Ryan has taught high school English Language Arts since 2007 and is also an adjunct professor in Providence, Rhode Island, where he teaches courses in English and Educational Studies, including *First Year Writing* and *The Teaching of Writing in Secondary Schools*. His coauthored work appears in the edited collections *Educators Queering Academia: Critical Memoirs* (2016) and *Acts of Resistance: Subversive Teaching in the English Language Arts Classroom* (2020).

Michael Cart is a columnist and reviewer for *Booklist* magazine as well as author or editor of twenty-five books including *Representing the Rainbow: LGBTQ+ Content since 1969* coauthored with Christine A. Jenkins. Cart is past president of both the Young Adult Library Services Association (YALSA) and the Assembly on Literature for Adolescents of the National Council of Teachers of English (ALAN).

Anthony Celaya is an assistant professor of English at Southeast Missouri State University where he works with undergraduate English teacher candidates. Anthony Celaya earned his PhD in English education from Arizona State University in 2020. His research interests include critical pedagogy, young adult literature, and teacher education. In 2017, Anthony was awarded the NCTE Early Career Educators of Color leadership award and was also awarded the ELATE (formerly CEE) Geneva Smitherman Cultural Diversity grant. Prior to higher education, Anthony served as an English teacher at a large public high school in Mesa, Arizona.

E. Sybil Durand is an assistant professor in English education in the Department of English at Arizona State University. Her scholarship is grounded in postcolonial and curriculum theories, which situate literature and education at the intersections of sociocultural, historical, political, and national contexts. Her research focuses on representations of youth of color in young adult literature, including multicultural, international, and postcolonial young adult texts, and how teachers and students engage such narratives.

Brittany Frieson is an assistant professor of literacy and anti-racist education at the University of North Texas. She is a former elementary and middle school literacy teacher of culturally and linguistically diverse children.

Lucy A. Garcia is currently an undergraduate at Elon University majoring in environmental and sustainability studies and minoring in policy studies and geographic information systems. She has a passion for writing and loves learning. As a member of the LGBTQIA+ community, she wants to fight for better representation both in and out of the classroom.

Megan Lynn Isaac is a professor of English at Elon University. She teaches classes in young adult literature, Shakespeare, and writing to both English majors and preservice teachers. Her most recent articles have been published in *Children's Literature*, *Children's Literature and Education*, and *The Journal of Teaching Writing*. Current projects focus on the representation and practice of surveillance in children's and young adult literature.

Tatyana Jimenez-Macias is an undergraduate English and language arts major, while obtaining a Teacher Certification for ELA in secondary education at the University of North Texas.

Joan F. Kaywell is a retired professor of English education at the University of South Florida (USF) where she won several teaching awards for her passion of assisting preservice and practicing teachers in discovering ways to improve literacy. She is past president of the Assembly on Literature for Adolescents of the National Council of Teachers of English (ALAN). She is highly published having one tradebook and fifteen textbooks to her credit. She was the recipient of the 2012 ALAN Hipple Award for outstanding service, the 2010 NCTE Conference on English Leadership (CEL) Exemplary Leadership Award, and the Florida affiliate established the Joan F. Kaywell "Literature Saves Lives" Book Award to honor her for her "deep commitment to FCTE, the profession, and her fervent belief in young adult (YA) literature." Kaywell is most proud of the Ted Hipple Special Collection of Autographed Books, a collection of over 5,000 titles she founded in honor of her mentor who introduced her to adolescent literature.

shea wesley martin is a Black, queer, gender-expansive scholar-teacher raised at the intersection of gospel and go-go. A product of public schooling and community college, they are currently completing their doctoral studies in Teaching and Learning at The Ohio State University. In their work, shea fuses queer pedagogy, Black feminist thought, and an abolitionist praxis to reimagine literacy instruction with teachers and students. A former classroom teacher, shea has taught the dopiest students in Texas, Florida, and Massachusetts. shea is the cofounder of Love and LiteraTea for LGBTQ Youth and the Liberate and Chill* Collective. A dynamic facilitator and writer, shea's work and writing has been featured in *The New York Times*, *Vox*, *Autostraddle*, and *Electric Literature*.

Summer Melody Pennell is a Lecturer in education at the University of Vermont. Her research interests include young adult literature, critical literacies, queer theory and pedagogy social justice education, and the experiences of academic mothers.

Kristin Rasbury is an undergraduate English and language arts major and student in the Teacher Education program at the University of North Texas.

René M. Rodríguez-Astacio is a PhD candidate in curriculum and instruction from the Pennsylvania State University. His area of emphasis is literacies and English language arts with a focus in children's and YA literature. His research interests fall within the intersections of Latinx LGBTQ children's and young adult literature. He has also coauthored chapters in *Does nonfiction Equate truth: Rethinking Disciplinary Boundaries Through Critical Literacy* (2018) and in the *Making the Invisible: Articulating Whiteness* *in Social Studies Educations* (2020) and has a coauthored article in *South Carolina English Teacher*. He is an active member of the National Council of Teachers of English (NCTE) and has presented his research at several NCTE Annual Conventions.

Jenna Spiering, PhD, is an assistant professor in the School of Information Science at the University of South Carolina. Before receiving her doctorate from the University of Iowa, she was a junior high school librarian in Iowa City, Iowa. Her research focuses on school libraries, graphic novels, issues of censorship and selection of LGBTQ materials, curation, and literature discussion. Her recent publications have appeared in *The ALAN Review, English Journal, Study and Scrutiny: Research in Young Adult Literature,* and *School Libraries Worldwide.*

Scott Storm is a doctoral student in English education at New York University. He has taught students English in urban public schools for thirteen years; he was founding English teacher at Harvest Collegiate High School where he served as Department Chair and Professional Learning Community Organizer. Scott studies disciplinary literacies, critical literacies, and social justice teaching. He focuses on adolescents' literary sensemaking across contexts—from traditional literary analyses in public high school classrooms to queer-led storytelling gaming sessions in community spaces. His work has appeared in *English Journal, Journal of Adolescent and Adult Literacies, English Teaching Practice & Critique, The Journal of Language and Literacy Education*, and *Schools: Studies in Education.*

Terri Suico is an associate professor of education at Saint Mary's College. She earned her EdD from Boston University School of Education and her MAT from Vanderbilt University. Her scholarly work has been featured in several books, including *Representing Agency in Popular Culture: Children and Youth on Page, Screen, and In-Between* and *Gender(ed) Identities: Critical Rereadings of Gender in Children's and Young Adult Literature.* Most recently, her chapter on using *Loving Vs. Virginia* to teach and contextualize the struggle for marriage equality appeared in the book *Breaking the Taboo with Young Adult Literature.* She currently serves as the book review and interview editor for *Study and Scrutiny: Research on Young Adult Literature.*

Joseph D. Sweet is an assistant professor of English education at the University of North Carolina at Pembroke whose research explores intersections among English methods, teacher education, gender, art, and philosophy. Among others, he has published in *Qualitative Inquiry, International Journal* *of Education and the Arts, Bank Street Occasional Paper Series, Men and Masculinities, Journal of Higher Education, Taboo: The Journal of Culture and Education,* and *Journal of Curriculum and Pedagogy.* Joe holds a BA and MA in dramatic arts from the University of California at Santa Barbara, an MA in English education from City University of New York, Hunter College, and a PhD in learning, literacies, and technologies from Arizona State University. Joe served nine years as a secondary English and theatre teacher in The Bronx and in Flagstaff, AZ.

LaMar Timmons-Long is an English teacher and an adjunct faculty member at Pace University, where he is also currently finishing his advanced graduate certificate in Teaching English to Speakers of Other Languages (TESOL). LaMar provides support to educators on the intersections between literacy, social justice, language, and students experiencing disabilities. He focuses on using culturally responsive pedagogical strategies and practices, centered around adding diverse voices and experiences, throughout his instruction. LaMar is a proud member of NCTE, where he serves as a member of the LGBTQ Advisory Committee. His writing can be found at the NCTE blog, the #31daysBIPOC project, and other sources. He often writes post centered around supporting BIPOC and LGBTQ youth.

Gabriel T. Acevedo Velázquez is an assistant professor in English education in the English Department at Arizona State University. His identities as a Latinx, bilingual, and Queer educator in Puerto Rico and the United States inform his research. Dr. Acevedo is fascinated by the expansive possibilities that diversity and social issues bring to conversations in the classroom, especially in English Language Arts. He is ever curious to understand how such conversations help make sense of teacher's and student's experiences. Acevedo prides himself on having interdisciplinary interests in teaching, research, and seeks to advocate for positive change among educators. In young adult literature, he focuses on LGBTQ Latinx texts and their impact as reparative forms of expressions in the classroom for both queer teachers and students.

Amanda E. Vickery is an assistant professor of social studies and anti-racist education at the University of North Texas. She is a former middle school social studies teacher.

Kyle Wright is an undergraduate English major getting their teaching certification in English language arts 7–12 at the University of North Texas.